"Perlov has written the kind of readable, insightful, and honest book that few anthropologists have the wisdom or fortitude to do. Chock full of real and often humorous accounts of what it is like to do anthropological fieldwork, *Driving the Samburu Bride* will remind readers of why anthropology remains the most humanistic of the social sciences, and also the one whose practitioners throw the most lively dance parties." — Peter D. Little, *Emory University*

"Samburu women are known for their elaborate traditional bead necklaces—individual strands laced carefully together, enhancing the effects of color and motion. Perlov has gifted us a book about the experience of fieldwork, presented as a string of vignettes that come together for greater effect. Each story rings true and is stitched to others to prompt consideration of the complex, intertwined concerns of culture change, gender roles, personal growth, and the important but often neglected effect of the fieldworker on the local people." — *Paul Leslie, University of North Carolina, Chapel Hill*

"Perlov recounts tales of fieldwork and friendship among the Samburu in this passionate, informative, and deeply amusing work that will touch your heart. With a comedic eye, she recalls her stumbles on the path to becoming an anthropologist, discovering only decades later the unexpected and moving effects she had on Samburu girls. Her charmingly written, illuminating, and refreshing work demonstrates how the candor and narrative quality of the memoir can enrich the study of anthropology. Beautifully done!" — John G. Galaty, *McGill University*

"*Driving the Samburu Bride* is an excellent introduction to the joys and frustrations of anthropological fieldwork. In parts humorous as well as thoughtfully self-reflexive, it is a perfect book for introductory undergraduate courses in cultural anthropology." — Nancy Lutkehaus, *University of Southern California*

"This book is one of the most captivating and riveting accounts I have ever read of an anthropologist in the field. Perlov is a masterful and provocative writer—witty and perceptive. In a fresh and nontraditional ethnography, she borrows from narrative techniques of ethnographic film and museum exhibitions to tell the multilayered story that is fieldwork. In vivid and riveting prose, Perlov connects anthropological theory and practice, and reveals the complicated reality of fieldwork for the anthropologist as well as for the people—the subject of her study. Her book elegantly walks that fine line of being academically thought-provoking, heartwarming, and at times laugh-out-loud funny." — Shahla Haeri, *Boston University*

"Authenticity comes through in each paragraph and chapter. Beautifully written and very engaging, this book will not only resonate with undergraduate students, and those about to undertake fieldwork, but it is also an important contribution to the literature on East African pastoral peoples and anthropology. I teach a large introductory class on East Africa and would definitely assign this book for the class." — J. Terrence McCabe, *University of Colorado*

"This vivid and accessible ethnography by a gifted storyteller offers fresh insights into several decades of cultural and economic change among Kenya's Samburu people. With rare candor, wit, compassion, and insight, Perlov demystifies ethnographic research in a captivating narrative that will appeal to both introductory and advanced students—as well as to anyone who has ever wondered what it is like to do anthropological fieldwork. *Driving the Samburu Bride* combines scholarly excellence with a novelist's flair. It will be a valuable text for students and professionals interested in the overall craft of anthropology, as well as in topics such as social change, cultural economy, gender relations, ritual, research methods, and Africa." — Angelique Haugerud, *Rutgers University*

"Anthropologists often tell us how their first fieldwork has affected them. Perlov's account of how her fieldwork affected the lives of the people she was living with, while she was there and after she had left, is far more interesting. An excellent contribution!" — Johan Helland, *Christian Michelsen Institute*, Bergen, Norway

"Perlov's thoughtful, engaging, accessible, and funny memoir of her research, relationships, and friendships among the Samburu of Kenya is insightful and also a delight to read. Her journey allows us to understand why connections to other cultures and experiences are part of what makes us *homines curans*, caring humans." — Robert Gottlieb, *Occidental College*

"Perlov takes us through the complex relationships, and the often unexpected and extraordinary experiences of anthropological fieldwork. This is an important read for both students and a larger reading public who are interested in cross-cultural relationships that have consistently made anthropology so appealing." — Elliot Fratkin, *Smith College*

Driving the Samburu Bride

Driving the Samburu Bride

Fieldwork among Cattle Keepers in Kenya

DIANE C. PERLOV
California Science Center, Los Angeles

WAVELAND

PRESS, INC.

Long Grove, Illinois

For information about this book, contact:
Waveland Press, Inc.
4180 IL Route 83, Suite 101
Long Grove, IL 60047-9580
(847) 634-0081
info@waveland.com
www.waveland.com

Cover photo
Left to right: Samburu bride, *Ichapukera* ("best man"), and groom.
Unless otherwise noted, all photos by the author.

10-digit ISBN 1-4786-4561-X
13-digit ISBN 978-1-4786-4561-0

Printed in the United States of America

7 6 5 4 3 2 1

For my beloved Dale,
Noah and Maria,
Matilda and Leo

*May green grass grow around your home
and rain fall wherever you go.*
— Samburu blessing

Contents

Part Three   Promise

Preface

My mother was a master storyteller. And while this does not explain how I ended up in Kenya, it plays a pivotal role in how I experienced it. Mom never lived a day she could not improve upon. Our family trip to a trout farm was an adventure at sea. An overheard conversation in a Las Vegas casino became a glamorous tale of international intrigue. And to inspire our sense of adventure, she would expound on the life of Vladimir Bogoraz, the renowned father of Russian anthropology and our alleged relative through her mother Olga Bogoraz. My mother didn't invent stories; she used them to make a point. Her tales conveyed the meaning of things, the first-person experience behind real-life events. She saw powerful lessons and humor in this truth. So did her audience. Everyone, that is, except her children.

My memories and my mother's stories merged together, and in the end I have no idea what my actual childhood was really like. Like my brother and sister, I grew up craving—for the lack of it—a concise and agreed upon family history. And I often wished that my mother's stories were more firmly tethered to a short rope of chronological events. However, because of her, I also saw the world through the lens of a storyteller and grew to value the truth it could reveal.

Mom came by it naturally. Her mother Olga had managed a harrowing escape from Stalin's Russia, bringing with her every Russian superstition and dark tale she ever knew. Known as "The Countess" among her friends, she read Tarot cards and dragged my mother to every illicit gambling den within driving distance of Salinas, California, her new American home. I remember her as the small, stout, loving grandmother who always arrived in heavy perfume, fox stoles, and long red fingernails. She taught us to gamble at cards, told spooky stories of Baba Yaga, and delighted us with vivid accounts of her worldwide cruises from Egypt to the Far East.

We grew up in a little house in Los Altos, on the San Francisco Peninsula, a close-knit family of individuals. We each did our own thing and lived in our own cerebral worlds. My older sister was the bookish one, my brother was a budding inventor like my father, and I was the storyteller—destined to carry on the family tradition. When I was in the fourth grade I created my own library of short stories in a shoe box. I'd write and fully illustrate them, fold them into neat squares, cataloged by topic, and stack them vertically and neatly in place. I remember them being complex adventures and mysteries. My mother remembers that they all had happy endings.

My world opened up considerably when my Aunt Helen came to visit in the mid-1960s, fresh from her safari in Africa. Helen was my father's older sister who lived in Chicago. On this memorable visit, all I could think of was the elephant-hair bracelet she said she was bringing me. I imagined a dark grey, hairy bangle, made of the soft hairs delicately cut from the tail of a grazing elephant. What Aunt Helen in fact brought me was a thin, black, wiry wisp of a bracelet, something that didn't look like it came from an elephant. It didn't look African. It didn't even look like hair. Although Aunt Helen regaled us with stories of cultural and natural wonders, this odd little bracelet is the major thing I recall of that visit these 50 years later. It was my first introduction to Africa, and it left me with nothing but questions.

I left for college in 1970, and the first course I signed up for at UC Davis was an African anthropology class. During class time the professor would put Africa in an academic framework, while during his office hours he would reminisce about what it was like to live and conduct research in the Cameroons. They were the types of stories I grew up on, and it slowly dawned on me that traveling, African studies, and my shoe-box stories could be the basis of a legitimate career. It was this same anthropology professor who first suggested I apply for the University of California Study Abroad Program. The program had two campuses in Africa, one being in West Africa where he had done his research.

"Hmm. I guess I could do a quarter abroad," I muttered cautiously.

"Don't be ridiculous!" he said. "You can't do anything in a quarter. This is for a year."

A year abroad terrified me. But, *what the heck*, I thought. *I can apply and always back out at the last minute*, which is how I ended up in quite a few marginally thought-out, life-changing situations, the first of which was at the University of Ghana for my junior year abroad in 1972–1973 and subsequently in Ghana and Kenya for the summers of 1976 and 1980.

The 1970s was a tremendously exciting time to be in Africa. Thirty-four African countries had recently gained independence, with nine more on the brink. The whole place was alive with political, economic, and social innovation and hope. Optimism was everywhere—the perfect place for a girl who loved happy endings.

"Mom, I have decided to officially become an anthropologist!" I informed her when I returned from my first year in Ghana.

"That's nice, dear." She was always supportive, especially when it involved college. And she was fine for my first few years of graduate study at UCLA—through my masters and doctoral course work. But when it came time for me to conduct my own doctoral fieldwork, to do my own two years of independent research on a subject of "significance to the field," it was another matter.

"Why can't you do anthropology somewhere nice, like Paris?" she pleaded.

"Anthropology doesn't work that way," I flatly stated. "You have to go someplace really, really foreign. They don't let you go to Paris."

Part of the allure was academic, the pursuit of knowledge. Part of the allure was pure adventure, to step into the unknown and carve my own path in getting to, navigating in, and exploring a foreign culture, just as I imagined my intrepid aunt, grandmother, and hypothetical Russian anthropologist forefather Vladimir Bogoraz had done.

Mom was not happy with my choice for exploration, but when I told her Nairobi had a Hilton Hotel, which it did, she was much relieved. "I will visit you anywhere as long as Conrad Hilton has been there first!" And she kissed me *bon voyage*.

That's basically how I came to spend two years in Kenya from 1981 through 1982. I lived among the seminomadic Samburu people of northern Kenya, collecting data for my doctoral dissertation in economic anthropology. I was 28 years old. My research focused on livestock marketing issues and the integration of the traditional and commercial markets. It was quite specific, as doctoral research needs to be. But basically it sought to make sense of shared beliefs and behavior in a way that resonated with people outside the culture. It was the most important and most exciting part of my academic career. I was finally living in a remote community, asking new questions, and exploring new conditions. I was investigating an important issue in a place where there were few existing written accounts. After years of academic training and short stints of fieldwork, this long-term project formed the basis of my doctoral thesis, and marked me, finally, as a real anthropologist.

The research was successful in that it led to my doctorate in anthropology from UCLA. And while I have no idea if I made a significant contribution to the field, I know that some people read it, because about three years after filing, I got my first and only royalty check for $3.38.

My mother was proud of my thesis, and even read it, but was not terribly impressed. "You left out the best parts!" she said as she dumped my 300-page manuscript at my feet. "What about the time the cormorant birds threw all those dead fish on your head? What about the time you herded goats and ended up with an extra one?"

"Mom, those have no academic value! I couldn't put those in my thesis!"

"Well, then write another book! I always told you to be wary of strangers. Yet if it weren't for the kindness of strangers, you'd be dead by now. Write about that."

"That's not interesting!" I cried in exasperation.

"Not yet," she said, with the confidence of a woman raised to read Tarot cards.

This is the book my mother always wanted me to write. It conveys the experience of anthropological fieldwork through stories of my journey, detours, and lessons learned among the pastoral Samburu of northern Kenya. The outcome—as you will see—has been far more than academic. Much like my mother, grandmother, and aunt did for me, I hope this story will inspire those who follow, that they may explore through a wide lens the strange and the familiar, revel in fortuitous adventures, and care about people on the far side of the world. Luckily, I kept good notes.

Driving the Samburu Bride

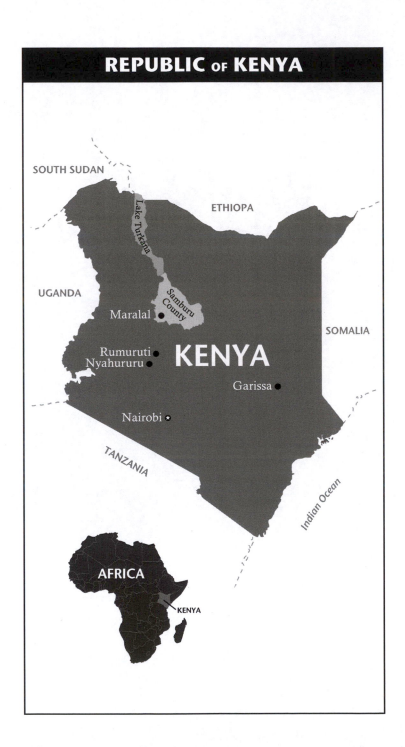

REPUBLIC OF KENYA

SOUTH SUDAN

Lake Turkana

ETHIOPA

UGANDA

Samburu County

Maralal

SOMALIA

KENYA

Rumuruti
Nyahururu

Garissa

Nairobi

TANZANIA

Indian Ocean

AFRICA

KENYA

Introduction

Luckily I kept good notes, because this is a story that takes place primarily over two fateful years that happened a long time ago. It's the story of my fieldwork as a young anthropologist finding my way, both academically and corporeally, in the days when fieldwork meant living off the grid. It's about experiencing the key stages of fieldwork: feverish anticipation, confusion, frustration, exhaustion, unrelenting boredom, regret, despair, drunkenness, dogged determination, sporadic euphoria, promise, and profound gratitude (not necessarily in that order). It's about the unwritten partnership between the observer and the observed as each tries to understand what on earth the other is doing and what the world is like for them. And since I have written this many years after the initial events, it includes something that rarely occurs to the fieldworker immersed in the moment. It's about what we leave behind and the impact we have on the people we study. For as much as fieldwork transforms the life of the anthropologist, it also forever changes the lives of the local people who welcome a complete stranger into their homes—a stranger who asks bizarre questions and who just won't go away.

The world I describe takes place in Samburu County (Samburu District at the time of the study), northern Kenya, primarily during 1981 and 1982. This world doesn't exist anymore, at least not like it did in the early 1980s. The events I describe all happened, but not necessarily in this order. The names of some people and places have been withheld or changed to protect privacy. Some of the dialogue is real, recorded in my field notes. Some of it reflects unspoken conversations. Some of it was originally in English, some in Swahili, and some of it in a mixture of Samburu and Ndorobo. It seeks to convey the truth of the experience. Some of it may even be accurate. The customs and practice of the Samburu were garnered from my surveys and field notes, library research, daily journals, letters home, interviews, and memories. On the off-chance I messed up, I asked my former Samburu assistant, Symon, and other Samburu friends to review the manuscript and set the record straight.

"I remember everything," Symon told me when I approached him with my plan. *Uh oh*, I thought. *This is going to take way longer than I planned.* While Symon and I were engaged in many of the same events, in the same places, at the same time, we were often living very different experiences, his steeped in growing up Samburu and mine born half a world away. In honor of the participants, I worked with Symon, his daughter Diana, and others to correct any glaring errors. In honor of my mother, who believed no one should be deprived of a good story for the sake of expedience, I left in all the best parts.

Notes on Language

Samburu is a dialect of the Maa language, spoken by the Maasai and Samburu peoples. During my fieldwork, Swahili and Samburu words were often thrown together in the same sentence, which is noticeable throughout the text. These words are defined and written in italics on first appearance and words used frequently are listed in the back glossary.

I have withheld the name of the local area to protect privacy. In its place, when I speak of the area where the Samburu and I worked and lived, I use the Swahili term for settlements, *bomas*. It is the term Samburu participants and I used when speaking English or Swahili.

Part One

Anticipation

Remember my dears, it is never really that simple.

—Hilda Kuper, anthropologist
personal communication, 1979

Chapter 1

Wasting My Time

"**H**urry!" she cried, barreling through my front door and straight into the bedroom. I jerked up in bed and immediately collapsed back onto the thin, sheetless and pillowless mattress. I stared at the familiar figure rummaging about in my room and tried to remember who she was, where I was, and why every muscle in my body ached.

"The bus is just here, and if you want a good ride down to Nairobi, this is the only one!" It was 3:00 a.m. The scene looked as if I had broken into and was squatting in an unfinished tract home. An industrious Luo woman was urgently stuffing clothes and toiletries into a canvas duffel bag like a criminal accomplice with the cops on our tail. I lay there holding my throbbing head, fighting through the fog to uncover the recent memories of my life. By the time she was done, I remembered everything.

The industrious Luo woman was Josephine, my dear Kenyan friend who lived down the hill from me in Maralal, northern Kenya. She was there to send me off to the hospital. After pulling off the African cloth I used as a blanket and jamming it into the duffle bag, she helped me out of bed, handed me my shoes, and gently pushed me out the door. I was still wearing the same clothes I had on the day before.

I leaned on Josephine as we stumbled down the hill and up the steps of the dusty vehicle while the bus driver revved the engine to hurry us up. After a quick goodbye, I fell onto the first available seat just as the self-proclaimed "Luxury Bus" pulled away from the side of the road. For the next few hours I lay on a hard, unpadded, and loosely attached wooden bench. With my arms wrapped tightly around my body, I cushioned my ribs from the stabbing pain as the driver found every pothole between Maralal and Nyahururu. I tried not to whine. It was 165 long miles to Nairobi, and I knew this "good" ride would only take me part of the way. Nevertheless, I welcomed the forward progress. To take my mind off my bruised and battered body, I gazed into the dust dancing off the floor and tried to sort out where I had gone so very wrong in just two short months.

It was January 1981 when I first landed in Nairobi, Kenya, to start my doctoral fieldwork in anthropology. I was filled with purpose and all the delusions of competence provided by my graduate studies and a minimal National Science Foundation research grant. I had arrived to study the Samburu, seminomadic cattle herders living in northern Kenya. But before I could do anything, I had to register with the government, secure my in-country institutional affiliation, obtain letters of introduction, and meet with government livestock market officials.

I remember my first day of institutional office visits. Like any recently arrived American anthropologist, I packed an engrossing novel and my favorite brand of granola bars in my shoulder bag in case I had a bit of a wait. Needless to say, my granola bars and that novel were soon depleted, and what I thought would be an extremely hectic afternoon of office visits took nearly a month.

I was frustrated by the delay, but not discouraged, perhaps because I was not alone. My boyfriend, David, a fellow graduate student from UCLA, had arrived before me. He was in Kenya studying the Maasai south of Nairobi. When he wasn't in the field, he shared a house in Nairobi with an ever-expanding group of expats, which now included me. They made good use of my time by advising me on everything from con artists (*they'll be the nicest people you'll ever meet*) to essentials (*batteries if you ever find them*) to lodging (*don't live behind a bar or in a mission*). Eventually I assembled all the necessary permits, affiliations, and letters of introduction, along with a few bonus ones I thought might come in handy depending on where I ended up living.

While I was still at UCLA, I pinpointed Samburu District for my research on livestock marketing. The Samburu, particularly highland Samburu communities, were at a fascinating juncture. They were subsistence-based pastoralists, but they were also tied into the commercial live-stock market. I was going to study the pastoral economy in transition, that pull of the commercial market and what it means to traditional economic institutions. What determines how people gift, loan, and sell their live-stock? How do nomadic pastoralists, who occupy a huge geographic terri-tory, fit in with the national livestock market? The hope was that the study would be useful, not only for regional development, but for national eco-nomic planning.

But where should I focus my energy? Samburu District was a big place, covering 8,000 square miles. After talking with colleagues in Nai-robi, studying maps, and poring over recent pastoral studies, I narrowed my focus to the plateau region around the district capital of Maralal. Deciding which communities I would study and where I'd live were com-pletely up in the air. I couldn't decide those issues from Nairobi. I had to determine them locally. It was time I headed the 165 miles up-country to Maralal. And as anyone familiar with Kenyan public transportation knows, this first step was no easy feat.

At 8:30 a.m. on a bright Thursday morning, I boarded a fairly decent bus from Nairobi to Nanyuki. I was traveling light since I was planning on being away for only a few weeks to select a specific field site and find hous-ing. Once that was settled, I'd return to Nairobi to pack up my equipment and supplies and move in. The bus to Nanyuki took about three hours with no delays or mishaps. So far so good. There I waited two hours for a *matatu* (Swa.) up north.

Matatus are privately run, multipassenger taxis. In the early 1980s these vehicles were neither regulated nor licensed, yet they were widely used to fill the pressing need for public transportation. Various kinds of cars were used: station wagons, minivans, pickups with converted cargo beds, anything with ample space. And every square inch of that cargo space, both inside and on top, was used. A common matatu at the time was a covered pickup truck where everyone was crammed onto three wooden benches in the bed, two lining each side and one resting cross-wise behind the cab window. Some had a metal roof over the cargo bed. Others made due with a canvas tarp that, in theory, protected the passen-gers and cargo from pouring rain. While the engines usually worked, the basic accessories we take for granted such as operable windows, doors, lights, seats, and brakes too often did not.

I never found out how one got the coveted and spacious shotgun seat next to the driver, but it looked like a dubious honor in any case. You had legroom, but then again you had to contend with the advances of the driver. And of course, you'd be the first through the windshield in an accident, which seemed imminent at every sharp turn and crossing every narrow bridge. The back of the taxi was even worse. Matatus—like the one I boarded—seated about eight to 10 people comfortably, but 14 or more people and baggage were generally crammed into every conceivable "seat," a word I use loosely. The vehicles were decorated with plastic ornaments, tassels, and charms. Slogans painted on the sides evoked the death-defying attitude of the driver, such as *Whatsoever It Takes* and *Waste No Time*, although some slogans were positively unnerving, such as *God's Will Be Done* and *Liquid Biopsy*. Each matatu was operated by two people: the driver and *makanga*, often an adolescent boy, whose job it was to hustle business, collect fares, and pack the vehicle. The makanga was the one precariously hanging out the back of the vehicle, calling out its destination.

"Nyahururu! Nyahururu!" shouted the makanga of an approaching matatu. That one being my next destination, I signaled the makanga, who pounded the roof to direct the converted pickup to stop, and he moved aside to let me squeeze in.

As we left the matatu stop, the radio was blasting "No Woman No Cry," by Bob Marley and the Wailers, and everyone was in a patient mood. The driver had that glassy, red-eyed glaze of someone who had been up for several days without sleep, not necessarily due to driving. But he didn't look too drunk or doped up, which was a tremendous comfort. He had one hand loosely on the wheel and the other on the back of the shotgun seat occupied by an aloof Kenyan girl. As he sang along with the songs and chatted her up, she smiled, stared out the window in a putting-up-with-it sort of way, and offered just enough conversation to maintain her first-class seat. It was as if they were riding in a different vehicle than the rest of us. Back in coach, even with the back door open for the standing makanga, there was the pungent odor of exhaust, sweat, and beer. No one stared at each other or talked much, and since we were sitting nearly on top of each other, everyone was on their best behavior. That is, except for the makanga. When the song "Get Up Stand Up" came on the radio, he not only sang along but also punched his fist in the air.

"Stand up for your rights!" And he laughed as he sang, because of course no one there could possibly stand up. He bounced around in the open back doorway, completely oblivious to the feet he stomped on or the legs he kicked. I didn't need to know much Kikuyu or Swahili to understand what was being said. However, no amount of hand gestures, swearing, or reasonable complaints from the passengers did any good whatsoever. The makanga just kept on singing and bouncing, and having his own private party. The car, which was filled to the brim at the bus stop, stopped again at the next street corner to squeeze in one more woman and her three huge sacks of maize meal. Then we were off to another part of town, where the makanga shoved in two more rather large women and a few live chickens.

"Ah! That is enough!" cried one woman squished painfully into the corner. "Are you trying to kill us? There is only so much air in here!"

I don't know exactly how many people one can squeeze into a small matatu. But the carrying capacity seems to be determined this way: In the beginning of the journey, the car careens through town with the makanga swinging on the back door frame or hopping in and out of the car calling out the next destination in search of more passengers. At the same time, the already seated passengers grow increasingly hostile, delivering hisses, tongue clicks, and a few choice words and gestures. Only when it appears that the passengers will break into outright rebellion and pummel the makanga to death is the matatu full and ready for departure. At some point, we reached this level. I could not even tell you how many people were in my matatu, because I couldn't turn my head to count. Finally, at last, we headed out on the highway toward Nyahururu.

I say "toward" Nyahururu, because we didn't actually get there. Thirty minutes into our trip, the car broke down. We all spilled out of the matatu and waited by the side of the road to flag down another one. Several people, including the women with the chickens, decided to walk. I probably should have joined them; it was only another 34 miles to my next stop. As it happened, the rest of us were able to catch other rides. My next ride, also a matatu, was much like the first, except I was more on top this time and closer to the back door. This matatu was much better than the first one because it actually arrived in Nyahururu, where I waited another hour for a third matatu up to Rumuruti.

We reached Rumuruti 30 minutes later. There the road ended. From Nairobi to Rumuruti is a lovely paved highway, the last bit having been laid only in the few years before my arrival. At the edge of Rumuruti, the tarmac abruptly ended and the long, rutted, dirt road up to the north began. I intended to catch the next northbound bus or matatu to Maralal, but by the time we reached Rumuruti, the last public transport had left, and this driver had no intention of going further north.

After much cajoling, I finally got the driver to take me another mile to a government office at the edge of town where I might catch a ride with workers going north. Naturally, by the time we got there, the office was closed. It was there I had what you might call a significant misunderstanding with the matatu driver. In my defense, I had been crammed in various matatus for eight harrowing hours. I was filthy, tired, and my right foot felt as if someone had been jumping on it repeatedly. Moreover, for driving me a mile up the road, where he—by the way—picked up an additional passenger, the driver wanted to charge me twice the going rate.

"What?! That's robbery!" I cried.

"That's a fair price. I didn't even want to go there. You are wasting my time," he pointed out dismissively with a wave of his hand.

Further words were exchanged, but no money, and I ended up being dropped unceremoniously by the side of the dirt road while the little matatu sped off without me.

As I limped back to Rumuruti, all I could think was, It's going to be a long two years unless things start to pick up a little bit.

A curious thing about rural Kenya is that you can be out in what appears to be the middle of absolutely nowhere, on a dirt road with no town in sight for miles and miles, and find all kinds of people walking. *Where are they going? Where did they come from? Can they possibly be walking 50 miles to get to the next village? Are there houses out there in the bush that I can't see?* As it happened on this day, I soon found myself on the road back to Rumuruti with two very nice Somali girls who were walking my way. We struck up a conversation, even with my broken Swahili, and by the time we got back to Rumuruti they had invited me to have dinner and spend the evening at their home while they helped me find a ride up north.

The girls, Sara and Asha, lived in a small house behind the main road in Rumuruti. There I spent the evening with them and seven or more other family members including their *mira'a*-chewing mother. Mira'a (Swa., or *khat*) is a stimulant, an herb that is legal in Kenya but illegal in many countries. It contains a psychoactive ingredient similar to amphetamine and is used like caffeine to help drivers and others stay awake for long hours. With the mira'a at work, we spent the next few hours talking and listening to the radio, all 10 to 12 of us crammed into that small sitting room. Cozy groups were sitting on two single beds, leaning against the walls. Others were sitting on the floor or in plastic chairs brought in for the occasion. In the midst of all the talking and singing, someone brought out bowl after bowl of stew with *ugali* (stiff cornmeal porridge, Swa.) from the back room. It was unbelievably welcoming after a long day of travel!

At some point Sara and Asha were able to contact a Somali friend who was driving a large lorry full of don't-ask-what and was heading in my direction. I have no idea when or how the girls secured this ride for me up-country, but by 8:30 that evening they hurried me out the door, around to the main road where I met up with Mahamed the truck driver as he rolled into town. I quickly climbed into the shotgun seat, so as not to waste his time, and leaned out the window to reiterate my gratitude to the girls and their family.

With their colorful scarves and wraps billowing in the breeze, my two generous saviors and several of their friends and family stood by the dusty road, waving and sending me off as the truck headed north. Meeting them had been the best thing that had happened to me all day, and I waved and waved in turn until they disappeared from view.

Three hours later we rolled into Maralal, the district capital. Maralal was a well laid out town that looked like it was designed for a cowboy western. The town center consisted of two parallel roads that curved and met at each end, forming a well-defined dirt-road donut. Dry goods stores, a butcher shop, hair salons, restaurants, Bholla's car repair shop, and for a short time an open-air cinema lined the streets. At one end was the local Catholic mission and clinic, at the far other end was the local den of iniquity, the Buffalo House Bar and Hotel. A small road to the north took you to the post office, school, hospital, and government offices. Further north was the only other lodging in town, the plush Maralal Safari Lodge where passing tourists stayed. Further still was the wildlife department complex, and beyond that lay the northbound road to Lake Turkana. We rolled in from the south; I thanked Mahamed profusely and had him drop me at the Buffalo House Bar and Hotel—ignoring the advice from anthropologists to *never live behind a bar.* By 11:30 p.m. I fell soundly asleep, oblivious to the raucous fun being had by everyone else in the popular establishment.

My first challenge in the morning was to find a place to stay that was quieter and not so sticky. I had been told the Catholic mission had some spare rooms for visitors. So, ignoring the second piece of anthropological advice to *never live in a mission*, I marched to the other end of town and, looking as respectable as I could, knocked on the Catholic mission's front door. A small, old, and severe-looking European nun opened the door and introduced herself as Sister Florida. Over her shoulder I could see a central courtyard flanked by two neat rows of white cottages lined with flowers. I could almost smell the fresh linen and lavender. Hat in hand, I explained my situation and inquired if there was a spare room I could rent while I was in town, even on a very temporary basis. Closing the door gradually, Sister Florida informed me in no uncertain terms, "There is no room here. Go away."

"But . . . But . . ." I said to the closing door. Rats!

Luckily, there was a Kenyan tending the front garden who heard my plea and motioned me over.

"You will get no charity from that woman," he informed me and suggested I contact a gentleman named Pascal at the wildlife department. "Pascal is a very Christian fellow, and I know he will assist you if anybody can."

I thanked the kind gardener, reminded myself to stick it to weasel-faced Sister Florida if I ever wrote a book about my days in Samburuland, and headed in the direction he had indicated.

The wildlife department occupied an entire compound on the hillside north of town. It was hard to take in the full scope of the place because it consisted of dozens of single-family homes snaking around the hill. Some looked new, built of concrete walls and tiled roofs. Others were simple wood-and-plaster homes. Following the gardener's directions, I found Pascal's home on the southern slope of the hill. It was one of the older wooden homes, but it had a corrugated tin roof, concrete floor, covered porch, outhouse, and a water spigot a short distance away. Pascal, who was there, quickly told me that Sister Florida was a 100 percent wicked woman who had lied to me.

"They have plenty of rooms there. That woman is not to be trusted," Pascal said emphatically.

"Ah . . . well, is there any room available up here?" I inquired sheepishly.

"Here we have plenty of room, a house even."

Well, it wasn't as easy as all that. But with Pascal's help, I eventually did get to use a house that was in the final phase of construction in the wildlife department complex. No furniture. No drapes. A few unfinished walls. Sure. Why not? I only needed it for a week or so, until I got settled in my field site. As it turned out anyway, whenever I was in Maralal, I spent most evenings with Pascal, his gracious wife Josephine, and their high spirited young children: five girls and two boys.

Pascal and Josephine were both Luo from western Kenya. They had been living in Maralal for the past few years where Pascal worked for the wildlife department. From our very first meeting throughout my entire stay in Kenya, they were so welcoming that it was hard to believe their home did not become completely overrun by itinerant anthropologists. I was never sure exactly what Pascal did for the department, but he went down the hill to work every morning, in a suit worn thin and shiny with age, carrying a similarly well-used briefcase. While Pascal was at the office, Josephine took care of the children and their small two-room home. I don't think I ever saw her without a broad smile and a pleasant greeting for everyone. And although her English was limited and she was not well traveled, she was always interested in the wide world around her.

That first week the nights ran long, and I spent a lot of time hanging out at their home with my maps spread out, learning about who lives where and how I could get around. When we weren't discussing the Samburu, Josephine would dig into a trunk she kept in the living room and pull out a prized stash of old *National Geographic* magazines. Sitting beside me on their front porch, she carefully turned each delicate page, and we'd share the wonders of the world together.

"Tahiti is an island," she informed me. "And is completely surrounded by water!"

During the next few days I met with range officers, county clerks, and various livestock-marketing officials. I was getting the lay of the land, an overview of livestock sales—talking and listening—so I could find the right community to live in and research for the next two years. Since I didn't have a car, I was dependent on the generosity of government officials taking me around, or hitching a ride from anyone going my way.

One community I was considering for my study was located about eight miles south of Maralal on the Lorroki plateau. It was known to be

Josephine with her youngest children.

home to about 300 households with most people engaged in livestock marketing to some extent. This made for a workable sample size for my research. Better yet, the area had an elementary school with teacher housing, and there was a good possibility I could find lodging there. One overcast afternoon, a large and jovial officer from the Maralal livestock office said he was not particularly busy and was happy to give me a ride so I could check out the place. With little formality, Mr. Otieno, four other people who came along for the ride, and I joined a driver in a soft-top, short-wheelbase Land Rover and off we went for what was expected to be a short sightseeing expedition. *Brilliant!* I foolishly thought.

The Lorroki plateau was an extensive highland plain that was home to the Samburu and their livestock, as well as herds of Burchell's zebra and the occasional Grevy's zebra. Although I never saw them in great numbers, the plateau was also home to a variety of other residents including gazelle, ostrich, lions, cape buffalo, and—as I found one crawling up to my thigh one day—the large and hairy but generally harmless huntsman spider.

We crossed the Lorroki plateau and stopped at the base of Naibor Keju, a large rocky hill in the heart of the plateau. There we took a short hike to the summit for a grand view of the region. To the south we could see five Samburu *nkang'itie* (settlements). To the northeast were another six nkang'itie occupying the grasslands between Naibor Keju and the Karisia Hills, the large old-growth forest reserve. The reserve designation meant the Samburu had permission from the forest department to gather firewood, but were prohibited from cutting green trees. The restriction was probably a good idea; Naibor Keju, which is now primarily bush and rock, was evidently once covered with trees before it was deforested for the production of charcoal sold in Maralal. Beyond the forest to the east was the beginning of the vast, dry lowlands. West of Nairobi Keju was Kisima, a small trading town, and beyond that the road that led north to Maralal.

I was extremely grateful that Mr. Otieno was able to take the time to show me around the region at such a leisurely pace. He didn't seem to be in any hurry to get back to town, and the other four passengers looked quite satisfied just riding around looking at stuff. The only person who seemed a bit out of sorts was the driver, who was visibly struggling to keep the car on the road. In addition to having to contend with poor road conditions, the steering wheel behaved as if it wasn't securely tethered to the steering column. The driver would rotate the wheel, making big turns to the left, then big turns to the right, just to get the slightest turn. If I wasn't having such a good time, I might have recognized this as the ill omen that it was.

But I certainly didn't want to turn back now. Our next stop was the Karisia Hills to explore the forest. This particular forest was home to the Ndorobo, a clan among the Samburu who are descendants of hunters and gatherers. These people speak both Ndorobo and Samburu and are known to be the beekeepers of the forest. After driving about 50 yards further than I ever thought we could manage, the driver parked the car in the middle of the path and we continued on foot. I thought it was significant that we not only failed to meet any residents, but we never even saw any evidence that anyone had ever lived there. What we did experience was a lush forest of ferns, strangler-figs, podocarpus, and cedar, alive with bright green-headed beetles, starlings, crested guinea fowl, and countless insects and birds we heard but never saw. And while we missed the larger animals, we saw evidence that they had been around, including a jumble of porcupine quills and part of a lower elephant mandible.

Far too soon it was time to leave, as Mr. Otieno needed to get the vehicle back to the office. With tremendous luck, the driver turned the vehicle around and we picked our way out of the forest and back onto the Lorroki plateau for the return trip to Maralal. If the drive out made me nervous, the return trip seemed even more precarious. Our driver—who was an idiot—was driving way too fast and refused to take my suggestion that he should slow down, especially given the kinky steering wheel.

Suddenly, as we rounded a curve, I felt one side of the car rise off the ground. Rather than flop back down on the road, it kept rising in flight. And it continued in very slow motion, higher and higher. Suddenly it dawned on me that we were somehow airborne, and that this was potentially a very dangerous situation. My thoughts were so deliberate and important, as if I were trying to decide if this was actually happening and how by thinking hard enough I would be able to control the inevitable outcome. Slowly I thought . . . *This is not a good thing. This is definitely not a good thing. We might get hurt here. We might really get hurt. I think we ought NOT to be in this situation.* I continued to tell myself how *not good* this was as I felt my whole body lift off the seat and hover in midair within the confines of the car. I had no awareness of anyone else around me or any noise or directional movement whatsoever—just a slow, peaceful floating inside a car capsule. Suddenly, as if I jumped forward in time or was yanked out of a dream, I landed hard on my stomach, taking the force of the fall on my forearms, elbows, and thighs.

There I lay, quite awake and alert, trying to focus on my immediate surroundings. Although I thought my eyes were open I couldn't see anything, as if my head were in a sack. But from overhead I heard grunting and felt people climbing over me as liquid pooled under and around my body. I had no desire to move as I was concentrating on figuring out *something of importance.* That something was a sound. It was odd that I knew there was a sound I needed to understand before I actually heard the sound. Slowly it seemed to gain substance and become increasingly more defined. It was a long, low tone at first, without any source, like a ship's horn you think you hear in the fog. As seconds passed, it got louder and sharper until I realized it was screaming, and it was coming from just in front of me. All at once, I smelled the pungent odor of gasoline, felt it pooling beneath me, and my mind instantly snapped into focus. The sound I had been listening to sharpened into the recognizable and continuous screams of a person. It turned out to be the driver, whose head had smashed clear through the front windshield! I jerked up, but there was nowhere to go. My head hit something directly over me, and my lower body was pinned under something immovable. Seconds later, the car was lifted up and someone grabbed my ankles and pulled me along the ground, out and away from the Land Rover.

I got up and felt just fine, as if nothing had happened. I pulled off my scarf and wrapped up the driver's head after he was similarly pulled from the vehicle. Then I took stock. I was feeling a bit shaky but certainly in no pain, until I turned to get a good look at the vehicle. There, flipped over on its soft, flat, top were the ruins of our Land Rover, flat as a pancake. That anyone, no less seven people, crawled out alive seemed impossible. And whether it was because of the shock of being alive when I should have been dead or it was just the adrenaline kicking in, I suddenly crumbled and began to shake all over and sob uncontrollably. In this state, I followed the others and slowly walked the few miles to Kisima, the nearest town, where we caught a matatu back to Maralal. When we were in route, Mr. Otieno broke the silence to casually suggest that perhaps it would be best if we said nothing about this incident to the authorities, as it seemed he didn't actually have any official permission to take the vehicle out. Sure. Whatever. I was a bit disappointed that I never found out how he explained the flattened Land Rover to the authorities, because I'm sure it was an interesting story.

Once in town, we silently split up and went to our own homes to lick our wounds. I shuffled up the hill toward Pascal and Josephine's, thinking, *If the driver lives, I wonder if it would be appropriate to ask for my scarf back.* I was also trying to remember the path and put one foot after the other to get to the warmth and safety of Pascal and Josephine's. I headed there like a wounded child. Thank goodness they were home to look me over and assure me that I wasn't badly hurt.

"Ah, yes, yes, a car accident," Pascal replied after seeing that I was walking, not bleeding profusely from any punctures, and thus not badly hurt. "Happens all the time." And he shrugged, chuckled, and turned back to the transistor radio he was trying to repair. Huh? This was not the response I had anticipated. Josephine was equally warm yet unconcerned. And that was where we left it. Soon afterward I gingerly washed up and joined them for a nice dinner of rice, beef stew, and a fistful of aspirin.

After dinner, Josephine and I mulled over the giant pandas featured in that evening's *National Geographic* and talked about whether they were more or less vicious than the American grizzly bear featured in last night's *National Geographic*. Later that night, I found one comfortable position in bed and fell asleep, wondering if perhaps I neglected to inform them that I had just been in a car accident!

We come to a place and to a people with so many assumptions. What made me so certain they'd respond to the car accident as I would? It occurred to me that evening that once again I was taken by surprise by my own unconscious expectations. There's nothing like participating in the daily life of a foreign people to learn what we take for granted. Behavior we think is unique to us turns out to be shared by the most unlikely people. Behavior we think is universal isn't. And the things we do know, we know so incompletely.

When I woke up the next morning, I was dizzy and nauseated. Every breath brought a stabbing pain. My whole body ached, every single bit of it. I felt as if I had been run over by a truck. As I lay there I suddenly laughed, which also hurt. *Oh yeah*, I realized. *I HAVE been run over by a truck!* It was time to get back to Nairobi and see a doctor, even though nobody else was terribly worried. After all, I was coherent and walking around.

My first thought was to call David. He had a good friend with a Peugeot sedan that David could borrow for emergencies. I was hoping that this incident would qualify as one. The only working phone I knew of was at the home of the wildlife department's director, whom I had met only once. Pascal took me to the director's home that morning, and he graciously let me make the call. While David worked outside Nairobi, he spent a great deal of time in the capital, and I was counting on this being one of those times. I was also counting on the call going through. Luckily for David, I never found out if he would have tried to borrow the Peugeot for me, because the call never went through after numerous tries. Nearly in tears, I let the handset drop back on the hook. Pascal, Josephine, the director, his wife, and three of the children peeked sheepishly around the corner.

"So, so sorry!" Pascal exclaimed, seeing that the telephone experience had not been to my complete satisfaction. But, he knew just how to help. "It seems we need to get you a bus, isn't it?"

The trip to Nairobi naturally proved to be far easier said than done. And the first grueling part was that it started at 3:00 a.m. the next morning, when Josephine came running up the hill to my house.

"Hurry!" she cried, barreling through my front door and straight into the bedroom. The bus is just here, and if you want a good ride down to Nairobi, this is the only one!"

So that's how I came to find myself lying on a hard, unpadded and semi-attached wooden bench, bouncing around inside the Luxury Bus for three long, excruciating hours, feeling every bump in the road. I had plenty of time to think.

Where had I gone so wrong? My mind raced through all the fieldwork advice I had been given, all the words of encouragement and wisdom from those who had come before me: meet with the elders, cross-reference your notes, and don't live behind a bar or in a mission. All of that assumed I could *get to* and *stay in* the field. Clearly this was easier said than done. All my plans for fieldwork vastly oversimplified the initial task of getting up-country. And I now realized my advisors had left out a critical step in the process: *get your own car!* As I was transported south, along the same route I had taken north, I carefully considered which four-wheel drive luxury vehicle I was going to buy with the zero money I had set aside for this essential item. Clearly, a reallocation of my meagre funds was in order. The bus stopped in Rumuruti, then in Nyahururu: bus to matatu; matatu to other matatu. *My new vehicle will have windows with glass in all of them,* I dreamed. *It will have brakes, automatic air fresheners, double-padded seats, tires with tread all the way around, and lots and lots of shock absorbers.* In Nanyuki I caught another matatu. *It will have a radio and a built-in cassette player, and both of them will work! And it will have a roof, a hard roof, maybe a double roof!* After two other matatus I finally reached Nairobi.

I was dropped about a half-mile from my requested stop because the matatu driver had somewhere else to go and I was wasting his time. As my bag was summarily tossed after me onto the chipped tarmac road, I said an emphatic goodbye with the foolish conviction this would be the last time I would ever ride in a matatu again! It would not be the last time my delusions would see me through the night. To the sound of the matatu's impatient horn and squealing tires, I picked up my bag and slowly, painfully, shuffled the rest of the way home.

Chapter 2

The Curse of the Maasai

I came back from Samburuland with a concussion and bruised or cracked ribs. "Who's to say?" the doctor informed me. "Either way, the treatment is the same. We can do nothing for you. Go home and rest. Do not ride camels or horses." Sound advice. I was dizzy, nauseous, and could barely lift my arms. For the next few weeks I stayed in Nairobi to heal and build up my courage to get back into a car. While there was no way I could buy a comfortable, reliable, and sturdy car like a Toyota Land Cruiser, I decided to focus on finding the closest thing to it I could afford. There is a saying among anthropologists that the three primary causes of death in the field are: (1) relentless boredom, (2) a horrifically fatal bite or illness, and (3) a road accident, which is the most lethal of all. As to the third option, if I were to die in a road accident, I wanted to be the one driving. But the car would have to wait at least until my body healed.

For my two years in Kenya, I had a much-appreciated second home in Nairobi with David and his two colleagues. The house was provided by the International Livestock Centre for Africa (ILCA), a research organization that in 1994 became part of the International Livestock Research Institute (ILRI). David and his colleagues all worked at ILCA while they conducted doctoral fieldwork among the nearby Maasai. David was studying land use issues, Frank from Florida was doing an economic study similar to mine, and Christie from England was studying the Maasai management of goats.

My Kenyan affiliation was with the Institute for Development Studies at the University of Nairobi, where I prepared a series of papers and lectures on livestock marketing as a part of my two-year study. I was fortunate to get the affiliation, but it did not come with housing.

David was the first of his colleagues to arrive in Kenya. He was tall, skinny, and the life of any party. He was also quick and bright with so many innovative ideas, schemes, and dreams that it was impossible for him to sit down or stop pacing for more than a quick recharge. But for all the space that David commanded, he brimmed with a youthful sweetness that made him endearing even to those—such as myself—he occasionally annoyed.

In contrast, Frank was short and reserved, with black-framed glasses, curly dark, brown hair, and a trimmed moustache. He tried to keep to himself and his Kenyan friends, but David invariably drew him into the household escapades through music and beer.

Christie completed the trio. British and proper, she had sensible shoes and short brown hair; she took no guff from anyone, especially from those she loved. As for her demeanor with strangers, they say good breeding shows, and that was certainly the case with Christie, who could remember her manners in any situation she found herself. She once fended off four street thieves by thrashing about and gripping tightly to her purse strap while politely shouting, "Let go of my bag, PLEASE!"

Other colleagues became close friends as well, including Johan, a Norwegian anthropologist born and raised in Ethiopia and now working with Turkana pastoralists in the far northwest of Kenya. He was ending his ILCA tenure just as David arrived. Among his many admirable traits, Johan owned a Peugeot sedan and shared our love for English-language spy novels. Both were hard to come by and expensive. And it spoke to Johan's generosity that he loaned us both the books and the car for emergencies, on condition we treated them with care. The car was a lot easier to keep clean than the novels, which traveled long distances from person to person, and from city to field, until the cheap paper softened and the pages were more stuffed in than bound in numerical order. In fact, when any friend or acquaintance got hold of a paperback novel, it made the rounds in the same way. We loved those novels. We relied on them to fill the downtime during fieldwork and to divert our attention from mosquito bites, some unidentified rash, or any other temporary discomfort. Turns out they did so much more. I recall one evening in Nairobi when David,

Christie, Frank, Johan, and I were sitting around the house discussing current events. It was 1981, the USSR had recently invaded Afghanistan, President Reagan had taken office, and both he and Brezhnev were rattling swords that threatened an already shaky detente. As we discussed the international situation, we were very impressed with our collective knowledge of Cold War international politics, until Johan wisely pointed out that everything we claimed to know was based on spy novels and the expertise of Robert Ludlum, John le Carré, Martin Cruz Smith, and Ian Fleming.

Another Norwegian anthropologist friend was Frode, who had already completed his doctoral fieldwork among pastoralists in Sudan. He was now working in Turkana with his anthropologist girlfriend, Vigdis. They came to Nairobi rarely and always seemed to wear stainless white linen. They made a dashing couple. And together or apart they were the subject of endless tales of adventure and bravado. Anthropologists always exchange outlandish stories from the field. One of the best came from Frode—the elephant story, which goes something like this: The Sudanese ethnic group Frode lived with hunted in the nude, which is a great way to start off any story. One day the warriors invited Frode to accompany them on an elephant hunt. Frode, embracing the bonding opportunity, grabbed a spear and stripped down to join them. This event might have gone no further than tribal folklore if not for a fortunate coincidence. Frode's academic advisor—who happened to be visiting him in the field—drove by at just the right time and reported seeing the most unusual sight—a group of Sudanese warriors with spears in hand running after a frightened elephant. In the midst of them all was his graduate student Frode, tall and pale, wielding a similar spear and running in nothing but his white Adidas tennis shoes. The news went viral and is no doubt circulating throughout East Africa to this day.

The only mythology circulating about David, Christie, Frank, and me was probably our legendary dance parties. Whenever we all came together in Nairobi it was the rare occasion for a grand party. Christie and Frank moved out the living room furniture; Christie and I prepared the food, which included homemade guacamole; and David selected the music. In terms of invitations, I would draft a short invite at the ILCA office, make a few copies, and pass them around. How they made their way around town is a pre-Internet mystery. We had no reliably working telephones, and cell phones had yet to be invented. Nevertheless, we always had a full house of expats and Kenyans, and the parties lasted well into the morning. We knew most of the people attending, but certainly not all. It was a chance to celebrate, meet new people, and catch up on everyone's work. But those celebratory events were yet to happen.

On this trip, beat up from my car accident, I did not feel like dancing. What I felt like was a failure, a failure without a car. So after a week of this, when David invited me to spend a few days with him at his field site in Maasailand, I eagerly accepted. *Why not?* I was still healing, but he worked only an hour away on a paved road. *Besides*, I thought, *maybe I'll learn something. Maybe I'll see what a real anthropologist does.*

For that particular week, David was starting a new study near Kisamis, a small town near the Ngong Hills southwest of Nairobi. Only a handful of people lived there, but the place included the popular Tokyo Bar (and res-taurant), a butcher shop, and a kraal for animals on market day. David had a field house further south, but for this visit we stayed in the home of his assistant's father, a small, tireless, brick-of-a-man named Apollo. David's Maasai-Kikuyu assistant Peter was Apollo's beloved son, tall, and like his father, he was as gregarious as he was charming. Peter was not only well connected in this part of Maasailand, but he lived with a Danish aid worker in Nairobi, so he knew how to handle European researchers. He was quick and articulate and had little trouble convincing David he had his thumb on the pulse of the Maasai people.

On the day we arrived, we were to meet a Maasai woman in Kisamis and then walk with her to her *nkang* (homestead or settlement), which lay a few miles south of town. She never showed up. So late in the day, while I took a nap, David and Peter set out for the nkang on their own. I was sur-prised to see them return a short two hours later. They explained that after crossing the river and walking for about an hour they realized they'd never make it there before the rains came. Figuring they would be stuck on the far side of the river with no provisions for the night or way back across the river, they decided to return and try again another day.

So this was what fieldwork was like?

The next day we all reconvened for the big meeting—the *baraza* (Swa.)—where Peter would introduce David to the elders so he could explain the next phase of his work and ask for cooperation. It was impor-tant, and David wanted to make sure it came off without a hitch. The baraza was to take place mid-morning at Ole Kumwasi's nkang, and David had paid for a large roasted goat to be served. Somehow Peter had notified all the pertinent elders, or perhaps they just smelled the roasted goat, or perhaps they were meeting there anyway about something entirely different. These things were rarely clear, and I was told you soon grew used to it.

When Peter, David, and I arrived, the goat had already been roasted and was being consumed. There wasn't a lot of conversation as far as we could tell. But the goat was going fast, which meant we should start the meeting very soon. Then, just as the goat was finished, people started walking away.

"Peter!" David said in a fluster. "Where is everyone going?"

"When the meat is gone, they leave," Peter explained.

"What about our baraza?"

"I think they want us to go inside the nkang," Peter offered. But they didn't. So without any apology, or alternative explanation for what just happened, Peter suggested we were wasting our time because no one was left to talk to and it would be better if we returned another day.

"This isn't going at all as I planned," David muttered as we drove back to Kisamis.

Later in the week, while David had yet to hold his introductory baraza, he decided to start conducting the surveys anyway. You don't expect to get totally accurate information from the first survey, but it was a starting point. So off we went to the first nkang.

"Peter," David began, "What's this guy's name?"

"We call him the Fat One."

"I can't call him that. I don't even know him. What should I call him?"

"I don't know. We all know him. We all call him Fat."

"Well, can you introduce me and ask him what I should call him?"

"I can't ask him his name!" Peter spat out, horrified at the suggestion. So, with a heavy sigh David wrote FAT ONE on the survey sheet, called him *apaiya* (father), and proceeded with his survey.

"Ask him how many cattle he has," David continued.

"I can't ask him that either." Peter said, as if repeating the obvious.

"What exactly can you ask?" David inquired of his assistant sarcastically. This started a long conversation about the questions Peter wanted to ask, which had nothing to do with names, livestock, or any of David's work.

Now really, this can't be how fieldwork is supposed to go.

A few days later, David finally had his baraza with the elders at Ole Nena's nkang. It went well, especially when they spotted David's small

four-wheel-drive vehicle, a little green Suzuki with the ILCA logo bla-
zoned on the sides. A company car meant that David didn't pay for the
petrol, something not overlooked by anyone at the meeting. David agreed
he was willing to help them out with transportation if they had emergencies, and then proceeded to introduce his work, his goals, and he thanked
them for their cooperation.

"Yes. Yes. We have many emergencies," they replied. So far, so good.

Things did not go as smoothly with the women of the nkang, who
demanded money or some sort of compensation for doing what they considered was Peter's job.

"We give you all the information and he [meaning Peter] just writes it
down. He does nothing but write and for that you pay him!? Why should
he get all the money? We are the ones with the information!"

Peter explained he had the
pencil and the proper forms and
they didn't. Moreover, he explained he had to follow David
back into Nairobi and do all
kinds of office work that the
women didn't know how to do,
so they should not bother him
anymore about the money.
After a while this seemed to
work, but it had certainly taken
its toll on Peter.

"Don't make me go back in
there and talk to those women

Peter, David's assistant.

again!" he cried. "We do not
need them!"

Back in Nairobi, things were not going much better. David had left a
new questionnaire with Eunice, one of the ILCA secretaries, to type up.
For the rare moments she was actually in the office, Eunice always seemed
to have something much more important to do when David asked about
his questionnaires. He had taken to bribing her with Coffee House meat
pies to get her to pay any attention to his work.

"And where is my meat pie?" she asked indignantly as David walked
into the office after this latest trip to the field. He held up the bag with a

confident grin to prove he had not been slacking off. "Hunh," she snorted and took what was rightfully hers. In response to David's queries about the questionnaire, she reassured him, "Just now." She then picked up and waved around David's questionnaire as proof she would get to it "just now." However, what she meant by "just" and "now" might be something entirely different than what David had in mind. All David knew for sure was it would cost him considerably more meat pies.

Which brings me to the topic of field training. It occurred to me during this expedition that, as official anthropologists, shouldn't we have had some training before being turned out into the field? Did we get some training and I just wasn't paying attention?

We learned a number of quantitative and qualitative research methods, something about statistical analysis, and how to write a kinship chart. We read oodles of ethnographies describing cultures from all over the world. We fantasized about wading waist-deep in leech-infested rivers to reach the most isolated and remote communities. We endlessly debated the big questions: Which came first, language or thought? What is the origin of money? What is the ideal size of a human community? Are there

Maasai elders waiting for the *baraza* to begin.

basic traits that unite people of all cultures? But did we discuss how to introduce ourselves into a community? Not so much.

That's not to say information wasn't available. E. E. Evans-Pritchard's classic 1940 ethnography *The Nuer* painted a more accurate picture of fieldwork in East Africa than any of us suspected at the time. Especially noteworthy is the humorous aside in the Introduction where E. E. describes his efforts to get a warrior to tell him his name.

Then there was the advice we got from returning anthropologists. But many had been in the bush for so long—four, six, 10 years—that we didn't really hear *from* them but *of* them. One colleague was out so long that her thesis advisor told her he was planning on dying and if she didn't get out of the field there would be no one to sign off on her dissertation. Another fellow got circumcised in Khartoum, but that's all I really knew about doing fieldwork in the Sudan.

Our academic advisors did give us some field tips. And while I wouldn't call it training, some proved to be surprisingly useful. Hilda Kuper was a legend in our field. She was a brilliant and generous woman who produced groundbreaking work on culture and ethnic relations in pluralistic Southern Africa. She also knew King Sobhuza II of Swaziland on a first-name basis. A colleague and I house-sat for her and her sociologist husband Leo Kuper one summer, where she gave us several pieces of advice.

"You must learn to hold your liquor," she told us earnestly. "In Swaziland, I ate a pat of butter before attending any function where drinking would occur. It worked quite well."

Yuck, I thought. *I'd have to get drunk before I could eat a pat of butter.* And whether we were discussing theory or practice (or how to operate her dishwasher) she would cryptically warn us: "Remember my dears, it is never really that simple."

My main advisor, Walter Goldschmidt, suggested I cut holes in my tennis shoes to let the water drain out properly, and to take lots of pencils. He also suggested I meet with the primary anthropologist who had previously studied the same people. This being the one piece of advice that clearly seemed worth following, off I went.

In my case this meant a visit to Paul Spencer, a British anthropologist at the School of Oriental and African Studies (SOAS) in London. So, before arriving in Kenya, I made a stop in London to interview the renowned scholar face-to-face. I was incredibly intimidated by the prospect of meeting the great man. When I arrived on campus in search of the faculty lounge, I half expected someone to block my path and direct me to go away. And I would have. But no one seemed to notice me, so inertia drove me indoors to meet Professor Spencer, who was sitting, as I recall, in a tall, imposing velvet chair in the corner.

Professor Spencer had written the classic ethnography on the Samburu in 1965, a mere 17 years prior. I had exchanged a few letters with him and had sent him a coveted English–Maa dictionary I bought on an earlier visit to Nairobi. But this was my first meeting with the man. After some brief introductions, I whipped out my notepad and began to run down my list of questions, preparing to write down everything he said. Perhaps it was me, but I had a hard time understanding exactly what he was talking about. It seemed to be about . . . dancing. Evidently, his current research focus was the social significance of dance among the Maasai, something that sadly none of my questions even touched on. Moreover, he seemed profoundly disappointed once he learned I had not actually completed my fieldwork and I was there not to tell him about my experiences but to ask him about his. He did give me a copy of a verb chart he felt was missing from the English–Maa dictionary, which I kindly thanked him for.

I eventually left for Kenya with a bunch of pencils, holey tennis shoes, a 17-year old ethnography, a Maa verb chart, and not much else in terms of prescribed equipment. In short, we got essentially no field training. Hence the fits and starts I witnessed at Kisamis may be pretty much par for the course.

David, however, had to deal with another obstacle, something he called *the curse of the Maasai*. As opposed to the traditional Maasai or Samburu curse, which was a commanding power held by elders, this curse was entirely made up by David to explain his severe procrastination. The curse went something like this: *You may study and live among us as many have done before you. But few will publish anything.* There were various explanations for this curse: (1) the Maasai are so accessible you never stop collecting data; (2) there are so many researchers, many of whom are Maasai themselves, you fear getting it wrong and never finish; and (3) the curse is real. But I favor a fourth explanation, (4) Nairobi.

The Maasai territory covers about 39,000 square miles across central, southern Kenya and northern Tanzania, with the Maasai themselves divided into between 18 and 22 sections or *iloshon* (Maasai autonomous political units) depending on who you ask. For those studying the Keekonyokie Maasai or the Loodokilani Maasai, Nairobi is only about 50 miles away. Unlike many capitals in sub-Saharan Africa, Nairobi has a large expat community, a well-established and cosmopolitan tourist trade, and the services that cater to them. It could be tough for anthropologists, especially the ones afflicted with acute time-management problems, to compete with the many distractions of the city. How could you leave for the field today when they were starting the Truffaut Film Festival at the French Cultural Center? French actress Catherine Deneuve was spotted recently at the famous Norfolk hotel. And River Road had the best Indian restaurants in the country. If you missed America, you could always hang out at Buffalo Bill's restaurant with its wagon wheel decor, Pepsi lampshades, Neil Young music, and saddles for counter stools. The only indication you were in Kenya was that the place was filled with Kenyans and non-US expats eating their hamburgers with silverware.

Best of all, if you had a home base as David did in Nairobi, there was a place to hang out with friends, drink Kenyan coffee, and read the morning paper. Then, there was always a household project that kept you from returning to the field, such as a really challenging jigsaw puzzle.

As for me, I was distracted in Nairobi, not just by my injuries, but by two very important projects I took up in earnest during the last few days of my recovery: (1) searching for a vehicle I could afford; and (2) organizing and labeling all the household music cassette tapes.

During my convalescence I noticed the cassettes were in a complete jumble and people came by to borrow them and never returned them. Seeing a clear solution to this untenable situation, I typed up The Master List of cassette titles in alphabetical order, assigning a number to each. Then I attached a corresponding sticky number to each cassette and arranged them numerically on the shelf. I also typed up a checkout form so we could record who took what tape, when it was taken, and when it was returned. It wasn't a perfect system because it depended on voluntary compliance. But I just couldn't figure out any way around that. I also had my doubts it would be properly maintained when I wasn't there. For one thing, when I explained the procedures to David and his housemates over breakfast, they just stared at me in silence. And it wasn't the kind of silence that precedes a sudden burst of applause. It was the kind of silence that precedes an uncomfortable ride to the Shady Pines Home for the Bewildered.

"This is what you've been doing at the typewriter all this time?" David asked, looking a little worried.

I could tell it was time for me to leave the big city and head back to Samburu District. My body had adequately healed, the music tapes were in perfect order, and as you will see, I had acquired my own vehicle. Moreover, I had actually learned a few things about fieldwork, the two most important being these:

1. Be wary of working with a community that has cursed incoming anthropologists.
2. This is clearly going to take longer than I had planned.

Chapter 3

Samburu in a Nutshell

I may not have been prepared, trained, or well equipped, but I was nonetheless confident and eager to return to Samburuland and begin "doing fieldwork." Correction: "doing fieldwork" and driving my own car!

Before leaving Nairobi, I finally bought my very own used, white, long wheelbase Land Rover. It belonged to Aude Talle, a universally beloved Norwegian anthropologist who was getting ready to leave the field and needed to sell her car. I was able to afford it because it was in the country under somewhat dubious customs declarations, which brought down the price considerably. I loved that car. It was huge. I had to jump up to get into the driver's seat. I sat high on the road and could easily carry four jerry cans of petrol, plus passengers. Who knew those great qualities were going to cause me so much trouble? Not I. For now, the car meant freedom, and I couldn't buy it fast enough.

A few days later I was on the road, packed to the brim with field supplies and country music singer Crystal Gayle blaring from my portable cassette tape player on the passenger seat next to me. Driving through pounding rain, I reached Thomson's Falls three hours later, decidedly more tired than when I had hit the road so cheerfully that morning. T-Falls and the recently renamed town of Nyahururu were at a major milestone, where the tarmac ended and the dirt road began.

While the rains were a blessing for the Samburu, they caused me no end of trouble. And while the locals prayed for rain, I secretly cursed it.

Nothing stayed dry. Water poured into the Land Rover through the poorly sealed windows and for some reason from underneath the dashboard. My feet, legs, and the left side of my body were soaking wet, and I periodically wondered if I could be electrocuted through the headphones of my cassette player. Outside the car, the dirt road north of T. Falls had turned to mud and the black cotton soil was nearly impossible to drive in. How could soil be as slippery as ice one moment, and gain the suction power of quicksand the next?! I could hardly steer the car straight when the rains first hit. And when the soil formed mud, I risked being stuck like a bug in the thick, sticky gumbo. Several people recounted how a small Volkswagen had sunk completely below the surface in a matter of minutes. (Other people swore the story was ludicrous! *Who on Earth would import a VW Beetle into Kenya? It's got no ground clearance!*) After 25 miles of this, I was cold, wet, and sorely in need of a break.

Cora was the daughter of white Kenyan farmers who owned a farm and cattle ranch in Rumuruti. I met her during my first month in Nairobi, and she had invited me to stop by the farm when I got up north. Bone-tired as I was, and finding myself just outside her town, now seemed like the perfect time for what I thought would be a short diversion. While their home was only a few miles off the main road, the soil was so rain-slick, potholed, and rutted that it took me nearly an hour to get there. One problem with the Land Rover was that to get it into four-wheel drive, I needed to pull a lever inside the car, then exit *outside* the car to adjust a knob on the front left wheel. Each time meant slipping down and fumbling in the rain, mud, and muck. Moreover, I had yet to learn any tricks to driving in the slippery-sticky black cotton soil. I swerved, slid, sunk, stuck, and finally slunk up to Cora's front door—only to find that my friend was out of town. Needless to say, after taking one look at my drowned-cat appearance, her mother opened wide the door and insisted I stay for dinner and spend the night. She didn't have to ask me twice. I sat on her couch wrapped in a blanket and Cora's dry clothes, feeling much relieved to be off the road. Before she could bring in the tea, I had fallen sound asleep.

When Kenya was colonized in the early 20th century, the British Crown Lands Ordinance of 1902 declared that all Kenya belonged to the Queen and promptly evicted the Maasai from their traditional lands in the fertile central highlands to make way for an influx of European settlers.

The relocation of the Maasai (by treaty), along with farming subsidies and other programs created to support immigrating British farmers, established what became known as the White Highlands. Since Kenya's independence in 1963, much of the land has been sold back to Kenyan nationals through various means. However, the process has been hotly debated for—among other things—favoring particular ethnic groups, the wealthy, and British loyalists. The unresolved land question continues to haunt Kenya today. And politicians, up to the present leaders, are repeatedly pressed by citizens to address what many consider to be Kenya's continuing unjust land tenure system.

In this environment, Cora's family had stayed on. They had deep roots in this central highland community and by 1981 were farming the land jointly with Kenyan co-owners. They kept cows, goats, and chickens, and made cheese to sell in the market. But for someone so well-known in her small community, Cora's mother struck me as quite lonely. She seemed like a woman whose friends had all gone away, or perhaps she was too tired to visit them. She made it clear she was not happy with the way the farm was being managed, but there was nothing to be done about it. Her husband was a man of few words, and he seemed to guard them judiciously. Cora, their only daughter, was in love with a South African big game hunter and had plans that clearly did not include staying in Rumuruti. I left after breakfast the next day, thanking her profusely for the hospitality and the armful of cheese she insisted I take for the road ahead. She gave me a long, firm hug, and I made plans to visit again on my next trip north.

While the weather was a bit better that day, the road conditions were worse. Dense, churned up mud filled the dirt road from Cora's farm all the way to Maralal. It was so hard to control the car, slipping through that mud. And when it wasn't slipping and had finally gotten purchase of the road, I was haunted by the cautionary tale of the buried VW Beetle. I had been driving like this for about two hours, when something caught my attention in my rearview mirror. With a disorienting sense of vertigo, I first thought my car was tipping over backwards, but I quickly realized it was the Land Rover's back ladder, detaching itself and falling away from the car! I was losing my ladder! Slamming on the breaks, I slid across the road to a stop, jumped out, and watched as the ladder fell completely off and sank slowly beneath the unforgiving black mud until it was gone, gone, mostly gone.

I stood by the side of the road in the now pouring rain, letting the water run out through the holes in my shoes. *Is it too early to quit?* I asked myself. A part of me tried to muster the strength to carry on: *You are almost there!* But another part of me was quick to respond: *Who are you kidding? This is the easy part—driving to the field. How are you going to cope with the hard parts of fieldwork?* A third voice in my head pointed out, *You don't have to do this. Nobody is forcing you to be a field anthropologist. There is no shame in good, honest library research!* The final voice came from way in the back. *If you quit now, do you have to return the grant money?* I was beyond frustration, beyond anger, and just bone tired, completely incapable of mediating between my combative inner voices. But it didn't matter. In actuality, quitting was never an option for me. I had wanted this for too long—this completely arbitrary career choice. I wanted to be an anthropologist. My whole life I had dreamed of doing my own fieldwork, or so it seemed at the time.

After dragging the ladder out of the mud, I threw it into the back of the vehicle on top of my bags and jerry cans—mud, water, and all—thinking I could perhaps reattach it later, and slammed the door. (I eventually gave the ladder to Pascal, who felt he could use it for something, and I never missed it.)

Northward I plowed for another hour and a half until I reached Maralal and Josephine's front door. I was worn out, shaking, and caked with mud. Words were screaming in my head: *What happened to the drought? There is supposed to be a drought! I was promised a drought!*

But as soon as I saw Josephine's open face, with that warm, embracing smile, I calmed down to simple exhaustion. Here was Josephine, who didn't know when I would return and had no way of expecting me, welcoming me with open arms. She took one look at me and started to boil water so I could take a warm shower and then change into dry clothes. Together with her seven children we dined on *githeri* (a traditional boiled maize and bean dish), and after dinner I sank into the low wooden chair on the front porch to catch up on the news. Pascal was off in Wamba, on the other side of Samburu District, seeing a doctor about his stomach ailments and was not due back until tomorrow. So tonight it was just Josephine, her exuberant children, and *National Geographic*. She picked the magazine off the top of the pile and skimmed through it to find her place.

"In New Zealand, they have porous and nonporous rocks, isn't it?"

Suddenly, her daughter Regina cut in with a question for me.

"Do you ever comb your hair?" Before I could answer, Josephine responded for me, "Of course not! Now go to bed!" It was clear that Josephine wanted some adult time, alone with me and *Nat Geo*. With all the kids tucked into bed, Josephine and I talked about New Zealand, our families, and our work, as the moon rose high, the cicadas grew loud, and the mosquitos grew fat because no matter how tired we were, neither of us wanted to go to bed.

"Best of all," cooed Josephine "you brought the rain. We are all so happy you brought the rain!" And through her sweet eyes, that damn rain began to look like an almost blessed event.

Finding a Samburu assistant was my next big hurdle.

"No problem, no problem," Pascal told me. He had returned from Wamba and was going to help me 100 percent. "We will find the best person for you, someone who is 100 percent!"

Josephine and Pascal immediately sprang into action, sending out the word, screening all applicants, and running background checks. They nearly set up a desk and sign-in sheet in their front yard. The few candidates that met their approval were interviewed by the three of us.

"This one is a friend of a friend of George. You talk to him; ask him anything." Turns out it didn't matter what I asked because he didn't speak English except for, "Money. How much?" The second applicant was pushed in front of us by his father. He so convincingly showed his contempt for the job that even the ever-optimistic Pascal got exasperated.

"No. No. He is not fit!"

Next! But there was no next.

"Pascal, these can't be the only people interested in the job?!" I asked plaintively.

"Well, you know it is difficult."

"But you said it would be no problem!"

"No problem. Just one problem. Samburu men go to the Air Force. The pay is much better. Just that problem."

I nodded in silence, pondering my next move. Luckily, I didn't have to ponder long.

The next day, Pascal delivered one last applicant. I wasn't about to ask where he came from because he was perfect. One hundred percent! He was a wildlife ranger's son and had completed his form three education. Good English. Manners were great. Plus he had Samburu relatives in the nearby countryside. After ascertaining that he wasn't on furlough from prison or otherwise currently engaged, we proceeded to the next step, asking his father for permission. His father and mother lived in the complex up the hill behind Pascal and Josephine's house, and they were waiting for us outside when we arrived. In a country with no working telephones, news sure traveled fast. Anyway, after meeting me, receiving assurance from Pascal that I indeed owned a working vehicle, the father quickly agreed to let his son take the job. "Not so fast," said an elderly relative who was either living there or visiting at the time. This Samburu gentleman wanted more information about *my* family. With the son translating, the old man began, first repeating the previous question that he either hadn't heard or had forgotten.

"Do you have a vehicle?"

"How can you stay here alone without your family?"

"Does your father have cattle?"

This last question was a big one. When they found out my father had no cattle, they had a hard time understanding how a white person could be so poor, and how could I afford to then pay an assistant. In an attempt to lighten the mood, which I felt was beginning to sour, I mentioned that I had two cats. I knew the Samburu also had cats to keep away rodents and snakes, and I thought that in the context of pastoralism they'd find this amusing. They did.

"Ah, your family herds cats!"

"How many cats?"

"Do you eat them?"

"How much does a good fat cat go for?"

In fact, they found it extremely amusing. On the plus side, it got me an assistant. On the negative side, the joke was so good it quickly spread throughout the region. And unbeknownst to me at the time, I was known for the entire two years of my stay as the *cat herder*. I suppose I've been called worse.

So Joseph was hired! I finally had my field assistant. As it turned out, he wouldn't last long. But I'm getting ahead of myself.

The next task was to decide where to set up a home base. I identified a location on the Lorroki plateau that seemed perfect. It was situated close to both seasonal grasslands and forest resources, with chilly winters and mild summers. Kisima, a secondary market along the main road to Maralal, was only an hour's walk away. It was home to the seminomadic Samburu primarily of the Lmasula clan, with the Lpisikishu clan nearby and some Ndorobo people in the adjacent forest. This provided some diversity to be able to study clan relations as they related to livestock marketing.

In the foothills of the forest were a Catholic church and a primary school. A Samburu blacksmith lived nearby. Over 80 percent of the nkang'itie had a small garden plot in addition to their animals: cattle, sheep, and goats. While there was no electricity, running water, phone connections, or services of any kind, there was a reservoir and creek that supplied water throughout the year. And with a borehole for pumping water nearby, all the community needed were the pipes laid to bring water to a central spigot. The pastoralists were primarily subsistence based, but not exclusively so. In terms of livestock market participation, this region had been a key supplier of immature livestock to be fattened down south, yet little was known about the private trading sector (the internal system of exchanges) or the reasons for the considerable fluctuations in commercial livestock sales. Here was a traditional Samburu community with emerging market opportunities on their doorstep. It was just what I was looking for in order to explore the incentives and constraints to commercial livestock marketing. Now, if I could just find a house to rent and get people to talk to me!

The primary school was run by a group of about four Kikuyu teachers and one Samburu teacher. This ratio was not unusual, as few Samburu at the time went beyond primary education, and fewer still went into education as a profession. There were all kinds of explicit and implicit barriers and incentives for one's career choice in Kenya just as in any country. Samburu men who left the pastoral sector usually became security guards or went into the Air Force. There were other options, but those were the roads most traveled and well-greased. Being educated by Kikuyus—an ethnic group resented by many in Kenya because of their large political influence—could cause significant tension in a non-Kikuyu community. I saw a great deal of that during my two-year stay, but not on the day when Joseph and I drove up to the school to inquire about housing. The Kikuyu headmaster greeted Joseph and me warmly, and after an easy discussion about my work, he let me stay in a spare room for free.

The room offered to me had mud and cow dung walls, a corrugated tin roof, dirt floor, and shared walls with the two adjacent rooms. Across the central courtyard was the one-room elementary school and adjoining storehouse. Down the dirt track toward the reservoir was an outhouse. It was perfect, and after two days of cleaning out the cobwebs and purchasing some basic supplies, I moved in my trunk, cot, desk and chair, barrel for water, paraffin gas stove with a pot, two bowls, two mugs, a knife, and two spoons. The first act in my new home would be to boil water for tea and celebrate with Joseph and the school headmaster, provided that one of them brought his own mug.

Day One: Acquire a Cat

That evening I drove Joseph back to Maralal and spent the night with Josephine and Pascal. As it turned out, I would spend many evenings with them throughout the next two years, as they became amateur anthropologists themselves, analyzing my experiences with me. The next day I woke up early, picked up Joseph, and sailed up to my new home. Sure, I noticed a few bumps as I crossed into the schoolyard, but the road was so rutted that I didn't give it another thought, and I would have preferred to keep it that way. Sadly that did not happen.

As soon as I stepped down from the car, local boys surrounded me. This happened to me nearly every time I arrived. But on this occasion, they were excited to tell me the latest local news—the latest news being that I had just driven over two little kittens and crushed them to death.

"WHAT?!"

"You killed the kittens. Dead. *Kabisa* [completely]."

"Oh my God. I am so sorry. I feel just awful!"

"Why?"

"Because I killed all the kittens!"

"No, not all. There is one you did not kill. If you want kittens, take this one." By now a much larger crowd of children and adults had gathered around us, and all agreed that I could and should take the kitten.

"No. I don't want any kittens; I just don't want to kill them," I protested.

"No problem," Joseph kept saying, translating the conversation to me continually even though it was all said in English and I didn't need to hear over and over how I had killed two kittens. Yes. All agreed. They were nobody's animals and they were just kittens. Yet, seeing as I was still feeling quite sad, they insisted that I hold the remaining black and white kitten, no more than two months old.

"Here, you take this kitten. Very alive. Very good kitten. Will make fine animal. Your father will be proud." This last bit was in reference to the fact that by now the entire community seemed to know about my father The Cat Herder. *How was this possible? How could this story have spread so far so fast? And yes, Daddy would be so proud.* That is how I acquired Bruno the cat, who was to live with me in highland Samburu throughout my fieldwork. When I eventually left Kenya, I found a very nice home for Bruno with the nine-year-old daughter of a prostitute working in the Starlight Lounge in Nairobi. She adored him. So there is no need to worry about Bruno. Things turned out quite nicely for him.

Day Two: Meet the Chief (or at least the subchief)

After acquiring the cat, my next step was to introduce myself to the local chief, show him my permits and papers, brief him on my work, and ask for his cooperation. In this region there was only a subchief, a very warm and agreeable fellow named Lekar. We drove out to his modest home on the Lorroki plateau and were very fortunate to find him at home and able to see us without delay. He welcomed us into his living room and offered us a seat on the comfortable sofa while he sat across from us in a large, wooden arm chair. Over a nice cup of Kenyan tea, I presented my papers and explained that my work involved gaining a better understanding of Samburu pastoral economic decision making.

"Anthropologists in general study culture, those shared values, beliefs and behaviors we learn and practice as a member of society, as well as the social relations of that society. My focus has always been on economic practices in tribal societies, that is, societies that are only loosely tied into the national economy and depend primarily on trading with one another. What cultural norms and social ties guide these practices of gifting, trade, loans, and other economic exchanges? How do people and a culture change when the economy changes? What are the core cultural beliefs, practices, and social relations that give life meaning and that support socioeconomic change over time?"

"Do you have a vehicle?" Subchief Lekar asked me after listening attentively and nodding approvingly over my research permit.

"Why, yes I do."

"Then proceed." I was pleased that the subchief understood the difficulty of transportation in such a huge region and wanted to make sure I was taken care of. How thoughtful. So, I proceeded to explain what brought me to Samburuland.

"Traditionally, the Samburu do not sell their cattle on the commercial market but accumulate them in great numbers for social and cultural purposes. The interesting thing about the Samburu is that while they do not raise cattle primarily for sale, they do use them for socioeconomic transactions within their community. I probably don't have to tell you that the very word *capital* is, after all, derived from *cattle*. One theory of pastoralist society is that they do not think of their livestock in economic terms, do not respond to market forces the way rational capitalists do, and they never will. Another theory holds that pastoralists are rational capitalists and respond to the normal market forces of pricing, infrastructure, and investment opportunities. If markets are developed, the pastoralists will sell their stock, and this market economy can work in conjunction with traditional pastoralist culture—that cultures evolve. In short, if you build it, they will come. Of course there is nuance to both these viewpoints, as I'm sure a man of your position appreciates." At this point in our conversation I noticed he was distracted by something on the floor, or perhaps he was falling asleep, so I cut to my big finish.

"In a nutshell," I explained, "highland Samburuland is at a perfect economic stage for study, and a community near Maralal is the perfect location. The nearby district capital has a post office, shops, two hotels, a local elementary school, a hospital and health clinic, and plans for a bank. In short, it's a place that could support further economic growth. And while there has been no petrol over the past several years, a brand new petrol station speaks of even better times to come. More importantly, the infrastructure to buy and sell livestock is also emerging. There is a cattle kraal in town with a daily marketplace open from 8:00 a.m. to 4:30 p.m. There is demand for beef from the growing urban centers, and the main road to the capital has recently been graded, making it passable year round. This could accommodate competitive buying and efficient transport of cattle downcountry. The question among cattle buyers and the

Kenyan nation is, in what ways will the pastoral Samburu respond to market forces and become integrated into the greater Kenyan economy or remain marginalized? With increasing economic choices available, what guides Samburu economic decisions, and what is the cultural impact on these pastoral communities?"

"Good! Good!" responded the subchief supportively, jolted awake by the sudden lull in the conversation. "And you will give me a ride in your vehicle from time to time, isn't it?"

Seeing me nod in agreement, he stood, promised to call a baraza of the leading elders, and vowed they would all cooperate.

"*Hakuna tabu* [No problem, Swa]." And with that the subchief abruptly stood up and walked outside, leaving Joseph and me sitting alone in his living room to conclude the meeting.

"I guess that went well, right?" I asked.

Day Three: Meet the Elders

Sure enough, a few days later, we got word that the subchief had called a baraza and we should wait at the designated clearing on the designated day under a large shade tree. And there we waited, and waited, and waited, until someone who was wandering by told us that while we could wait there, there would be no baraza, and we were just wasting our time. Why he knew this and we didn't was beyond me. But I was beginning to see this as a recurring pattern. The random fellow passing by seemed to know my schedule or what it should be better than I did. Always.

"OK. Joseph, you have family here. Can we talk to them? I'd really like to talk to someone today." As luck would have it, he had some cousins living nearby and we ducked into their nkang for an impromptu chat. A nkang consists of a group of one to four (or more) houses built in a rough circle around a central area left clear for livestock. The settlement is surrounded by a thorn bush fence to keep out predators in the evening. Each herd owner has his own gate in the fence that is opened every morning to let the animals out to pasture.

It was through the gate of Joseph's family that we entered and walked over to the short dome-shaped house of his relative. Joseph announced us, and after we were invited to enter we walked into the home's low, dark opening and through a switchback entryway. The entire *nkaji* (house) was made of wooden poles and sticks, lined with leaves on the inside walls, and roof. A layer of livestock dung sealed the roof and inside walls, and hardened to make a perfect plaster. Once inside, I could see absolutely nothing. It was pitch black, and I was thankful when someone reached out to lead me to my designated seat. When my eyes adjusted, I could see that the entrance hallway emptied into one room that served as living room, kitchen, storeroom, and bedroom, with a side space that was fenced off for young stock when they needed special attention. There was a fire circle near the middle of the room with only a tiny window high on the wall close to the ceiling for ventilation. While the smoke took some time to get used to, I understood that the system was very successful at keeping the flies out. On either side of the fire circle were two platforms made of stretched hides that served as seating areas by day and beds by night. Thatched interior walls gave the beds privacy on three sides and made for an intimate conversation area around the fire. And the whole place was swept so clean that the dirt floor didn't seem to kick up a bit of dust.

It was a typical size for an nkaji, no more than 100 square feet and 5'5" from floor to ceiling. Looking around, I was very impressed with how much stuff the family had squeezed into such a small space. Pots and utensils hung from wooden hooks on the wall behind the fire. Underneath each bed was a storage space stuffed full of wood, trunks, and other belongings. As I sat on the bed, the room steadily filled with women and children. In fact, I felt a bit like a clown in one of those circus cars, with the addition of a fire blazing in the middle.

After the customary greetings, they dug right in and started peppering *me* with questions, mostly about who I was and why I was there. Then with everyone relaxed, and warm tea in our bellies, they asked me what seemed to be the main thing on their minds: "How can you live all alone away from your family? Aren't you terribly lonely? Aren't you afraid?"

It was the same question I was to get over and over, and one I found very touching. It was a question you could imagine being asked of any lone traveler visiting any community at any point in time. Finally, they warmly told me I could treat their nkang as my home. And it would certainly be nice if I could give them a ride to Kisima and Maralal in my vehicle from time to time.

"Of course," I replied.

Leaving the smoke-filled nkaji, I said good evening to Joseph and his cousins and returned to the school and to my new home. The teachers were gathered in the schoolyard drinking beer and chatting, so I excused myself and retired to my little room. Lying on my cot, I looked at the ceiling and tried to reflect on this issue of being alone. Instead, I got distracted by a more pressing question: *WHERE IS THAT ONE DAMN CRICKET?* The chirping was endless from sunset to sunrise, and I would never find him. But looking up, I noticed for the first time that the mud walls did not extend all the way to the metal roof; there was a gap joining all four rooms in the row together. *That's unfortunate*, I said to myself. It was another reminder that while I was alone, and often lonely, I longed to be alone, because I was never alone!

Day Four through Day Eight: Try to Complete Day-Three Work

The subchief assured me all would be taken care of, and sure enough, on the new designated day under the baraza tree there was a crush of elders. The meeting started with important business about the upcoming election, and why Lalaikiar is running again when even his own father will not vote for him and isn't it time for others to step forward? I knew I was on the agenda somewhere, but I could not take my turn until I got the nod. More speakers, more business, and two hours passed. All the while and one-by-one, elder after elder was "pushed asleep." The expression is apt, because just as it sounds, an elder would suddenly fall over where he sat on the grass and pull his blanket over his entire body. There he would lie on his back as if newly deceased and waiting for the coroner to arrive. By the time it was my turn to talk, the macabre scene had grown to an entire field of sleeping elders, all supine, covered by their red blankets, still as corpses. The few elders who remained awake sat staring at the ground or into space. Through an appraising eye, one elder asked Joseph, "Does she understand any Samburu?"

"No. She doesn't understand anything," he replied.

"Well, I understood that!" I reminded him. But I understood not much else. So I communicated in rudimentary Swahili with a few Samburu words sprinkled about, filling in the rest in English. Lord only knows what

Joseph translated and what the elders heard. I presented my papers and my authority to conduct my study, told them about my work and what I would be talking to them about. The ones who remained awake responded cryptically, "*Ashe* [thanks]," before wandering off in search of, most likely, alcohol: *muratina* (honey beer) being a locally brewed favorite. The only person who came up and expressed any real interest in assisting me was Lekaso, who agreed to show me his *shamba* (garden, Swa.) after which, I could invite him to a meal, which he would graciously accept.

I'm not ashamed to say I jumped at the opportunity since it was the best offer I'd had all day. His shamba was close by and no bigger than his nkaji. We stood beside his harvest: carrots, green tomatoes, and a gigantic orange pumpkin. I felt like I was hallucinating. I knew the Samburu in this area (excluding the warriors) had recently added ugali (cornmeal porridge) to their diet of milk and meat. Some people were also eating vegetables such as beans, cabbage, and potatoes to "become educated" as one elder told me. But do they now eat this variety of vegetables?

"Take whatever you want," Lekaso generously offered. "Maybe you want this gourd."

"Well, if you are not going to eat it, what are you going to do with all this?" I asked.

"*Maiyolo* [I don't know]," he shrugged. "Maybe sell it to somebody."

The Samburu were indeed experimenting with agriculture to supplement their diet and income, with seeds provided by the government. The results were mixed. Some people were successful on a small scale, others not so much, especially those like Lekaso who were given seeds without adequate instruction. In addition to not knowing how to grow the crops, he had no idea what part of the plant to eat, if it was to be cooked or eaten raw, picked green or red. His garden was infested with aphids, something was nibbling the leaves, birds ate his tomatoes, and then there were the elephants.

Forest elephants were a real problem in this region. More aggressive than the bush elephants, they trampled gardens, destroyed crops, and at times killed children who failed to get out of their way. The Samburu had little recourse, as the elephants were protected by law and could not be harmed. Compounding the problem, the Samburu understood elephants to have many human-like qualities, such as their ability to act individually with intent. This meant the Samburu took the destructive behavior of individual elephants quite personally. To protect the elephants from angry

Samburu and to compensate the farmers for their loss, the government had a policy of paying the Samburu compensation (if the policy conditions were met) for both loss of life and loss of crops. The result was that you could see Samburu planting a very interesting assortment of crops and why I could occasionally secure locally grown delicious tomatoes, squash, and other vegetables, as long as I could get to them before the bugs, birds, and elephants.

Day Nine: Give Up Keeping a Schedule

From time to time I would be a guest lecturer for the primary school kids. On day nine I gave a lecture about American livestock to the two highest primary grades, bringing in some *National Geographic* magazines I borrowed from Josephine. Despite my efforts to stick to my notes, the students prevailed with their own agenda, and I spent the hour just answering assorted questions about America. They were fascinated when they saw the photos of the tall skyscrapers in US cities. One boy asked me if a person could fall off when climbing up those tall stairs. Another boy asked if we eat donkeys or bugs. Everyone wanted to hear about the wild animals of America. They thought the rattlesnake was terrifying because it spoke to you before striking. The most fearsome of all was the bear because it had huge teeth and claws like a lion but could run on two legs like a man! Nearly everything I said elicited cackles of laughter. All my lectures went that way, and I was always greeted with enthusiastic applause. No wonder my fieldwork was getting off to a slow start.

Another group I met with repeatedly was the local government officials in Maralal, who were eager to give me the big-picture view of Samburu economic behavior. While they were not Samburu, they had lived there a long time and were happy to tell me all about the Samburu even though *it was all very simple and I was wasting my time talking to a bunch of Samburu for two years.* In a nutshell it was this: *The Samburu have little use for cities or money or the things in life that we value. They don't sell their livestock because they like to keep them around. These Samburu are like that. It's just the way they are.*

The district official thought I was further wasting my time examining past years' market sales receipts, but I was free to review the ledgers if that was how I wished to pass the day. And he graciously had an assistant bring the ledgers to a desk I could use in the corner of one of the district offices. The ledgers—and I use the term very loosely—were slips of receipts. Some years were bundled together with string and stored in boxes. But it didn't take long for this system and string to break down. I reached into a box of paper and let the first batch of handwritten receipts fall from my fingertips. Sticking his head in the office as he left for the day, the district official offered a few final words of advice.

"I should mention that these receipts are not all complete."

No matter. This was a start. So, deep in concentration I sat, sorting and recording receipts, and providing humor to those in the office who walked by me for days on end, shaking their heads in amazement.

Whether complete or even accurate, I told myself that, through volume, I was gathering a rough idea of the pattern of livestock sales—what kinds of animals were sold, for how much, and when. Now, I only needed to find out *who* sold stock and *why*. Also, I probably should get a more accurate picture of the *what* and *how much*, and while I was at it, I really had no confidence in the pattern of *where* and *when*. My next step was to map out the territory and start my household surveys. For this I focused on my next task—putting together a map and questionnaire.

Census Begins

The first questionnaire was fairly straightforward. This was something I actually knew how to do. I had a map of the region I wanted to survey. On this I would identify all the residents, select a random sample of 98 households, and conduct a livestock and household survey along with a short interview. The purpose of this initial set of interviews was to introduce myself, figure out who lived where, get an overall impression of the composition and size of people's herds, and see where I wanted to follow up. To start me off, the district official gave me a list of the region's 335 group ranch members and their livestock holdings. The group ranch was a land tenure system established in Kenya's pastoral districts in the mid-1960s. It subdivided the pastoral areas into communally owned rangelands. The government's intent was to link pastoralists by membership to a specific grazing area to encourage settlement, environmental stewardship, and commercial marketing. With the membership list and holdings to check my data, I could see this was going to be a piece of cake.

The next day, Joseph and I started work at the crack of 2:00 p.m. because Joseph didn't show up until then. I spread the geographic map on my table and, with the list of the local group ranch membership, attempted to plot where people lived. It was a good idea and would have been even better if Joseph could read a map, knew any local families beyond his own, or if either of us knew the neighborhood. But clearly we could collectively do none of those things. No matter. We would start the old-fashioned way, walking the territory, home by home, plotting the households on the map as we went, which was exactly what we did. Along the way, I was able to engage two more local Samburu young men, John and Symon, who agreed to help me with the census.

Symon seemed the most promising. His father was one of the leaders of the community, and Symon himself was a warrior with a side job teaching in the adult education school of Maralal. His Swahili was excellent and his English quite good. Moreover, he was a well-respected and responsible young man. So naturally, he already had a lot of stuff to do and was not available to work as my assistant beyond this one project.

Many anthropologists rely on a local assistant or two, depending on the nature of the study, time constraints, and translation needs. Local assistants can also be helpful for access into a segment of the community. That said, I had no idea how previous anthropologists went about finding an assistant. THEY NEVER TAUGHT US THAT IN SCHOOL. For me, it was a matter of trial and error and a few blunders until I finally just got lucky. But at this point, I was oblivious to the rocky road ahead, and I felt secure in the belief that I had hit the jackpot on my first try. And why wouldn't I be? Within a month we completed the census and a whole slew of interviews. Everything was going along swimmingly, until one evening after a long day of work, as I sat in my little room reading over the day's notes, there came a gentle knock on the door. I opened it and there stood Joseph holding in his hand a neat white envelope. *Uh-oh*, I thought. *This sort of thing never goes well.*

"For you," said Joseph, and he pushed the envelope in my direction. I knew it was bad news, and I didn't want to take it—no less open it and read what was inside. But he stood there, looking at me. What could I do? I opened the envelope and took out what felt like the weight of the world.

I could tell it took him a long time to write it; it was three pages of small, tight handwriting on lined paper. I can't recall any of the specifics, for I only read it once. It was a love letter, a sincere and sweet love letter from him to me. *Darn!* He had been such a good assistant. Head down, I scanned the entire letter, all the while frantically thinking: *Is there any way I can make this go away and pretend nothing ever happened?* If there was, I couldn't come up with it.

By the time I finished reading the letter, I had composed myself and figured out how I was going to handle this. I looked him straight in the eye and said, "Joseph, I am so very flattered. But I have to tell you the truth." And I proceeded to lie. I lied about having a husband in Nairobi. I lied about not being able to keep the letter for fear my husband would find it. And I may have left the slight impression that David would beat us both mercilessly if he heard anything about this letter. In sum, I told Joseph, "For both our sakes, we must never speak of this again." I only hoped he would never see the film from where I got that line. He left the next morning without saying goodbye, and I later found out that he joined the Air Force. It was certainly a move up, and I was comforted by knowing he would at least see a significant raise in pay.

Luckily, John was able to step up his hours, and I quickly promoted him to Number One Assistant. If anyone could be the exact opposite of shy and diligent Joseph, it was overly confident and charming John. While not the bookish model of responsibility I was looking for, he was standing right in front of me, and available. *Why not?* I thought. *What's the worst that could happen?* Well, it turns out that the worst that could happen did happen. Behind my back, John was extorting money from the households we were interviewing. It was a kind of bizarro pay-to-play scheme that didn't even make sense to the Samburu. Yes, sly old John turned out to be a crook. After I fired him, I spent the next few weeks wandering around apologizing to everyone I had met. Amazingly enough, no one ever seemed to hold me responsible, as they believed John had charmed and duped me. Let's face it, I was not having much luck with assistants. At this point, I'd run out of locally available young men, and I was starting to worry that I might be getting a slutty reputation, or at least a reputation as a real dimwit.

On the plus side, I was now enjoying the Third Month Delusional High, common among anthropologists, which stemmed from the belief that I finally had it all figured out. Everyone was friendly and answered every question with a response that sounded pretty darn good. My charts were filling up with names and numbers, and my brain was forming all this information into neat and meaningful patterns.

In a nutshell, the Samburu do not sell more cattle because the livestock are more valuable in the nonmonetary economy.

"What use is money?" one elder told me, "Money runs through the fingers like sand. My cattle serve me throughout their lives, and when they die, I can eat them."

Much has been written about how cattle are mainly used as bride-price and that a Samburu man cannot marry without them. In terms of bride-price, the father of the groom gives a negotiated number of animals to the bride's father in compensation for his losing a daughter and her future offspring. But cattle are exchanged in other ways too. Quite often cattle are loaned or traded. Cattle are traded for ritual purposes, to change herd composition, or to secure a certain animal to pay a bribe. Cattle are borrowed for many reasons including milking and breeding. What's in it for the lender? He can gain labor, information, a way to hide his assets, safe grazing away from raiders or a local disease outbreak, and a loyal political ally. What's more, the owner doesn't even have to provide the actual animal to get all that. He can promise a future loan, trade, or gift of cattle for milking rights, inheritance rights, breeding rights, and so forth. In these ways, cattle are essential for not only subsistence but for valued goods and services including building a network of alliances essential for thriving in the traditional community.

This pastoralist culture, where cattle form the backbone of social and economic activities, has been called a "cattle complex" in the anthropological literature. And as the highland Samburu demonstrate, in an underdeveloped market economy, it makes perfect sense to keep your cattle out of the marketplace. Why would you sell off your capital? While a single animal can be sold only once, that same animal can be loaned out many times, gaining valuable assets each time. As soon as the market develops a stable infrastructure and investment opportunities that can compete with livestock, the Samburu—as rational capitalists—will increase their participation. The shift from a traditional to a commercial economy was inevitable with development. Done! I had built a tight framework out of the information I had obtained to date, and with just a bit more fieldwork I could fill in the remaining gaps. True, my first two assistants didn't exactly work out, but I was sure there were other candidates out there, and my Swahili and Samburu language skills were getting better every day. I was more confident than I had been in months.

Anthropology professor Sally Falk Moore once warned me that graduate students tend to commit to their initial hypotheses like a person clings to a small boat in a swift current, ignorant of the obstacles around the bend and unwilling to see any other way down the river. Clearly that wasn't true in my case. I was solid. Thus, I climbed into my three-month-old theoretical boat, fully prepared to ride that baby downstream for the next two years, gathering and sorting neat little packages of data as I went. I lay back, feeling exceedingly proud of myself, oblivious to the tiny holes everywhere, slowly taking in water.

Part Two

Dogged Determination

One finger cannot kill a louse.

—Samburu proverb

Chapter 4

Year 1
Life at the Center of the World

Thank God Symon's father, Lentoijoni, took pity on me. After my first assistant Joseph abruptly resigned and John was run out of town, Symon stepped up his hours and was promoted to Number One Assistant.

"Symon," I began ceremoniously. "Due to your hard work, I am now promoting you to Number One . . ." But before I could finish, he interrupted me.

"My father says I must help you. He feels sorry for you."

"Works for me!" I cried. And so my life with Symon and his family began.

Symon's family had the nkang next to the primary school where I lived, which made collaborating a whole lot easier. Moreover, Lentoijoni was an amazing man who impressed me from the moment I met him. He had the dark, penetrating eyes and the quiet face of a man who knows what's going on. When I arrived in 1981, he was in the firestick elder sub-age grade, which is a social stratum of middle-aged men who are the political and ritual leaders of the community. As such, he was one of the key decision makers for traditional rituals and local policies. This included advising government bureaucrats and school officials, and influencing community opinion. When I spoke with him, which I did as often as I could, he would settle in and be utterly present as if he had nowhere else he needed to be. When I asked him a question, he would think carefully before he spoke and give concise thoughtful answers. I felt honored to have become close to him and his family.

In addition to being a successful man with over 340 cattle, Lentoijoni was a prophet. The Samburu have many different kinds of prophets whose exclusive knowledge is revealed early in life. Some prophets interpret the calls of the hyena. These men can predict the behavior of hyenas and whether they will attack a herd. There are prophets who read the stars to predict the rains, prophets who can read the thunder to predict if lightning will hit a man or an animal, prophets who read the colors of cattle to predict the future of an animal's life, and prophets who read illness in people and predict future illnesses. Lentoijoni was another type of prophet—one who reads the color of faces. These prophets can predict the future of individual people.

Lentoijoni was born a prophet, or it was conferred on him at an early age. It was probably a power that was handed down to him from his father. Each prophet may anoint one person (and only one) from the next generation. Lentoijoni's position was embraced by everyone except one person, himself. Oddly—at least with me—he brushed aside this power of prophecy, saying he didn't believe in such a thing. Personally, I never saw any convincing evidence of his powers. While he accurately predicted I needed Symon's help with my research, it hardly took the gift of prophesy to interpret my woebegone face and high turnover of assistants. However, I did witness the influence his reputation had on others.

Early one morning, I drove to Maralal on a routine market trip, accompanied by as many people as could uncomfortably squeeze in the Land Rover. As usual, I had several stops to make in addition to the marketplace, including lunch with Amer, a local Somali who owned a restaurant and who made the best *mandazis* (fried donuts, Swa.) in the territory. Amer was a good friend who often gave me extra mandazis in a to-go bag, and I loved my talks with him. Sometimes Samburu even showed up at my doorstep with mandazi presents sent from Amer. After this particular visit, I spent about an hour with Josephine and Pascal, then loaded the car with provisions and passengers and headed back home.

We arrived without mishap, and I leisurely unlocked my padlocked front door and entered the small room. My eyes immediately went to the sunlight shining through the open back shutters, along with the gaping hole in the wall around the window frame. While I was out, someone had chipped away the dung around my window to reach in and open the shutters. As in any tight community, it didn't take long to get to the bottom of the crime. Evidently, three schoolboys broke in through the window and reached in to take a few pencils before the school guard noticed them and chased them into the forest. I wasn't too worried, knowing the only things I valued—my field notes and portable Smith Corona typewriter—were probably the last things anyone would want to steal. But here was my chance to find out about crime and punishment. How did the community deal with such behavior without a local police force, jail, or formal court system? I knew that for the Samburu, as with many indigenous communities, theft was considered a very serious crime. While you may be justified in beating someone who wronged you, there was no justification for stealing from your neighbors. The fact that these were young boys and that they stole from a non-Samburu was no excuse. As soon as I reported the break-in, Lentoijoni spoke with the father of each boy. Symon said that because I was considered Lentoijoni's daughter, the theft was a direct insult to him personally as well as to the community.

"Really?!?" I responded brightly. "I am considered a daughter of Lentoijoni?"

"The boys will be given a very severe punishment." Symon continued, trying to get me back on topic.

"Like what?" I asked.

"They will be beaten by their fathers."

But first the elders had to find them, I thought. Finding the boys turned out to be no more trouble than waiting for them to return home, all because of the curse. The curse was considered the ultimate means of social control within the Samburu culture, and, with a few exceptions, it was a power tightly held by the elders, such as Lentoijoni. In invoking the curse, Lentoijoni called God's wrath down on the boys for disrespecting the property of another. This claim would have to be justified to God, but no one doubted that Lentoijoni had God's ear. The curse would only be lifted if the boys returned and received their punishment. It took less than 24 hours for the matter to be resolved in just that way and for my shutters and wall to be repaired. Needless to say, no one messed with me from then on. I didn't even need to lock my door.

Not surprisingly, Lentoijoni's son, Symon, was similarly well respected in the community. Positioned in the junior warrior age-grade when I arrived, he was tall and lean with short hair that he kept cropped due to his teaching position at the Maralal adult school. The first thing one noticed about Symon was that he was always so cheerful. But as cheerful as Symon was, this young man was no goof-off. His posture was perfect and he had boundless energy, which he certainly needed to manage his work on the plateau and in town. While he often wore the traditional Samburu cloth when he was around the *bomas* (settlements, Swa.), he always wore a Western shirt and trousers when he was in town conducting classes, and he seemed equally at ease in both. When I asked him if it was difficult to bounce between these two worlds, he shrugged it off. "This is what we do," as if the question made no sense. He was a born leader with a focused and problem-solving mind, and we quickly developed a great bond.

In Samburu culture, the father retains ownership of all his family's livestock. So while Symon was a young adult, he helped manage his father's herd and remained tightly integrated into the nkang of his extended family. As a warrior, Symon slept in his mother's nkaji, or in the home of another married woman of his mother's general age. It was convenient because I could usually track him down. The Lentoijoni nkang included a nkaji for each of Lentoijoni's two wives as well as *nkajiji* for two other relatives: elderly Leshomo and his wife, and cousin Hitler and his young wife.

"Excuse me?" I stammered when Symon introduced us. "Did you say this man's name is Hitler?"

"Yes." Hitler confirmed that this was indeed his name and smiled sweetly.

"Symon," I whispered. "Why is that man named Hitler?"

"Oh, don't you know?" he explained. "Hitler was a very big European president. He was a very important man."

"I certainly know who Hitler was. But he was a very, very bad man."

"Is it." Symon asked. But it wasn't really a question. It was more of an expression that meant he thought I was probably wrong about Hitler, but it wasn't worth arguing over.

One of the best things about Symon was that he valued efficiency and was a quick study, so I felt we could ramp up the pace of work right away. It was a strategy that was not without a few bumps along the road. For instance, take our first interview with Lenairo. I probably did not explain my game plan to Symon well enough in advance. There is an arc to the

Hitler and his wife in their later years.

process of field interviews, and I wanted to make sure the initial interviews went well. The goal of the first meeting was to build rapport and trust. I was focused on establishing a mutually agreeable relationship. The specific information gained would be refined and corrected over time. Symon was focused on something altogether different. Moreover, I don't think Symon much liked Lenairo. So, there was that.

We met Lenairo at his nkang late in the afternoon—a good time when men get together to socialize. I began by exchanging pleasantries, such as commenting on the recent rains and the beauty of his animals. I should have suspected that things were about to head south fast when Symon didn't bother to translate my opening statements but rather shot me a look that said, *Are we here to work, or what?* Symon, with his matter-of-fact, get-the-job-done work ethic, was there to complete the question-naire, or rather make Lenairo complete the questionnaire.

"She needs to know how many cattle you have," Symon began.

"Why?"

"Because it is her work. Weren't you at the baraza? She explained it to everyone."

"I don't know how many cattle I have."

"Yes you do."

"No I don't."

"YES YOU DO!"

"OK. Twenty-five."

"Ha!"

"Fifty-six."

"What?!"

"One-hundred-thirteen."

"I know you are lying. Tell us the truth!"

"I'm not going to tell you anything."

"YOU HAVE TO TELL US. STOP LYING!"

"SYMON! SYMON!" Finally, I got his attention. "We'll get the information we need later. We don't want to make enemies. I'm trying to build rapport here."

But by now it wasn't even about the questionnaire. This was one of our first interviews, and matters were quickly spiraling out of control.

"Symon, forget it. We don't need to know his number of cattle."

"Then why is it on the form?!"

"How about if we accept his answer, you let him know that you know he is lying but that you'll let it pass for now. Maybe you can wink at him, or tap your nose, or something."

"You want me to wink at him and tap my nose?"

Symon was not only exasperated but now totally confused by my bizarre gestures that had absolutely no meaning in the Samburu culture. Thankfully by this time Lenairo had simply wandered off.

As we returned home, Symon and I recovered from the Lenairo visit in part by teaching each other various Samburu and American hand gestures. While it was enormous fun, Symon reminded me, to leave no misunderstanding, I was not to use any of those gestures with the Samburu, and I also needed to revise my questionnaire if I had any hope of getting anybody to talk to me. Furthermore, maybe a good idea would be to take a break and teach him how to drive my Land Rover. As he pointed out, no one for miles around could drive a vehicle but me, and we should prepare for the day when I get really sick and delirious and need someone to drive me to the Maralal hospital. It made perfect sense at the time.

When you grow up with cars, play with cars, and sit behind the wheel from the age of three, learning to drive at 16 is no big deal. When you have rarely even been inside a car, it's not so easy. This was the case with Symon. Moreover, the Land Rover put the teacher at a distinct disadvantage. The manual stick shift separated the driver from the front-seat passenger, making it difficult for the instructor to reach over and grab the emergency brake in an emergency. My Rover was even more awkward in that it had the steering wheel on the left side (like USA vehicles) in a country that drives on the left side of the road (like in the UK). If the Lorroki plateau had one thing going for it in terms of driver training, it was the open grasslands devoid of moving vehicles and big stationary objects to run into. I positioned the Land Rover in a clearing outside the school grounds and began the first lesson. I started with the basics of steering-wheel control and what all those knobs and buttons were for. Then we rolled through how to shift gears, accelerate, and stop. Then we reviewed how the mirrors worked and how you could look through the side mirrors, which were angled so you could see behind you. "Too confusing," concluded Symon quickly. "I will only go forward." Good choice.

I was very impressed with Symon's concentration and his ability to use each independent element, when he operated them one at a time. But the task of working his hands on the stick and the wheel and managing the three foot pedals at the same time was a daunting challenge. Nevertheless, it was time to try driving a moving vehicle. With Symon seated behind the wheel, I—for some reason which eludes me now—thought it was a good idea to run over to the driver's side and clarify which pedals were the accelerator, break, and clutch—since these were confusing—and have him practice a few more times *before starting the car.*

There was evidently a misunderstanding on this last part. Because as soon as I exited the vehicle, Simon turned the ignition and somehow had taken off, driving my Land Rover all by himself!! *HOLY CRAP! WHAT HAVE I DONE!?*

Luckily he wasn't too hard to catch since he immediately ran into a thorn bush and stalled. After extracting the Rover from the bush, I moved firmly back into the passenger seat, and we tried again. Each time, Symon could work his hands and one foot well enough, but never together. And he never did get the rhythm between the clutch, the gear shift, and the accelerator. With each lurch he got more and more frustrated.

"Ah! What is this?!" "This is no good!" Finally, Symon threw up his hands in disgust. "Your car is no good!!" And he walked away, leaving me to worry, *just who will drive me to the hospital when I get sick and delirious?*

Symon was a straight-talking and impatient person—which I could totally relate to. In that sense I felt like I understood him. Arguing with Symon often seemed like I was bickering with myself. We respected each other and, after a few rough interviews, we began to function as a fairly efficient team. We took more time planning interviews in advance, discussing my goals, and I indeed revised my questionnaire with Symon's help so that people would talk to me. That's not to say we always followed the script or were always on the same page. Take the day we interviewed Lekulishi's younger wife for the first time, managing to alienate her in under five minutes.

"Have you received any gifts this past year?" I asked. Symon translated.

"No. Nobody gives me anything."

"Have you given any gifts?"

"Yes. I give away everything. I have nothing left. I give milk to my children every day."

"We're not interested in that!" Symon barked. "You call that a gift?!? That's not a gift!" For good or bad, that was the last time she spoke to us. Unfazed, Symon walked out and decisively informed me, "We don't need the woman!"

Another time, I inadvertently divulged an illegal activity to the worst person possible. It's illegal in Kenya to cut green trees down to make charcoal. It sometimes happens, but as far as I know I'm the only one who inadvertently ratted out a confidential informant to the head of law enforcement. I did it by asking Subchief Lekar about the Somali charcoal seller, only to hear from Symon that Lekar knew nothing about him until I mentioned it.

"You should not have mentioned this to the subchief. The man will be severely punished." *Oh no*, I thought. *Not the severe punishment again.*

"If it was supposed to be a secret," I asked incredulously, "why did you translate it to Lekar? And why did you tell me the Somali charcoal seller had received permission?"

"Did I?" Symon asked. But it wasn't a question.

Fortunately, the subchief said he would "forgive the Somali for today," and Symon reassured both me and the subchief, saying, "We will be more careful from now on." I did a mental eye-roll and decided to save my further questions for the walk back home.

Then there was the first time we walked to Lekar's nkang. It wasn't far—through a patch of forest, past the reservoir, and across the Lorroki plateau. We arrived and had a good chat. When it was time to leave, Lekar casually remarked how brave I was. *Oh gosh, I'm not all that brave.* But he kept talking about it.

"Symon, what is he talking about?" I finally asked.

"He says you are very brave because that part of the forest where we walked has many dangerous buffalo. Many people are killed."

"What buffalo?! I didn't know there were dangerous buffalo on this route! Why didn't you tell me?!? I would have driven the Land Rover!"

"I thought you knew. Everyone knows this." And to fill the tense silence Symon added, "I think you are very brave too."

The worst part was that we had to walk back the same way! We almost made it, too. As we approached the last turn before the school, at the edge of the path, we came upon a lone buffalo, head down, staring at us. Lone buffalo are renowned for their ferocity. Unlike other game, which tend to leave you alone if you don't bother them, a lone buffalo that has left the herd is just as likely to charge you as not. All this information was playing in my head, when suddenly from behind me, Symon hurled a rock that bounced off the buffalo's head like a grape.

"Symon!" I hissed. "Don't throw rocks at the buffalo!!"

Luckily the buffalo didn't charge. But he didn't step back either. Slowly, we crept past the glaring, head-down buffalo, with Symon's spear at the ready. I only let out my breath when we reached the school grounds and knew we would live to tell the tale. I don't think Symon broke a sweat.

That night, as I lay on my cot staring at the ceiling, I was pondering not the cricket but my second brush with death and the big questions of the day: *Why are these people so darn aggravating?!? Why all the evasive answers and the lack of communicating REALLY IMPORTANT INFORMATION!?* In highland Samburu of 1981, where there were no modern modes of communication, information traveled from person to person, and it was valuable. Samburu exchanged information to find out where the rains were, where disease was, where cattle raiders were passing. Even before small talk, people exchanged vital information about where they had come from. Information was something one invested in and gained through social relations. It was something that could help you and harm you and was not something one gave away frivolously, or without calculating the consequences.

Anthropologists come into the field understanding the role of "information," so we expect evasive answers, especially at the beginning. For instance, the number of livestock an elder owns depends on who wants to know, what the inquirer intends to do with the information, and, unless there is a reason to inflate the number, what is being counted. Do I mean to include outstanding loans, inheritance, and promises? Do I mean the number of cattle in the subsistence herd and/or the surplus herd? Am I referring to the animals in this nkang with this wife or the animals in the nkang where the second wife lives, or both?

While I knew this explained some early interactions, it was not the whole story and wouldn't be the main issue with my communications with Symon. I didn't believe Symon or any of the others close to me were trying to mess with me any more than I was intentionally speaking in riddles. We just didn't always understand each other. Because we were fluent in the same language, communicating seemed deceptively easy when it was anything but. Symon had never come across anyone who knew so little about basic things, like where the dangerous buffalo grazed. Nor had he ever met anyone who asked such difficult or nonsensical questions, like what time you left home this morning.

I guess you could look at it from another perspective. Why did people help me at all, when it was so time-consuming, so unimportant, or important enough that you didn't want information falling into the wrong hands? Sure, I had a car and I had medicine, and who knows what other stuff they could possibly use. But there was something else I heard over and over again, it was the value of education for people like me. In the early 1980s, education, to the Samburu, wasn't universally accepted, accessible, or risk-free. There was the free, centrally located primary school, but at that time parents needed to buy uniforms and contribute for chairs, pencils, and other supplies. And classes took children away from herding sheep and goats and other family duties. Moreover, while the first three years were taught in the Samburu language, the next two years were taught in Swahili, and above that in English. For this expense, trouble, and loss of labor, it was said that school was best suited for "dull boys" and for girls who had poor marriage prospects.

Few Samburu in the highlands went on to the secondary boarding school because it carried a steep tuition fee and meant paying for room and board. The closest secondary school was in Wamba, 67 miles away. Furthermore, it took quite a commitment, as high school was taught in English. Another cost of school was that boys who were away from home risked being shut out of access to the family livestock, which was a real career killer if you aspired to succeed in the traditional pastoral business. Girls were educated if the father felt this was their best option, but it was a mixed blessing. An educated girl brought a higher bride-price when married into a more progressive family. It was said that this compensated for all her father had invested in her. As one elder explained to me, "I have put much money into my daughter's head." However, it was also said that when you educate your daughters, they get their own ideas about things, become headstrong, and difficult to control. Hence the mixed blessing for the family patriarch.

University was even more remote. During my first two years in Samburuland, I was told there was only one Samburu to have graduated from college, and he worked in the government office in Maralal. Regardless of the significant cost and risk associated with gaining an education, many children wanted to attend primary school, and a wealthy pastoralist certainly saw the advantage of sending some of his children to school as a means to gain access to new types of information and assets (such as wages from a son's job).

But for me, the benefits and cost of education were calculated differently. Elders told me over and over how important it was for me to complete my education. As the elder Leshomo succinctly explained to another elder, "She needs to know about us for her education, and we must help her." To be perfectly honest, I think they saw education as my *only* path to success, since I was clearly useless for the herding life.

That evening, all these thoughts were rolling around in my brain. You can't possibly do this work and not deal occasionally with complete and utter frustration. I don't know how the Samburu dealt with their frustration. But I dealt with mine by writing it all down in my hidden diary and drawing cartoons of my Samburu friends. So that night, after I wrote all this down, I got out my stash of hidden drawings and went to work. The cartoons were to be my little secret, my outlet. But of course, since I had absolutely no privacy whatsoever, it should not have been a surprise when Symon came by my room that evening to see how I was doing and found me hard at work, drawing pictures of Samburu warriors.

"What are those?" he asked.

"These are nothing. I'm just drawing pictures to pass the time."

"What are they about?"

"Um . . . They are about warriors and elders—funny things about life here."

Symon took his time looking at them, reading them, and then handing them back to me with an odd look. It wasn't an upset or alarmed expression but one that said once again, *I don't understand anything you white people do.* Three cartoons I managed to save are on the facing page.

The existence of the cartoons became common knowledge shortly after I gathered them up and buried them deep inside my trunk. The next day, Symon invited me to join him and the other warriors at a goat roast down by the river, and to bring along my drawings. I accepted, clearly with mixed feelings.

When I arrived, about half a dozen warriors were casually standing around an open fire, and the cartoons were hidden deep inside my shoulder bag. I timed it perfectly, for right behind me was another warrior with the goat that he took aside and began to kill in the bush nearby. This served as the perfect distraction.

The process of killing the goat involved slitting its throat while suffocating it with its own chin hair. It was effective, but not particularly quick or silent. So as not to waste the nutritious blood pouring from the goat's neck, the warriors pulled out the neck skin, catching and pooling the blood. Each warrior stepped up and took a drink of blood, after gallantly offering a drink to me first. The warriors then cut out the kidney from the now definitely dead body of the unfortunate goat and offered a piece of it to anyone who wanted one.

Once the kidneys were eaten, two warriors helped each other skin the goat, removing other organs as they went. They then cut the goat into chunks for roasting, while another few warriors were laying out wood on top of the fire. The chunks were then spread evenly on top of the wood to

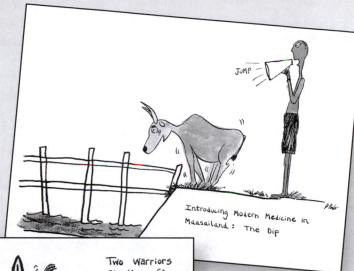

Introducing Modern Medicine in Maasailand: The Dip

Two Warriors Starting off on a Lion hunt

I must say Jeki, you look absolutely stunning this morning.

I know the nickname represents a life-long fraternal bond which is an integral part of Samburu social life. I just don't think it's funny — that's all.

cook. When the meat was well roasted, the warriors would use their long knives to slice off pieces to share around. Some would stack slices onto their spears. I saw one warrior use his spear in just this way. Biting on a large piece of skewered meat, he then took his long knife blade and sliced off a bite-size piece, missing his nose by inches. If he was merely showing off, it worked; I nearly fell over laughing.

There I sat, stuffing pieces of delicious goat meat into my mouth, making small talk and waiting for them to begin interrogating me about my cartoons. To my great surprise and relief they were not interested in my cartoons, but they were feeling comfortable enough to ask some very pointed questions. As it often was, a bold younger warrior spoke out first, asking me how I could live alone and what I do in my room all by myself. "It's very strange," he explained, "and not entirely safe." As the Samburu proverb says, *mulo miata lesomwa* (don't go without someone to help you when something enters your eye). I conceded he had a good point. "All the same," I added, "it's OK to be alone sometimes, isn't it?!"

He went on, wanting to know what it was like living in the middle of nowhere, so far from the center of the world. It took me aback when I realized he wasn't talking about Samburu District.

"How can you live in Europe, so far away from everything?" he repeated. (The Samburu knew I lived in America, but there was no important distinction between America and Europe and they used these words interchangeably.) It was a question shared by all of them. They assumed Samburuland was at the heart of the world, a viewpoint that oddly never occurred to me. Sitting there, I realized how people all over the world consider their home as the center of the world.

I wondered how much of "the world" these young men knew, and I used the opening to talk about what lay outside Samburu District. Taking out a pencil and one of my cartoons, I flipped the paper over to the blank side and drew a map of the world. It was quite abstract and more like a series of blobs, but I was actually quite proud of how well it turned out.

On the map I located Kenya, Africa, and what lay beyond Africa and Europe. People who are not used to reading maps have a hard time interpreting them, but the warriors immediately focused on the relative size of the spaces. Surprisingly, Asia turned out to be the main topic of conversation. They were shocked that there was such a huge part of the planet filled with unknown people who did not fit into their two available categories:

"African" or "white" (which included those from India). It was the perfect time for me to discuss "race" as a social construct, an opportunity I sadly missed when the warriors fixated with alarm on a different spot on the map. They suddenly noticed how incredibly small Great Britain was! No one could believe the *wazungu* (white people, Swa.) came from such a tiny island country that had so little land. I explained that there were wazungu in other parts of the world, too, but it didn't quite register.

"Is that all? The *mzungu* (white person, Swa.) lands are so few and they have all this power!"

"How is that possible?" they wanted to know. I was not sure if they were impressed or emboldened by that realization or merely doubted my assertion and map-drawing skills.

In any case, someone left with my map. So I definitely got the feeling they were not done pondering the implications . . . or my cartoon of warriors on the reverse side.

Other questions were equally profound in very different ways. Wherever I went, young children would often cluster nearby. I'd be standing and talking to someone when I'd feel a slight tickle on the back of my arm. I'd absentmindedly swat it away—thinking it a fly—to find out it was a brave child behind me, ever so gingerly stroking my arm. Other times I would feel a quick tug on my head and discover a child pulling out a single strand of my hair to examine. One time, when I was with Symon, I drew quite a crowd of children because I accidently cut myself on a knife. I was blotting away the blood on my shirt when the kids quickly pressed in very close to me. Sensing a kind of excitement in the crowd, I asked Symon what was happening.

"They want to see your hand."

"Oh, it's fine," I assured him, "Just a small cut."

"That's not it. They want to see inside you. They want to see what you look like inside."

Good Lord, I thought. *This is a bit creepy.* But it seemed like a teachable moment I could not ignore. So I tried my best to pry the cut apart just enough for them to see under the skin and discover that my blood and insides looked just like theirs. Naturally, they were disappointed, but I'd like to think at least some of them thought confidently to themselves, *I knew it!*

Besides Symon and his family, I made two other very good friends that first year—Jacob and his fiancé Dorcas. Jacob was slim, with soft, doe-like eyes. Dorcas was equally petite with a gentle round face and a sweet, quiet voice. Jacob was unusual in several ways. He was the only Samburu teacher in the elementary school, he was a Christian, and he always dressed in Western clothes. He lived at the elementary school in the building adjacent to mine and became my second very close friend. While Symon was a very practical, resourceful, and deliberate person, Jacob was a philosopher and an educator who loved to talk about big ideas. While he came from the region just southwest of Maralal, he seemed more at home in a classroom than in a cattle kraal.

One time, Jacob took me to his mother's nkang to meet her and his family. They kept a few camels, which was unusual for this region in the early 1980s. I'll never forget the day we were standing outside his mother's nkaji talking about the soul of humanity. Jacob had fetched us each a cup of tea with hot milk. It was lovely, and we stood there pleasantly chatting while drinking our tea. Jacob's mother was on top of her house throwing off chunks of old, cracked, cow dung and mudding in new ones.

His young sister was hanging around with the camels in front of us; they were the dromedary (one-hump) type. All of a sudden, the girl walked behind an enormous female camel, pulled tight on the tail, and, holding it as a rope, climbed up the animal's hind legs to sit comfortably on top of the hump! The camel didn't flinch. I dropped my jaw and nearly dropped my china teacup and saucer. My understanding was that female camels were generally agreeable creatures, especially milking camels such as this one, and that they only bit, kicked, and spit when they were annoyed. Well, I was no camel expert, but what I just witnessed seemed like the very definition of something that would "annoy" a camel. Naturally, I was both shocked and impressed.

"Jacob!" I interrupted. "Your sister just climbed up the camel's back legs!"

"Yes," he said proudly. "She does that. No one else can do that."

There we stood with the girl directing the camel to walk in circles around us; the mother was packing cow pies and whistling while she worked; and Jacob in his pinstriped suit and city shoes was holding a china teacup and quoting the Bible. Fieldwork was becoming full of such curiously odd juxtapositions. I recorded them all, cross referenced them as needed and filed them away for future reference. If I was lucky, a few would be useful, as this one was, for fitting into an anthropological puzzle.

I also spent a lot of time with Dorcas while Jacob was teaching. She spent hours tutoring me in Swahili and Samburu, and I'd tell her stories of California. We would also get water together. Getting water. What a pain in the butt that was. Our water came from a nearby creek behind the school. We'd each carry two plastic jerry cans down to the creek, fill them to the brim, haul the water back, and fill the big plastic water barrels in our rooms. Luckily it was a short walk. But it was equally challenging in drought or deluge. When it rained, the challenge was sliding up and down the muddy embankment without falling or sinking deep in the mud. In the dry season, the challenge was finding enough water. We knew it should be running water to be safe for drinking. But as the dry season progressed, our standards got progressively lower.

"Does that look 'running' to you?" I'd ask.

"Running enough," she'd reply, and we'd roll the dice. Needless to say, Dorcas was a much better water hauler than I was. Dorcas was better than me at almost everything. And she did it all neatly dressed in a skirt and plastic shoes.

On December 13, 1981, Jacob and Dorcas got married. The ceremony was in nearby Kisima—the small, one-street town on the road to Maralal. A priest presided, with Jacob dressed in a handsome grey suit and Dorcas in a long white wedding gown. The ceremony was held outside under an acacia tree with about 20 guests circled around. The weather was perfect except for the wind, which whipped dust in everyone's face and all around the hem of Dorcas' flying white dress. But nothing could dampen our high spirits. There were warm bottles of soda to toast the bride and groom, and quite a few long, heartwarming speeches to honor the blessed event. How could it be otherwise? The only person looking slightly distressed was the father of the groom.

"Jacob's father was just wondering why Jacob couldn't have had a Samburu wedding first and then the Christian wedding," explained Symon, who spent considerable time talking with him at the ceremony. And as I saw the old man pacing under the acacia tree, he looked like any other father of the groom, from anywhere in the world, who was living in a culture that was changing way too fast and in a direction he didn't fully understand.

I thought about Jacob and Dorcas a lot. They identified as Samburu, yet because of Jacob's education and profession, and their religion, they were outside the traditional norm. Moreover, there seemed to be no issue with demonstrating this through their Christian wedding, non-traditional dress, china teacups, and other behavior. I was intrigued with how they were accepted and integrated into community life and how they reconciled very different worldviews. Yet the more closely I looked, the more I recognized that all around me were people operating simultaneously in many different cultures and economic sectors: Lentoijoni the ambivalent prophet; Symon the pastoralist cum urban adult-education teacher; the Ndorobo hunter/gatherer who sold charcoal; and anyone serving as tribal subchief—a nontraditional position of community authority created by the British colonial government. Samburu women even wore Maasai-style jewelry, the traditional jewelry of a rival ethnic group. Why? "Because," one Samburu woman laughed, "the Maasai do better beadwork than we do."

Nobody was solely one thing. Every person absorbed and reflected a unique mix of influences—both foreign and domestic, traditional and modern—contingent on their life experiences and opportunities. This was even the case with the most traditional of Samburu weddings, as I was about to witness later that same month.

Chapter 5

The Samburu Bride

Around this same time, I got an intern. I first met her when she was dropped off at my home in the highlands.

"Diane, meet Kathy, your new intern. She's a college anthro major from Texas. Kathy, meet Diane, resident fieldworker. She'll tell you all you need to know. See ya both next month." The program coordinator didn't even turn off the engine. Kathy hopped out of the Toyota Land Cruiser, grabbed her bag, and the vehicle sped off in a cloud of dust. It was at the end of my first year, and I had agreed to host a young intern to shadow me and get an introduction to anthropological fieldwork. Kathy was participating in the St. Lawrence University Kenya Semester Program (which is still going strong). The final month of her semester abroad was a program of independent study, where the students work with a local host or organization in their academic field of interest. As an aspiring anthropologist, Kathy chose to learn from me, which she evidently thought was a perfectly reasonable idea at the time.

"This will be fun," I told her. "You will just love these people!" As I recall, Kathy didn't say a word, which should have been my first clue. Further clues were dropped while we prepared dinner that evening.

Kathy was about 18 years old, short in stature, with curly brown hair, small features, and a delicate frame. She didn't know how to drive a stick-shift vehicle, make oatmeal, and had no idea how to peel garlic. I opened the large metal trunk where I kept all my goodies, brought out a slab of raw meat, and swatted away a few flies that quickly assembled. Kathy visibly recoiled.

"Don't worry," I told her. "I bought this fresh from the market yesterday. This smell is perfectly normal. We just need to wash it off. Just like in Texas. You're from Texas, right?" Again, she was speechless and gave me a look that was both horrified and incredulous, as if to say: *Nothing about any of this reminds me of Texas. Not even the cows remind me of cows.*

The next day, Kathy was curious about how people lived, so I arranged for us to visit the nkang of Symon's family and then follow a young boy out goat herding. *This will be great*, I thought, because I had never observed the work of children closely and was as interested as Kathy was. Perhaps "interested" was overstating her enthusiasm, but she did consent and asked very thoughtful questions.

"Are there always this many flies?"

The nkaji we visited was that of Symon's cousin Hitler and his young wife who lived within the Lentoijoni family nkang. While I stayed outside talking with Symon's father, Kathy was led inside the nkaji to take tea with Hitler and his wife.

"Why is this man called Hitler?" she asked no one in particular as she disappeared into the darkened nkaji.

When I went in to check on her, it was quite a sight. Kathy sat on one of the beds, surrounded by the women and children of the family, Hitler having left after a short greeting. The women were talking nonstop. Sometimes they pointed things out instructively. Other times they laughed. Sometimes they looked gravely at her and spoke in hushed tones, as if they were recounting their deepest hopes and fears. Kathy understood none of it. Yet that didn't seem to be the important thing. She nodded and occasionally got in a few words herself, in a language none of them understood. All the while, the children stood by and stared. Sometimes she'd feel that soft brush on the back of her arm, as a small child was exploring what she felt like.

"Ow!" Kathy cried once in exasperation. "Someone keeps pulling my hairs out!"

We emerged about 30 minutes later. While I wasn't sure if Kathy appreciated how special that opportunity was, I could tell the Samburu women had enjoyed themselves immensely.

"Now we get to see how the children herd the goats!" I informed her, and out to pasture we went.

I don't know what I had expected, because I had never researched precisely how these herd boys actually herded. But whatever the process was, this one was clearly not doing it. The boy, named Kennedy, was about eight years old and only had about 15 animals to watch. But aside from getting them out to the designated field, he pretty much ignored them. The goats were going every which way. Some were climbing the acacia trees; others wandered one way to the forest; others ambled the other way across the road. Meanwhile, Kennedy wasn't doing anything I could remotely identify as "herding." He spent the entire time pretending he was a warrior with some kind of ninja moves. He put on my necklace and scarf, and when he wasn't waving around his six-inch knife at invisible cattle raiders, he was killing any bug or reptile he could find with his small bow and arrow. So who was watching the goats? Me, that's who! Like a crazy person, I was running all over the place while Kathy sat on a nearby rock, swatting away flies and calculating if she could make it to the nearest town with a hotel before dark.

While I probably should have spent more time mentoring Kathy, I had worries of my own. The Samburu family who owned the goats was very important to me, and I didn't want to be responsible for distracting their herd boy and somehow losing a goat or two on my watch. And those goats were not easy to herd, especially for someone from the city who had never seen so many free-ranging goats in her life.

Then, as I stopped to catch my breath and have a motivational word with this herd boy about his job performance, a miraculous thing happened. As I stood there, trying to get Kennedy's attention, the goat right in front of us started twitching and shaking. Out from the vicinity of her rear wiggled a slippery and wet newborn kid. At just the right time Kennedy leapt into action, and in one swift pull he yanked the newborn from between the legs of the mother goat. Both goats staggered around for a minute, and then the boy and the goats resumed their mutual disregard for each other. I stood there amazed. I had never seen anything being born before and here it had happened right before my very eyes. Not only that, but it seemed so effortless, so quick. I didn't even know this goat was pregnant. Kennedy seemed equally amazed at my amazement, and we stood there for a while laughing at each other, seeing each other with new eyes.

At midday we all returned to the nkang for lunch and a nap. I was the only one exhausted. I only hope that someone noticed we returned with every single one of those goats. We even brought back an extra one!

That night Kathy and I went to bed early in the relative comfort of my relatively private quarters. "Tomorrow, we need to get up at 5:00 a.m. for the circumcision," I reminded Kathy. I thought I heard a little whimper of anticipation, as she curled into a fetal position and eventually fell sleep.

I didn't know the wedding couple and hadn't even heard about the marriage until I was invited to witness the bride's circumcision that was to take place the day before the wedding. Only women could witness a female circumcision. So while Symon could not attend, I was able to bring along my young intern. Kathy didn't want to see the operation, but I convinced her that it was a rare opportunity to witness this veiled part of a girl's rite of passage. At the time, very little had been written about the Samburu female circumcision operation, and it was not yet the national and judicial issue in Kenya that it is today.

The Lmasula clan circumcise their girls at sunrise. Not wanting to be late, we arrived at the designated nkang by 5:30 a.m. We were each dressed in layers of clothing, I with my long pajamas under my skirt to keep warm. I never wore trousers in the field, but it was early and quite cold. The entrance to a nkang is closed-off by tall thorn branches each night to protect the herd inside from lions. Not having any door to knock on, or even being able to identify the opening, we waited outside for about 90 minutes debating the difference between first light, dawn, and sunrise. At 7:00 a.m.—which was definitely neither first light, dawn, nor sunrise—women appeared, removed the thorn branches from the nkang entrance, and welcomed us in.

As a side note, Kathy left the nkang before the cutting began. And while she slept more and ate more as the internship progressed and was always pleasant and thoughtful, she never seemed to fully engage with the interviewing or participant observing we were doing and left at the end of the month as quietly as she had arrived. I eventually found out that when Kathy returned to Texas, she changed her major. And for reasons that were fortunately never explained to me, I was never offered another intern.

Girls are not sedated for a circumcision, but this one did appear to be in a type of trance. The girl was prepared with some ritual blessings, and a mixture of cold milk and water was poured over her shaved head before she was led onto the hide of a male sheep—slaughtered for the occasion— and placed just outside her mother's nkaji. The women helped her sit on the hide with her knees bent and her feet flat on the ground. One woman sat on a stool behind the girl and clasped her firmly around her chest under the arms. Another woman sat next to the girl, holding her leg to keep it still and murmuring words of encouragement I could barely hear. The girl was not allowed to speak. Then an Ndorobo woman removed a razor blade from its wrapper, sat before the girl, and began her work.

The girl flinched a little but never cried, and blinked very little. She sat, staring down at her crotch with her mouth set strong and firm as the woman methodically, with a series of small slashes, removed the clitoris. Every few seconds the Ndorobo woman and the leg assistant would finger the girl's vaginal region, checking their progress, and then resume the operation. In one vision I could see the girl's stoic face and the bloody operation between her legs. The two images just didn't fit together.

Finally, with a single word from the Ndorobo woman, everyone visibly relaxed. They were done. The back assistant released her grip and the leg assistant cleaned the wound with a mixture of milk and water. Fat was then smeared over the entire region and inner thighs. With help from the leg assistant, the girl was led directly into the nkaji and onto her circumcision bed to rest. The whole operation took 30 seconds.

When it was done, I followed the attendants into the nkaji and had tea with the women who were celebrating as the silent girl sat wrapped in a blanket, shivering on a raised circumcision bed. Beside her was the back assistant who gave her a blood and milk mixture to drink and stayed with her to make sure she was kept warm.

As a part of the postoperative healing process, the girl was given cow blood to eat. It was prepared inside the nkaji, over an open fire pit. First a pot of cow blood was placed on the fire to heat up. Then a stick was swirled into the pot of blood like you would swirl a stick to make cotton candy. The blood-coated stick was then roasted for a few minutes in the fire. The protein-rich food, which by now looked like blood sausage on a stick, was then stuck in the roof rafters above the girl's bed for her to eat later. An uncircumcised girl was also there to periodically wash the wound with warm water and *sunoni* leaves (used only for this purpose). Another uncircumcised girl would help her later that evening, but she was not allowed to say anything to the uncircumcised girls about the operation.

I was to witness three circumcisions during my fieldwork, but this one was the only time it went off without any complications. The girl accepted the highly ritualized event, as did all the girls I talked with. They wanted to be married Samburu women, with all the rights and responsibilities that come with it. And while some expressed apprehension aloud, not one refused, or felt they could refuse, to be circumcised. For all the girls, this was the only avenue open to them within the culture for their social maturation from girlhood to adult woman and wife. For this girl, tomorrow she was to wed.

Among traditional Samburu, a girl's circumcision and wedding are usually intertwined and part of the same ceremony. Here is how it typically goes: prospective groom's father finds girl and negotiates with the girl's father; girl's father agrees; groom agrees; girl agrees. (The fathers are the key players and usually have a preexisting relationship. The girl is usually the last to be notified and to agree. Sometimes the deal is set before she is even born.) The bride-price is negotiated and the circumcision date is set; the cutting takes place at sunrise; a ceremonial bull is killed and the meat distributed; the next day, the bride, groom, and "best man" set out from the bride's nkang to the groom's nkang, where the ceremony is concluded. Symbolically and literally the bride leaves her father's lineage and joins the family of the groom. After that, she and all her offspring belong to her husband's lineage. The bride-price is given to the bride's father as compensation for the loss to his lineage.

The most critical part of the whole ceremony is the slaughtering of the bull. In fact, it is when the bull is slaughtered that the couple is considered wed. The groom cannot kill the bull but must begin the process, which takes place in front of the bride's mother's nkaji about two hours after the girl is circumcised. The ceremonial bull (called a *rikoret*) is lowered closely to the ground so that a mixture of grass and milk can be put inside its mouth. The groom points a knife four times at the nape of the bull's neck but does not pierce the skin. He then hands the knife to his *sotwa* (special friend) who inserts the knife sharply into the nape of the bull's neck, killing it quickly. Once the bull is dead, the local elders take over to butcher the bull and divide the meat. The first piece removed is one rich in fat—a piece of meat from the chest to the anus. At this same time, local married women come into the nkang through a small side doorway. They line up to get a piece of the fatty meat, leaving behind their shoes and walking sticks. Barefoot, they walk back to their homes to render the fat from their select portion. They keep the meat, but later that day they return the liquid fat and pour it into a special ceremonial gourd that the bride will carry with her to her new home. Once the women have returned the ceremonial fat, they are given back their walking sticks and shoes.

The rest of the bull is shared according to custom. The elders who carved the bull each take a chunk of meat and let the women of the bride's family give out the rest as follows:

- The back is given to the woman who held the bride's back during her circumcision.
- The hipbone is given to the woman who held the bride's leg during circumcision.
- The heart is given to young uncircumcised boys in the neighborhood.
- The women of the nkang get the small intestines and the liver.
- One kidney goes to the mother of the bride.
- The other kidney goes to the woman who circumcised the bride.
- The thighs go to the women who made the bride's dress of hides that she wears on the wedding day.
- Other portions are given out until the bull is gone. (At another wedding I sat next to an old woman who was chatting away with her relatives while chewing on what looked like a large blob of cartilage. It was the bull's nose, which she enjoyed thoroughly.)

While the bull is being slaughtered and divided up, women sing in praise of the bride's courage, warriors sing in praise of the groom, and the bride's family serves tea to all guests who wander in and out of the nkang throughout the day and night.

By nightfall on the day of the circumcision, the exhausted bride, her mother, the groom, and *lchapukera* (best man) sleep in the bride's mother's nkaji. Early the next morning they resume the ceremony, whereby the bride leaves her family nkang and walks to the groom's nkang.

On the morning of this particular girl's wedding, the bride and two girls from the circumcision ceremony gathered inside her mother's nkaji to prepare for the big day. The girlfriends washed off all the bride's old ochre decorations, carefully applied fresh ochre, and ate meat together from the ceremonial steer. The bride could do nothing for herself. Since she was recovering from her circumcision operation of the previous day, it was probably a small blessing.

When the makeup was completed, they all emerged, and the women of the nkang dressed the bride in an ochre leather cape, belted with a leather sash, and an over-cape. It was all quite serious and precise. The girl said nothing and could touch nothing as the women dressed her, making sure every piece of the garment was placed just so. In contrast to the bride's silence, the women of her lineage emitted a continual low, earnest mumble, punctuated with several emphatic words, as they gave her important marital advice. I couldn't understand what they were saying, but the gist of it was: *Do this. Don't do that. You'd better not mess up because we have no intention of returning the bride-price cattle.* I learned later that a big part of the advice was how she was to behave as a proper married woman, meaning: *forget about your no-good warrior boyfriend.* Since her husband was likely 20 years older than she was, that was probably an appropriate reminder.

As a final part of the ritual dress, the attending women strapped two gourds of milk and one gourd of the fat rendered from the ceremonial bull onto the bride's back. The fat was to be given to the women of the groom's nkang once she arrived. The milk was to be given to the children of the groom's family. The bride could take sips of the milk along her walk, but she was not allowed to swallow any; she must spit the milk out on her skirt. While she might eat before her long trek, she was not supposed to eat or drink anything else until she arrived at the groom's family nkang.

Once the bride was all prepared, the women stepped aside and the groom and his best man came forward and stood in front of her. It was time to begin the long walk from one nkang to the other. As they led her from her mother's nkaji up to the main gate of the nkang, they walked very, very slowly. And while neither the bride nor groom seemed particularly ebullient, neither did they seem particularly sad. I was told they were serious and walked extremely slowly to show that the bride was not too excited for marriage. Just inside the gate to her family nkang, the bride's father stood fanning a leafy branch over her head to bless her and say goodbye. All the other married men of the nkang formed a colonnade outside the gate, through which the wedding party solemnly passed. Much like the father had done, all those men similarly fanned their branches over the heads of the girl and two men, blessing them and saying goodbye. The best man then took the branches, stuffed them into a pouch carried by the girl, and they were off! Off at a snail's pace.

I had no idea how far they had to walk to the groom's nkang. This could be miles away, and they had to walk the entire distance. The groom led the way, with the best man behind him, and finally the bride (as depicted on the cover photograph). They stopped often to rest and sip, then spit out, milk from the gourds. Each time, the best man held the gourds for the bride and groom, and when they rose he used the branches to clear their path. The married couple could do nothing for themselves that day. I was there to take pictures and document this slow, painful process. After about 30 minutes, when they had gone all of a few yards, I could stand it no longer. Feeling for the bride, I had an idea. It was probably a bad idea, but *what the heck*. Casually, I sidled up to the groom and whispered in his ear.

"Ahem." I cleared my throat. "Excuse me," I began. "I don't want to interfere or offend you in any way. However, if you would like, my Land Rover is just here and I would be happy to drive you all the rest of the way." I said it in my elementary Swahili, so that's at least what I intended to say. It turned out that the message, especially when I pointed to my Land Rover, was received loud and clear. "You bet," he replied (in so many words). "Pick us up now!" The only caveat was that since they were not allowed to backtrack, I had to make sure the vehicle was in front of them. The bride was not even allowed to look back at her family's nkang. When I pulled up and swung open the doors, I never saw three people move so fast. They literally jumped into the car. Well, at least two of them jumped into the car. The serious young bride, who I never forgot was circumcised only the day before, needed a bit of help. The groom and best man weren't the only ones visibly excited; the family back at the girl's nkang were waving and encouraging us along as I drove away and out of sight.

The traditional wedding illustrates the pattern of Samburu culture as well as its dynamic nature. We think of important cultural traditions such as weddings as something stable, with ritual practices that are passed on, unchanged, from generation to generation. And if I had not come along to ruin this particular event, things would have unfolded a bit differently, but not necessarily as prescribed. At this time, in this place, there was no issue with dropping a modern convenience into the middle of the ceremony. The wedding party could not enter the car when it was behind them; that part of the ritual was critical. But evidently, the part about driving rather than walking was no problem at all. I considered the traditional rite that I was watching unfold. The rules and conventions were evident, yet not so rigid as to keep the ceremony from being relevant to the current situation. And when it came to implementing them, clearly some rules were more important than others.

At least one thing seemed certain; if you lived here you found a place in the community. And living in the community was a continual, dynamic process of finding that place and cementing the relationships that would weave you into the social fabric. As I drove these three young people, I realized that particularly the bride was both literally and figuratively in the risky and exciting state of transition from one position to another. We would soon arrive at the groom's nkang where the ceremony would resume. How well the bride negotiated the final steps of the process remained uncertain.

I glanced at the newlyweds in the back seat through my mirror. The girl was gazing out the window, wide-eyed and alert. She flinched when I accelerated, and I worried that she was still in pain. But she said nothing. Sitting ramrod straight, she stared out the window, with an enigmatic expression I could not read. I could not tell if she was looking outward or looking inward. Then, she did the most amazing thing. For the first time in this painful, two-day ritual, she followed a tree moving past her window and released a small but unmistakable smile.

A few minutes later the best man directed me to the nkang of the groom's family, which stood alone in a clearing just below the forest. I wasn't surprised that the groom's mother appeared to be expecting us to drive up in the Land Rover; by now I was used to seeing that news seemed to travel telepathically.

By tradition, the bride and groom are to reside in the groom's family nkang for up to a month, or until the bride sees the moon. (The Samburu only marry during a new moon). Only then will she be able to find her way to her husband's nkang. Practically speaking, this gives the women of the groom's family time to build a temporary nkaji for the newlyweds inside the groom's family nkang, and time for the girl to heal and regain her strength. At the designated period, the new husband shows up to walk his bride to their new nkaji, and "meets her"—as they say—for the first time. The couple will stay in this small nkaji until she builds her own house, either inside her husband's family nkang or in a separate nkang nearby, and the ceremonial house built by her in-laws is burned down. In this prescribed fashion, a new household is woven into the fabric of Samburu social life, built within or close to the paternal nkang, since a man's father remains the true owner of all his son's cattle until the father dies. A son may be able to gain some or all of his inheritance livestock before his father dies, but this is at the father's discretion.

According to tradition, when the wedding party first arrives, the bride does not enter her in-laws' nkang until the family coaxes her in with promises of livestock. The livestock she gains in this fashion belong solely to her. Because this is one of her few opportunities to gain livestock in her own name, the girl must know her in-laws' assets in advance and be adroit at getting the most she can while saying nothing. I'd heard of extensive standoffs at the nkang gate, with the women inside the threshold flattering a new bride and inflating the value of their offerings while the bride's supporters outside the gate shout out their opinions and advice. Finally the women of the nkang will cough up enough livestock to get the bride to move inside. This is what I was expecting. But this is not exactly what happened.

I stopped the Land Rover in front of the nkang gate, and the best man hopped out to open the car doors, since the couple still could not touch anything. As soon as the wedding party alighted from the Land Rover, the groom and best man nonchalantly entered the nkang without a single glance back at the bride, who stood outside the entrance on her own. Resolutely, the mother-in-law walked up to the girl and offered her one young female calf if she would enter the nkang—clearly not much, and not what the girl was expecting. Uncertain of how to respond and alone at this critical junction in her life, she just stood there in silence, thinking and waiting. Suddenly, she looked so young and vulnerable. She knew the rules, but without any family present to advise her, she was clearly at a disadvantage, and there were no do-overs in this game.

After much encouragement from the in-laws to *just go inside*, the mother-in-law moved forward to speak again. Would she increase her offer? Not likely. Acidly, the old woman spoke.

"Don't stand there like a fool. There's no one else living here but me and you, and I have no more animals to give you." With that closing argument, the mother-in-law turned abruptly and walked across the threshold into the nkang. Hesitating but a moment, the bride gave out an imperceptible sigh, hung her head and followed the old women inside.

At the time, I only knew the bride by her father's name, but her first name was Namayian, and it was 35 years before I heard her memories of that day.

"I was crying," she told me, as she described her confrontation with her mother-in-law at the gate of her new home. "I felt so alone. I didn't know anyone, this was my first time to see my husband's mother, and I was so afraid. She was not a kind woman. But as soon as I entered the nkang I saw some children near to my own age. They were my husband's nephews. They treated me well and I was able to play with them. They saved me in a way."

Namayian's new husband was about 20 years her senior. He was a kind man but from a poor family. Abiding by tradition, the bride and groom resided with the groom's mother for the first month while the couple's first nkaji was being built. For Namayian, that first month was excruciatingly long. The mother-in-law was extremely harsh, treated Namayian like a stranger, and beat her for the slightest infraction.

As life unfolded, Namayian never did get very far away from her mother-in-law. While the couple built their own separate nkang, it was situated "just there" to the south, with her mother-in-law forever in her daily life. "I got used to the beatings," she told me.

Chapter 6

Animals Blessed, Cursed, and Just Plain Trouble

With the marriage ceremony over, everyone had gone. I got back into my Land Rover and pensively drove home. I thought about the rituals I had recently witnessed, and the role of these rites of passage in bestowing Samburu identity. The Samburu know who they are—their transition from child to bride, from warrior to elder comes with clear boundaries in expected behavior, dictated by the norms and expectations of the age-grade system. This form of social organization, representative of the Maasai type age system, includes all members of the society from birth to death in a hierarchy of status positions and/or corporate groups. While women have just two status positions: girl and woman, men have three age grades: boy, warrior, and elder, with strong fraternal subgroups within the warrior and elder grades. For instance, a warrior will advance through two sub-age grades: junior warrior and senior warrior. When transitioning into the sub-age grade of junior warrior, a boy becomes a member of an age-set, a corporate group that advances as a unit through all the successive age grades in the system. It's a tight brotherhood of young men that spend nearly all their hours in each other's company, learning the ways of the *lmurrani* (warrior).

Once you cross that threshold, you cannot go back again. American teens may try on different roles, be it child one week and adult the next, but not so for the Samburu. Once circumcised, you leave childhood forever. The newlyweds cannot walk backwards. And once the bride crosses the threshold of her mother-in-law's nkang the deal is sealed. Each promotion ceremony propels you to a new identity, pushing you forward to the next stage of life, while it wipes out the option of retreating. At every age grade, a Samburu knows what his or her responsibilities are. And while, as I witnessed in the Samburu wedding, not all rules carry the same weight, and cultures are continually changing, the social network created by the age system is a stabilizing force in the society. It defines success, supports compliance, and illuminates the traditional path forward from birth to death.

By the time I arrived home, my mind had wandered from the Samburu bride and Samburu identity to the calf the bride had just acquired and the role it played in the marriage contract. Here, animals are everything. They cement social bonds, fuel commerce, symbolize success, and grease the wheels of bureaucracy. Throughout Samburuland, cattle are woven into every significant ritual and social relationship. Livestock—primarily cattle—seal a friendship and a marriage alliance and are the currency of divorce, civil suits, and bribes. They gain you access to information, prestige, loyalty, and power. And along the way, they provide a steady supply of milk, blood, and meat. The Samburu keep cattle, sheep, and goats. Some have camels, and some even keep a dog or cat to chase the snakes away. But cattle are king.

"In the old days," Lekimorian told me, "a steer was like the husband of the home. They were not sold, but stayed in the home until they died. If they died fat, that was good. If they died thin and sick, then a he-goat must be slaughtered."

Cows and steers are beloved, and some are named after their mother or a particular event or a trait. The Samburu claim the animals know their names, and I can honestly say that I have seen one come when called, but only when called by its proper name. One of the first things Symon did when we started working together was tour me through his herd.

"This one is tough; no one can milk her, so the calf goes to pasture with her and drinks all her milk. This one is so tame you can ride her." Symon smiled as he gazed over his herd, patting one, scratching another on the back. I instinctively reached out to do the same, but he lifted his hand to stop me.

"You no. Me yes. *Ana sema, mimi ni Baba yake*." (He says I am his father).

Lesambaini once had a cow named Love, given by a warrior friend. Even though Love died a long time ago, her calves are still alive and are also named Love. They are spoken of and regarded as that same animal originally given in friendship so long ago.

In addition to valuing each cow's individual personality and life story, the color and color pattern of each animal has meaning. In general, solid-colored cattle are good and a red or black spotted bull or steer is blessed. Also valued are cattle with a different colored patch on the right hip, white on the sides, and a different color all over; white on the back and belly; or black-and-white speckled. A man may brag when he's a warrior, "I have a red bull!" After that, he'll be nicknamed as such, and Red Bull will become his bull name for the rest of his life. But there are cursed animals as well, which pose a particular problem; misfortune—like fortune—is thought to pass through the male cattle's line. A prophet who reads the color of cattle knows how to read any animal, but I was told that even a child knows you don't want an animal with a spot behind the front leg or on the nape of the neck!

Beyond color, cattle are evaluated based on the shape of their horns, hooves, and tail, as well as health, heritage, milk yield, and breed. If lucky enough to have one, a warrior will brag, "I have a bull with horns drooping low." Then there is the herd composition. Not only are individual animals ranked, but the entire herd is valued as a unit. A herd owner will be known for and take pride in having a good number of red cattle and/or a variety of the desirable colors and markings. It's a lot to keep in mind.

When a boy is born, he is given a male calf. Three months later, he'll be given a female calf. At circumcision (around 15 years old) his family gives him more animals. When he becomes a warrior, his warrior friends will promise him stock when he marries. In these and other ways, as a boy grows, his herd grows with him. A girl will receive a few animals upon marriage and at other times, and the animals will remain her property. But cattle are mainly a man's business, the responsibilities of warriors, and the dreams of boys.

Maybe it was all the country music I was listening to, but the more I hung around these people, the more I saw interesting similarities between pastoralist warrior culture and cowboy culture. Both are shaped by the needs to feed, move, and protect cattle through often hostile territory.

Both value the nomadic life, confrontation over compromise, and the justice of the warrior's code over the laws of the greater society. And both sing endlessly about their dogies. Even their songs seemed interchangeable, singing about being in the open land, cloudy skies, moving along, and battles won. Naturally, this got me thinking. The warriors definitely preferred my country and western music over rock, particularly my cassette tapes of Crystal Gayle. So I offered to teach them a few cattle songs from America. Luckily, the days passed slowly, with lots of opportunities to amble along the prairie singing, or so I thought.

The first song I tried to teach them was "The Farmer and the Cowman" from the musical *Oklahoma!* Unfortunately, that started quite a long argument about why the parties should be friends: *Whose territory is it? What are the farmers doing in the cowman's rangeland in the first place? Haven't the farmers already taken too much valuable grassland that the cowman needs in the dry season?* Then I got to the stickiest part of the song about the cowboys dancing with the farmers' daughters. After I sang the famous lines, the warriors just stood in stunned silence, but not for long.

"Dance with the farmers' girls?! No, No, No! We would not do that!" *And what exactly did the song mean? Who is joining whose dance?* Needless to say, I had to abandon all hope of finishing the song. Knowing no other cowboy musicals, I switched to standards and sang a heartfelt chorus of "Home on the Range."

"There are parts in-between the chorus," I confessed, "but I don't know those words."

"We know all the words to our songs. But this song at least makes some sense. We have buffalo, and we also sing for the clouds to bring the rain."

But sadly, because this song didn't have enough words that I actually knew, they soon grew bored with it.

"Are these the only songs you know?"

Then, I pulled out my ace: "Rawhide!"

I think my enthusiasm and whiplash sound effects really sold it! They loved this song, even though I couldn't remember all the words to this one either. It was great to hear a sea of warriors singing the "Rawhide" song, each one singing his unique version.

"We like the shouting, but we never whip our cattle. We just tap our cattle with sticks and then they do what we want them to do. American cowboys should come here and we will teach them how to do it."

While many individual cattle were named and pampered, it's important to keep sentiments about cattle in perspective. Lentoijoni said it best. He was walking and talking with me about how pastoralists think of their animals, and how this lifestyle was so much better than being a farmer.

"The cattle take care of themselves. I do not have to take the grass and lift it up to the cow's mouth, I do not have to scoop up water and make the cow drink. They eat by themselves. They drink by themselves. They walk by themselves. And if one should die, I eat it! The farmer, on the other hand, has to work very hard to make his crops grow, and if they should die, he has nothing!"

Livestock were about the only animals that the Samburu were fond of. Beyond the settlements roamed buffalo, lions, leopards, and forest elephants to name a few of the big grumpy ones. Their experiences with these wild animals were often disastrous. Over the two years I was there, four people were killed or seriously gored by buffalo, and one little girl, Jacob's six-year-old cousin, was killed when an elephant came charging out of the forest. And that was just in my neighborhood.

The first time was in September 1981. I was away from the settlements in Maralal, interviewing livestock and land adjudication officers. That evening I spent time with Pascal and Josephine, playing cards (Crazy Eights) and relaxing with the kids. I returned to the settlements several hours later to hear that, while I was gone, a buffalo had gored a woman to death in the woods by the reservoir, just beyond the school. In a tightly knit community every death hits close to home. In this case, the daughter of the gored woman was a classmate of Jacob's cousin who had been killed by the elephant. The Samburu are forbidden by law to hunt any wild animals and are supposed to call the game department when something like this happens. The wildlife department soldiers are then sent out to find and kill the offending animal. You can imagine all that could go wrong—and it usually did. In this case, the soldiers came out to hunt the buffalo. Found it. Shot and wounded it. Lost it. Gave up. And returned to Maralal. They instructed the Samburu warriors that if they found the buffalo, they should let them know, and they would come back to finish the job.

"How do you find a buffalo and make it stay put until the soldiers come back?!" I asked.

"I need a ride in your vehicle," everyone else asked, but they didn't really phrase it as a question. Until the wounded buffalo was found, no children were permitted in the woods, and even warriors and adults stayed clear.

The next day was spent driving endlessly, because no one would walk in the woods, and I had the only vehicle for miles around. Knowing I would be driving hither and yon, I hauled out the extra jerry can from the school storeroom and filled my gas tank. I was driving across the plateau, skirting the buffalo-filled forest, when I hit a huge bump. By the time I dropped off my first customer, I noticed that my petrol tank was leaking badly! Not wanting to be stuck on the edge of the forest after nightfall, I headed straight into Maralal to Bholla's garage. Luckily I made it with plenty of petrol. Bholla took one look at my car and reported that the gas tank was just fine. I had just overfilled it and petrol had leaked out over the top. It would have been nice if he had mentioned this to me privately, but he did not. Having heard the news that the vehicle was fine, the remaining Samburu passengers erupted in complaints and expressions of indignation at my poor driving and petrol-filling skills. No language barrier could obscure their indignation. *Oh well*, I thought. As long as I was in town and they were upset with me anyway, I took a break and ran next door to Amer's café, telling them I'd be right back. "Right back" in Samburu can mean anything from two minutes to two weeks, so I knew I had some time.

"The usual please." I gave my order and sat down at my customary table with a view out the door. Amer filled me in on the family news and served his fabulous chai, mandazis, roasted meat, and plantains. Fortified, I headed back to the car and the waiting crowd. By this time, my passengers had swollen to about a dozen more, including some kids who I knew didn't live anywhere near my area and just wanted to take a ride.

"No, No, No," I told the nonresidents. "This is a school taxi. Only those going to the elementary school on the plateau. No stops!"

Not surprisingly, three more people squeezed in the back while I was talking.

As soon as we arrived home, we learned that the rogue buffalo had claimed another victim while we were away. This time it was a warrior, Lalaikiar's son, whom I had just spoken to the previous week. I felt guilty for taking so long in town, forcing him to walk across the plateau instead of getting a ride from me. Luckily, he was only wounded. It was Friday, and the game department was sending soldiers out on Monday to stay for a few days, or until they finally killed the rogue buffalo. Needless to say, people were on edge. As I got into bed that night, I heard the haunting sound of warriors singing in the near distance. I felt glad that at least I could help out with my taxi service. These people had done so much for me. I promised myself that I'd be a better taxi driver over the next few days, take fewer mandazi breaks, and be more tolerant of people spitting (profusely) inside my car.

In the morning, I caught up on the buffalo news. Lalaikiar said the buffalo that attacked his son was not wounded, so we were looking for two different lone buffalo. Late in the afternoon, we heard gun shots coming from the woods just by the school. Evidently someone was on the job, and no one was walking anywhere. After I completed my taxi rounds, I snuggled in my little room, remembering to bring Bruno the cat inside for the evening.

Five days had gone by, and the buffalo saga continued. One soldier shot at and wounded another buffalo Monday night. Then another soldier shot at a herd of sitting buffalo, wounding one and losing it. Now there were three or maybe four wounded buffalo in the forest—at least as far as I knew. *Lord!* I thought. *I wish the game department would stop helping us.*

The next day Jacob accompanied me to interview households in the region across the river by the non–buffalo-ridden part of the forest. We really pounded the beat, through driving rain and hailstones! On the way back, the game department soldiers were tailing us. Apparently we were going to the same place, which did not reassure me in the least. We got back home just in time to rush Lenairo to the hospital in Maralal, after a buffalo had gored him. Yes, yet another buffalo attack. I was losing count, but I thought that was five.

By now a whole platoon of soldiers was camped by the forest, drinking and determined to kill all the marauding lone buffalo they could find. Eventually the game department killed two large buffalo and enjoyed a delicious buffalo soup with the local adults, teachers, and children before declaring victory and retreating. The rest of us were left warily looking over our shoulders, not knowing what to believe. In any case, I got the strange feeling we had not heard the last from the lone buffalo.

Two months later the whole nightmare seemed to start all over, when a lion attacked a warrior in the same forest. Again the soldiers came out, this time late at night and already somewhat inebriated. Never a good start to a story. After a burst of whooping and hollering, they entered the woods, and in quick order they managed to find a lion, shoot and wound it, lose it, and drive back to Maralal.

Needless to say the elders were pissed! They immediately scheduled a baraza for the following morning to begin promptly at 10:00 a.m. At 11:00 a.m., elders started arriving, and somewhere around 12:30 the meeting began. Eighty-four local elders attended, gathering under the meeting tree. Across from them sat the government guests: the land adjudication officer and two livestock officials. Behind them sat about 15 local women representing their husbands who could not attend. First up was Lenairo, who read the minutes from the last meeting. When he asked for approval of the minutes, a heated debate erupted, moderated by Subchief Lekar, which lasted until 2:15 p.m. Part of the problem was that the elders spoke in a continuous stream of mixed Swahili and Samburu, with a simultaneous translation going on for the officials who spoke no Samburu. In the confusion, many things had to be repeated several times. With the minutes finally agreed upon, Lentoijoni opened the meeting with a greeting and statement that essentially declared, "The elders are very sad and disappointed that the game department officers did not come to the meeting to address the buffalo, lion, and elephant problem as requested, as that is why we are meeting." It was then the land adjudication officer's turn to formally greet the elders, which he did for one and a half hours until all the elders—those who were still awake—had had enough! Lentoijoni formally closed the meeting at 3:45 p.m., amid cries of rebellion that "one opening speech is no meeting at all!" And that this was "wasting our time!"

The next day, a committee of 13 elders was formed and walked to Maralal to demand that the district commissioner himself come out and talk to the entire community. This time, they hoped, he would state how he would precisely address their problems. The DC did come and some sort of meeting did take place. Unfortunately, this meeting was much like the last one, with the additional affront that Lentoijoni forced Symon to slaughter one of *his* goats for the meeting, which according to Symon (and I paraphrase) *was so totally unfair!*

It was a sobering thought that if you take away the roasted goat, these barazas were very much like any meeting I had ever been to, anywhere. Sadly it crossed my mind that "the meeting" might be a universal culture trait and one of the few distinctly human attributes separating us from other animals. I tried to think of more honorable and beneficial human traits, but somehow the meeting left me sort of brain dead and I drew a blank. Numbly, I staggered home to sleep.

I will never know if a third follow-up meeting would have been requested, because shortly after the second one, the warriors proceeded to hunt for the lion themselves. They assembled, and armed with nothing but spears, they headed straight over to my door.

BAM! BAM! BAM!

"DIANE!"

"GO AWAY!"

"We are going to get the lion. You need to come with us!"

"WHAT?!"

"Open the door!"

"NO! GO AWAY! I'M NOT DRIVING YOU INTO THE FOREST WITH ALL THOSE WOUNDED LIONS AND BUFFALO!"

"Ha! You can't drive into the forest. You'd never get the lion that way!"

"Then why do you need *me*!?"

"You have the torch [flashlight]." This was followed by a moment of silence while an alternate plan formed in my head. I opened the door a crack and shoved my flashlight into someone's hand.

"Bring it back!" I said and slammed the door. It occurred to me that I was just duped out of my flashlight or, more likely, the batteries inside the flashlight. In any case, I never saw my flashlight again. But from the warrior's singing that went on far into the night I could tell they successfully brought in the wounded lion. *Good for them*, I thought. *They can keep the batteries.*

Later someone explained that the warriors had a very good reason for commandeering my flashlight, and it wasn't just for the batteries. When a bright light is shined in a lion's eyes, it will freeze, making it easier to spear. I wasn't entirely convinced, but knew that a braver soul than I would be required to test that hypothesis.

Did I mention the black leopards? People knew of two in the region: one by the reservoir behind my home, and the other spotted occasionally near Maralal. I never had a close encounter, which was a shame, since I really wanted to see one—from the safety of my Land Rover. One night, however, I came close. I had just driven to Maralal for dinner. I had an English friend, Lesley, who lived above Maralal in a lovely little bungalow with a cement floor, private outhouse, and kitchen. She also had a solar heated shower, which was a real luxury. I had just arrived and we were settling down for a dinner of stir-fried vegetables and fresh bread when her neighbor, a retired British range manager, came knocking on the door. He was clad in his pajamas and dressing gown and sporting a very, very large rifle.

"Sorry to bother you ladies, but best to stay inside for a bit. The black leopard was perhaps seen just here, quite close to the homes."

Yikes! I thought.

"Cor blimey!" was exactly what Lesley said.

While it was occasionally scary and sometimes tragic, it was also a continual marvel to be living surrounded by such magnificent animals. And they didn't get any better than the zebras that roamed the region in great numbers. Two zebra species lived in the area: the more common Burchell's zebra, with wide black and white stripes, and the less common Grevy's zebra, which are larger and more muscular with narrower black and white stripes. Grevy's zebras don't live in harems, and I often saw them in pairs, while the Burchell's always traveled in large, closely packed herds. Their stripes make it hard for a predator to tell where one zebra ends and another begins, and in which direction they might run. When times got tough and I needed to get away by myself, I'd take my Land Rover out to the Lorroki plateau, roll down the window, and sit among the disinterested zebras grazing throughout the broad, flat plains.

It was a totally different story when I'd see the same zebras blocking the only road to the bomas, in the only spot where it was impossible to drive around them. There, I felt totally impatient waiting for them to move out of the way. They'd bray in that loud, coarse donkey way and just stand there looking at me as if to say *I'm eating. Go around!* But of course, I couldn't go around because the zebras were taking up the entire road. I'd creep slowly forward in the Land Rover and they'd move a leg about two inches. *There, is that enough?* they seemed to say. It was funny for about the first 100 times. Then it got a bit old.

But other than the stubborn zebras and the few times I had to avoid ornery animals that might kill me, the plains and the forest were breathtakingly beautiful, both day and night. The Samburu had a deep respect for their environment and the power it had over them. Although this was not a designated game park, there were national laws that prohibited killing game and felling trees. I was talking with Symon about this one day when we were walking near the forest, heading to an interview. He thought the law about trees was completely unnecessary, saying there was no way the Samburu could ever cut them all down. His perception was that the Samburu were so few compared to the vastness of the forest. Like elsewhere in the world, their perception of the human impact on the natural world has changed over time; and like other indigenous peoples, the Samburu have become some of the best conservators of their land, flora, and fauna. But back in those days, it was commonly thought to be inconceivable that people could conquer such a powerful natural resource, and not without reason. The forest was so big, so dark, and so magical, from the twinkling fireflies and prowling black leopards to the vibrant Milky Way overhead. The Samburu moved within this world, were a part of it, but were not the masters of it. Here they made their homes and tended their beloved cattle, navigating their way attentively between all of God's plants and animals—the blessed, the cursed, and the just plain trouble.

Top: Diane's Land Rover (left) at Samburu *nkang*.

Center: Warriors and bead girls (Symon in blue shirt); Diane outside her room with Bruno. *Photo by David Caddis.*

Left: Six of Josephine and Pascal's seven children.

Dorcas with Jacob and members of his family.

Opposite top: Diane with Jacob's youngest sister; *nkaji* of Symon's little mother with recently installed modern chimney. *Center:* Symon with some of his father's cattle. *Bottom:* Symon's younger sister; warriors at *Ilmugit* ceremony.

From top: Jacob's mother repairing the roof of her *nkaji*; Samburu girl; Burchell's zebra; Zebu bull with upward-sloped horns, which gives the male animal added spiritual value; Symon enjoying roasted meat with warriors at *ilmugit*.

Opposite from top: Bead girls watching warriors dance at *ilmugit*; warrior of Lmasula clan; girls and warriors dance.

Left: Women inside *nkaji* who shared stories with the author

Center: Lentoijoni holding a Teenage Mutant Ninja Turtle

Bottom: Diana at her college graduation, the only graduate wearing Samburu jewelry

Top: Diana and her mother.

Center: Diana (cap and gown) and Lucy (blue skirt) dancing during graduation party at their brother's home.

Bottom: After the party, from left: Joe holding Dale's flywhisk, Diane, Diana, and Malian who held her daughter's hand throughout the photos.
Photo by Dale Weaver.

Diane with two of Symon's grandchildren, and other friends. *Photo by Diana Lentoijoni.*

Chapter 7

Year 2
The Participant Observer

By now I was a fully invested participant observer. I was deep into the routine of conducting interviews and counting things amid the drama and distractions of daily community life. There was no such thing as a typical day, but there were typical activities and recurring issues with all the excitement and boredom, hope, and despair attached to this privileged work. This is what it means to be a participant observer.

January through February is the heart of the dry season in highland Samburu. So it was not surprising that January 1982 began with a fire. Or rather, it eased into a fire after a suspected animal attack. It started one Sunday when a lion chased a zebra across the schoolyard, right by my front door, and two lions were spotted down by the river behind the school. The elders quickly chased the lions back into the forest, but sadly matters didn't end there. Later that day it was discovered that four elementary schoolboys had disappeared from the school. With all the recent injuries from buffalo and elephants, people were on edge and quick to suspect the worst. Word spread that the boys were last seen where the two lions had been sighted, and the community sprang into action. Fanning out, warriors and elders searched the nearby woods well into the night, but the boys were not found. The next morning the search continued, and the poor mothers looked like they hadn't slept a wink. Into this tense and exhausted environment the four boys casually ambled back home, totally unaware of the lions or that they were even missed. They were also quite surprised at how pissed off everyone was!

By midday the boys had been punished and it seemed that everything was starting to settle back down to normal, when Lentoijoni noticed a small forest fire up in the hills. Apparently, the boys had gone off into the bush to burn out beehives for the honey. In their haste, they left some smoldering embers that ignited in the dry conditions. Immediately, all able-bodied men rushed into the hills to extinguish the fire. Within short order, the fire was out and everyone relaxed a bit, except—of course—the boys, who now had something else to answer for.

This time of year was tough, even beyond the threat of animals and fires. Nearby wet-season grazing had dried up, and the cattle needed to be herded to higher-elevation grazing. This was the work of the warriors and junior elders, not small boys. Men had to walk longer distances than they did in the wet season, and they returned late in the day tired, or they stayed with the cattle in camps at the higher elevations. And there were always the cattle raiders to contend with, who preyed on the herds grazing far from home. Because of this, Symon and I worked late as well, interviewing elders about dry-season herding customs and behavior, collecting milk yields, tabulating sales records, and more. And we were tired too. Symon, if you'll recall, had many jobs. He was a lmurrani, with all the singing, dancing, hanging around, and security work the position required. He was also an important dry-season herder for his father, and a teacher in the Maralal adult school. Finally, he worked for me as my Number One Assistant. All of this gave him a lot of responsibility and little free time. Without rain, the workload and stress level only increased. But Symon was such an energetic and positive person that he rarely complained, nor did he shirk any of his responsibilities.

I do remember one trip late in the day when he opened up about his frustration with his adult education class. In 1979 Symon had started a women's group. Once a week he convened about 30 women, often inviting guest speakers to discuss important issues, such as home economics, raising poultry, health, and education. This week he had two guest speakers: one woman from the British NGO Action Aid, and one home economist from the Ministry of Agriculture in Nairobi. The speakers were there to discuss the group's concerns and offer suggested resources. But it didn't go as smoothly as Symon had planned. From the moment the door closed, the 30 women confronted the speakers in, as Symon described it, a very disrespectful way. They wanted to know why they had received no aid so far. The officials said it was because they were doing quite well and needed no aid. *Au contraire*, said the women.

"We were promised free seed and money to buy hoes at 40 shillings each. We want the seeds and we want the money." In addition, some of the women were interested in opening their own shops where they could supplement their income by selling sugar, tea, beads, and other goods.

"No problem," the speakers suggested.

"Yes problem," the women countered. "Many problems!" And they were not shy about describing exactly what the problems were.

"To get a business permit, the shop has to be inspected by the health officer. But first we have to find the health officer. Do you know how hard that is? Then we have to get petrol and a vehicle to get him out to inspect the shop. And before any of that happens, we have to get the regulations for the shop. We have to get the whitewash, cement, wood, and all the other things and tools to build the shop. And no one helps us with any of this!"

It's hard to blame Samburu women for their frustration. They had very little authoritative power. They were regarded as children who must submit to their father's or husband's wishes, and their only real power was influential. In terms of work, they were overloaded with the heavy lifting. They had to walk, collect, and carry firewood and water. They had to cook, care for the health, welfare, and education of their children, and complete all the other homemaking chores. And by "homemaking," I mean they literally had to make their home from sticks, mud, cow dung, and water. Plus they had to routinely patch it up in the wet season when a wall caved in. They had very limited access to money or livestock, got the worst parts of the meat (the liver, sternum, and tail bone after the meat was removed), and even God didn't seem to be on their side. In the Samburu religion, there was one God, but he had many sons and daughters who lived everywhere so God could see everything. The Samburu prayed to God, but they didn't fear his wrath and they yelled at him when things went badly, especially in the dry season. When God was good, the Samburu praised him as if he were a male, because it was believed it was his sons, the warriors, who were responsible. When God was bad, it was his daughters who were responsible, so they yelled at him in a female voice. Add all this grievance to an underdeveloped marketing system, bad roads, inefficient bureaucracy, and empty promises and you get frustrated women!

"Symon, does this seem fair to you?" I asked.

"Ah!" he said, and waved me off. "I don't have time to argue with you about Samburu women!"

"Then why did you bring it up?!" I asked.

We drove on in silence, both fatigued and stewing in our own ill humor. I was glad to hear that the women in Symon's adult education group were so assertive and entrepreneurial. In previous graduate work, I had researched women's economic activities and knew what a separate income could do for women in communities such as this one. It could not only increase their general economic, political, and authoritative power, but having their own money could specifically advance the education, health, and welfare of their children. The shops and tools these Samburu women wanted could provide these and so many other benefits. I sympathized with their frustration.

I recalled a specific occasion when I had visited one of these rural *dukas* (shops, Swa.) in an area north of Maralal. I was with my friend Lesley, the one living in Maralal, who worked for a British NGO. We were driving a Samburu woman and the health inspector out to examine the woman's shop in pursuit of the required business permit. Throughout the trip, the woman recounted in excruciating detail the tremendous effort it took to get a shop built, approved, and opened. Once in operation, business was good, but profits were small. Women who ran dukas had to compete with their suppliers who sold direct to the public from the shops in town. On top of that, the Samburu merchant had to contend with clansmen expecting to buy on credit.

I was still deep in thought when Symon and I arrived home. I parked in front of my room by the schoolyard and turned my focus to the work ahead. We were both tired, but I had two more chores to accomplish before calling it a day.

"Symon, we have an early day tomorrow, so I'm going to fill the petrol tank now and then get some water."

"OK. I'm going down to the river to wash," he said.

I walked across the dirt yard to the school storeroom. Unlocking the padlock from the front door, I entered and lugged out a five-gallon jerry can of petrol. Lifting the 41-pound jerry can carefully over a funnel I filled the tank as my able-bodied warrior assistant strolled down to the river empty-handed. I took the empty jerry can back to the storeroom and locked up. Returning to my Land Rover, I then retrieved two empty plastic jerry cans reserved for water and followed a separate path to another part of the river. Slipping down the bank and over the rocks, I filled the water cans one at a time as efficiently as possible, listening for any signs of wild-life. And there I waited. Perhaps when Symon finished his bath, since NO ONE was around to see him, he'd help me lug the water back up the river-bank. I also wondered, not knowing how far away he was bathing: *Would I be able to hear Symon scream if he were attacked by a lion? Could he hear me, if I screamed?* It didn't take me long to calculate that I was more likely to be attacked by a lion than to have Symon help me carry the water home. So, as I had done countless times before, I dragged the cans up the hill and through the overgrown thorn bushes. I was outside my room, cleaning off my scratched legs, by the time Symon passed me on his way home, look-ing very content after his refreshing bath.

"AND ANOTHER THING," I yelled after Symon. "WHY IS IT THAT WOMEN CARRY ALL THE HEAVY STUFF?!!!"

I had just refilled the large water barrel in my room when BAM, BAM, BAM, someone pounded on my door with a familiar request—a ride into town.

My Land Rover was called upon not just when wounded animals were on the prowl or women needed to buy sugar and tea for a celebration. My scope of work seemed to include taking sick people to the hospital, ferry-ing people to town for government business, and apparently "other duties as required." People would knock on my door at all hours of the day and night, asking for a ride into town, especially when I wasn't doing anything at all, just sitting there reading, or typing on my typewriter, or sleeping.

Which brings me to the subject of time. It is often said that indigenous people have a totally different concept of time than Westerners. Because the rhythms of social life are tied so closely with the activities of herding cattle and the changing seasons, it is said that time for nomadic pastoral-ists is cyclical, while the Western concept of time is linear. As Evans-Pritchard wrote about the pastoral Nuer:

The Nuer have no expression equivalent to 'time' in our language, and they cannot, therefore, as we can, speak of time as though it were something actual, which passes, can be wasted, can be saved, and so forth. I do not think that they ever experience the same feeling of fighting against time or of having to coordinate activities with an abstract passage of time. (Evans-Pritchard 1940, 103)

Well, maybe. It's true that I could never get anyone to show up on time, or acknowledge we even made "an appointment." All the same, when it was their time that was in question, the Samburu could be in a pretty big hurry. "Let's go! Let's go! You are doing nothing. You can drive me into town." As people filled my car for a market run, the women would not let up until the car was rolling. "You can go just now. Now we go!"

But when I wanted them to check their watches, it was a totally different story. For instance, because I was doing an economic study, one thing I explored was what people did during the day and how long it took them to get around. And since wristwatches were the latest status symbol, I mistakenly thought they were used to tell time. Here is a typical exchange:

Me: "Where did you just come from?"

Him: "From just over there."

Me: "From near Naibor Keju?"

Him: "Yes, near that."

Me: "How long did it take you to get here?"

Him: "Not long."

Me: "By your watch how long did it take you to walk here?"

Him: "I don't know."

Me: "What time did it say on your watch when you left home this morning?"

Him: "I don't know. How would I know such a thing?"

Me: "Did you happen to look at your watch when you were leaving this morning or getting ready to leave?"

Him: "No. Why would I do that?" (Man looks bewildered.)

The unspoken sentiment was that if I had the time to ask such ridiculous questions, then I certainly had the time to drive them into town.

One small achievement was that by year two I had instituted my own "ride-share" program to help me get work done during my taxi runs. Only in this ride-share, if you wanted a ride, you had to participate in the conversation. It worked quite well as it was easy to instigate a conversation, and I was usually able to include someone fluent enough in English to translate for me. Similar to the talks I'd have around a roasted goat or an evening chat, they were casual. But unlike those conversations, no one stayed on one topic for long, and there was more lighthearted gossip. Because we were in transit, and together with a random assortment of people, the situation produced a distinct kind of interaction. There was a wonderful sense of freedom and transience about the conversations. The bonding and intimate conversations that often occurred were unique to the group composition and seemed to last only as long as the ride. It was also an additional method of hearing what was on people's minds. For instance, I learned:

- The development worker convinced Symon's little mother to put a chimney in her house, but he installed it crooked. She's afraid the rain will pour in during the wet season and the flies will get in when it's dry, but she's more afraid to touch it. So there it stays, a cautionary tale of what can happen when you try something new.

- Jumping on that theme, a senior warrior described how he got tricked into eating his first scrambled egg. Someone told him it was a cake so he ate it and found such a horrid taste. "Ah!! This is no cake!!" he cried!

- There's big trouble between the Samburu of the Lmasula clan and the Samburu Ndorobo who live across the river. Two nights ago, a few Lmasula warriors went to sing in Lorian where the Ndorobo live. As soon as they started singing, the local Ndorobo elders ran out of their homes, shooting arrows to chase them off! The Ndorobo claimed that the warriors were singing to attract the attention of their wives, whom the warriors were then seducing. The warriors denied any wrongdoing. The next day, there was a big meeting attended by Ndorobo elders and the Samburu warriors, along with some Samburu elders (including Lentoijoni) to settle the dispute. The warriors called the meeting to order by . . . singing. Everyone thought this was very funny except the Ndorobo, who—

according to the warriors—have no sense of humor. Matters are still very tense. *But things are always this way*, the Samburu tell me.

- The next Land Rover crowd said the Ndorobo may have a point about the singing. They said Samburu warriors don't just go and sing anywhere. They sing where there are lots of girls and young wives. The group had no doubt that the warriors were indeed there to seduce the Ndorobo elders' wives.

- Once when Symon and Lmariwan were in the car, they tried to explain how they were related. Symon started: "My father's brother is Lmariwan's mother's father's brother, er, I mean sister! Ah!" Lmariwan and others tried to help get it straight, and everyone was in stitches! Finally someone offered, "That's why Lmariwan calls him uncle," which only brought on more insane laughter.

As people got more used to me, I became more a part of everyday life. In addition to providing the periodic car service, I was also the local pharmacist and the neighbor who had a lot of extra stuff to lend out. The Samburu are a very generous people and will always lend you things you need. So I followed suit, lending my flashlight, tin cups, spoons, etc. to friendly neighbors. Unfortunately, the rules for returning borrowed items were never quite clear to me. I was told it was extremely impolite to ask for items to be returned, and hinting at it never seemed to make the slightest impression. I even tried asking to borrow them back.

Me: "Say, can I borrow a torch from you tonight?"

Him: "I don't have any."

Me: "What about the torch I lent you last month?"

Him: "The one you gave to me?"

Me: "I didn't give it to you; I lent it to you."

Him: "Yes, I will get that for you."

It was not clear if he just remembered that he did have my flashlight and would now go get it, or if the flashlight was at a friend's home and he had to track it down. No time frame was given for when he'd actually return it to me, and I didn't want to risk making a social blunder over a flashlight. So I let it lie. Maybe he was counting on that. Maybe he went to retrieve it and just forgot. Maybe he is still planning on getting it to me sometime. In any case, I never saw the flashlight again, or—as you might have guessed—the tin cups, the spoons, or the "etc."

I was also the resident expert on the weird behavior of white people, such as the disgusting things we eat. Every time I fired up the old gas canister and started cooking, the kids would crowd around the window to see what I was brewing up. Like Hansel and Gretel, they were innocently curious, but unlike the ill-fated children of the fairy tale, the Samburu kids would wisely never accept a taste of my supper. I don't know what they were expecting, but I usually ate oatmeal with a dash of salt and no milk, sometimes twice a day. During the day I'd open the shutters to get some light, and the kids would peer through the hole in the wall that was my window.

"What is that?!?" they asked as I slopped a glob of oatmeal into my tin bowl.

"Oatmeal, the same thing I ate yesterday," I responded, giving them the same answer that I had given them yesterday. As I spooned the lumpy, colorless mush into my mouth the kids squealed in disgust and gleefully ran away, the same way they had yesterday. We'd all get a kick out of this silly routine. When we started out, it seemed irrelevant that the dish was oatmeal; they would have squealed at anything. Then the fact that it was *always* oatmeal became part of the game. Sometimes I dreamed of cooking up something with dangling tentacles or neon colors to add an element of surprise. But, of course, I never did because I was such a lazy cook. And it hardly mattered. The kids remained enthusiastic no matter how many times we played, and so did I.

My most rewarding community obligation was as nurse and ambulance driver. The maze-like entrance of the traditional home helped keep animals out, but it also acted like a light and smoke block to keep it dark and smoky inside. There was only one small window high on the wall. The design kept the flies out, and worked very well at that. However, it was also difficult to see where you were walking as you entered from the bright outdoors. Add the fact that the open cooking fire was usually near the center of the room and that children ran in and out all day, and you can guess the problem. Unfortunately, burns were common in Samburu homes. Samburu mothers trained their children early in life to be wary of fire. I once witnessed a mother handing a small child a smoldering log from the fire. "Here." The child grabbed the log, burned her hand and recoiled screaming. "See, it's hot," said the mother calmly. "Don't touch it again." It seemed to be very effective. However, accidents still happened and they were hard to witness.

Before leaving for Kenya, I packed my trusty medical reference book *Where There Is No Doctor* by David Werner (first published in 1970 with many annual updates). I also packed instructions and medical supplies from my physician stepfather, including hydrogen peroxide, tetracycline antibiotic powder, and plenty of gauze. With these, and boiled, clean water, I could give emergency treatment for first- and second-degree burns. Nevertheless, there was always the open question: *Should I drive this person straight away to the hospital?* It was never simple. I was not always around, and even if I was, I could not be driving to and from the hospital every day. Moreover, the Samburu were very suspicious of Western medicine.

Take the day that Lekimorian came by with his daughter, who seemed to have malaria, and his son, who suffered from a *rungu* (club) wound. The rungu wound was pretty straightforward. I cleaned and bandaged the

Samburu children. The girl in front (with bead necklace) liked to accompany Diane and carry her notebook.

wound and checked for infection over the next few days. For his daughter, I left Camoquin and aspirin to fight the malaria. Her father had given her seketet fruit, a traditional remedy from the seketet tree found in the forest. The Samburu would grind the dried fruit, then mix it in porridge or tea for a tonic. It was commonly used to treat malaria, boost immunity, speed recovery, and restore the body's strength. He had also given her goat fur and fat to make her vomit. It was very difficult convincing Lekimorian of the value of taking Camoquin and aspirin and the importance of drinking clean water. He seemed pretty set on the goat fur and seketet, which he found to work just fine. Nonetheless, I pressed on. "You take three Camoquin pills all at once today, then the two aspirin tonight, and then the other two aspirin tomorrow morning. Don't forget to drink boiled water and see me tomorrow morning." Chloroquine, if it were available, would have been better, but would have been even more difficult to administer. The regime for Chloroquine went something like this: take four pills all at once the first day, two pills after eight hours, and two pills each day for the two following days. It's hard enough to get people who actually believe in Western medicine to take all their pills on a schedule. Moreover, my treatment sounded ridiculous if there were forest remedies nearby that "worked just fine."

The Samburu were even more suspicious of the hospital. To them, it was the place where people went and died. They treated most of their ailments at home with local remedies and with the aid of experienced women and local healers. If someone was taken to the hospital, it was generally after considerable time and after exhausting all traditional options. By that time, these patients were likely so far gone that nothing could save them, and they would end up dying in the hospital, fulfilling the prophecy. One particular case haunted me.

It was in February, at the end of another long day. I had been up late the night before and wanted to sleep in that morning. Symon and Letumba's brother abruptly changed my plans when they pounded on my door at 7:45 a.m.

"Letumba's wife is very sick! You need to drive her to the hospital immediately!"

On the way to her home, they gave me the lowdown. She had been sick for three days; the traditional healer had given her boiled seketet fruits and goat fur and fat; she had been given no other food; nothing was working. Friends had warned Letumba that if he took his wife to the hospital she would die immediately from the injections they would give her. But after three days with her condition deteriorating each day, Letumba felt he was out of options.

By the time I arrived at his nkang, all the elders were outside waiting for my car. Before my car even stopped rolling, they had carried her out and opened my back door. She immediately went into a muscle spasm, severely arching her back, stiffening her body, and locking her hands into claws. I had never seen anything like it before. But remembering the pictures in my health book, it looked like tetanus. Whatever it was, I saw it as another example of an illness that had gone on for too long without effective treatment. Moreover, it was surely aggravated by their practice of withholding water from those who are sick and instead giving them melted fat. They gently laid her out on the back seat. Then Letumba, Lenoppian, and a brother-in-law climbed next to her and into the far back of the vehicle. By the time we got her to the hospital, the spasms had worsened. The doctor suspected pneumonia with complications of meningitis or cerebral malaria and did not have a hopeful prognosis. However, by the time we left, he had put her on intravenous fluids, which was somewhat reassuring. We drove back home in silence—getting a flat tire on the way—each imagining the worst and not knowing what to tell her anxious family members waiting at home. "We'll see," I told them when we returned. But I could not imagine anyone recovering from that condition.

A few nights later, I had another illness to deal with—my own. The cold that I had been nursing for a week turned into something like pneumonia. I was coughing so badly that the noise woke up the headmaster, who pounded on my door in the predawn hours.

"Diane, it is time you drive yourself to the hospital, while you still can." He helped me into my Land Rover and sent me off with his mother's home address, which was very near the Catholic mission clinic, which was on the other side of town from the hospital. If I was not up for driving back that night, I should stay with his mother. She—for some reason—was expecting me. So with her address in hand, I set off for the same hospital I took Letumba's wife to, arriving just before sunrise.

Luckily, the hospital was staffed, and I didn't wait long before a professional-looking fellow in a white jacket showed me to a room. There he took my vitals and gave me a small paper Dixie cup with three large white pills.

"Here. Take these. They will cure your cough." And he left. Even in my feverish stupor I knew that three pills could not cure an undiagnosed cough. But I was still puzzling over these mysterious pills, and who gave them to me, when the doctor came in. Oddly, I sat holding the Dixie cup of pills throughout my whole exam without him asking about it. He diagnosed my illness as either a common cold or a bacterial infection. But in either case the treatment was the same, as they had no antibiotics in stock. He went on to tell me that they also had no aspirin or malaria medication. They did have insulin, which was not in any demand, and what he described as a pregnancy-test kit with instructions only in French. It was hard to tell because no one there read French, and in any case no one needed a silly kit to detect pregnancy. But back to my case. Yes, he was 100 percent certain they had no useful medicine.

"What about these?" I asked, holding up the Dixie cup with the three large pills.

"What are those?"

"I don't know. The fellow who checked me in gave them to me to cure my cough."

"Oh give me those!" And he snatched the pills from my hand while muttering, more to himself than to me, "I wish he would stop doing that!"

Needless to say, the whole trip did not inspire much confidence, and I made a mental note: *never again should I get sick up-country.* The doctor did recommend I try the Catholic mission clinic on the opposite side of town, as they often had a better store of medication.

The small Catholic clinic was packed with patients by the time I arrived. But as with the hospital, they were doing their best to see everyone. The nun who attended to me looked so tired that I didn't expect her to have an ounce of compassion left in her, and it wasn't even noon. But to her credit, she tried. Without much of an examination, she diagnosed pneumonia and gave me a rolled up newspaper cone filled with what she told me were antibiotics. So with my medicine in hand, I drove over to the headmaster's mother's house as he had instructed.

I was in pretty sad shape when I arrived on her doorstep. As she opened the door I saw that the headmaster's mother was an elderly woman in a printed skirt and white blouse, and her headscarf wrapped in the Kikuyu style. There I was, a bedraggled, ill, white girl, holding a newspaper cone of pills whimpering in a language she could not understand.

As it turned out, she spoke no English or Swahili. And I spoke no Kikuyu. To this day I still don't know how she could have expected me, or if she even did. I'm only guessing she understood me when I told her that her son had sent me. Nevertheless, she immediately ushered me into her home, made a bed for me in the back room, and mothered me back to health over the next three days. Each morning and evening she would tenderly mop my forehead with a wet cloth and bring me chicken soup she had made from one of her chickens.

On the afternoon of the third day I felt well enough to go to the post office to check for letters from home. There I found four letters from my mother that had been stacking up over time. My mother wrote me every single week for nearly 100 weeks, and I cherished each of those letters. The mail came sporadically, but never had I received so many letters at one time. I remember the day I sat in bed reading Mom's letters and crying softly when the headmaster's mother came in to check on me. She sat down on the bed and gently spoke to me. I held up the letters, and she appeared to understand without words that these were letters from my family. It had been a tough few weeks. I was sick and lonely, and I just seemed to break down. She didn't know me, and she asked nothing from me. She was just there for me, a stranger on her doorstep, and I have never forgotten it.

To this day, people ask me and my husband why we always seem to have a series of long-term houseguests. For me, it's partly because I always remember the headmaster's mother and others who opened their homes to me. I know how much it means to receive help when you are far from home. I thanked the headmaster's mother as best I could. Yet I don't think she ever realized how much her kindness meant to me.

At the end of three days, the headmaster came to visit his mother, and he and I returned to the plateau together. Back home, I couldn't help thinking about the contrast between the care I had received and what Letumba's wife was probably getting in the hospital. While the hospital provided a bed and medicine, when they were available, that was about all it provided. There were no linens, towels, or food for the patient, except that which was provided by the family.

As it turned out, Letumba's family rose to the occasion. Over the past week a female or male relative walked every day into town to see the young wife and care for her. Letumba was an important elder in the community and a significant actor in the livestock market. Since this was the end of the dry season and beginning of the wet season, he was extremely busy moving his livestock from dry- to wet-season grazing. But his close network of family was there to help him and his wife. When I asked how the young wife was doing, I was totally shocked to hear she was "fine." Amazing! I was anxious to see the family again and hear how she had been treated. But that would have to wait. For now there were wet-season rituals to prepare for.

Along with the early rains in March came the green grass, fatter cattle, milk, money, and ritual ceremonies, in that order. There were circumcisions, weddings, and this year the *lmugit* (age-set ritual) *lenkarna* (of the name), whereby the junior warriors move up in rank to join the senior warriors. The lmugit lenkarna happens when boys are about 20 years old, every five to eight years. In the first part of the ceremony a *launoni*, or ritual leader of the age-set, is chosen; in the second part of the ceremony the group receives an official name from the elders.

The lmugit rituals (and there were several throughout a young man's life) were promotion ceremonies of the Samburu and core to its age system. The *lmugit of the name* recognized that the junior warriors had advanced in maturity. In joining the senior warriors they would maintain their unmarried, warrior lifestyle, with a few new privileges that began to prepare them for elderhood. When you became a senior warrior you could father children, as long as the girl was circumcised, and you gained a certain amount of power over your younger siblings if your father died. But you still could not marry, nor did you have any authoritative power to influence the elders over important issues, such as selecting a husband for your younger sisters. Fundamentally, the ceremony relieved some of the pressure created by the group of growing young men pushing to advance against a group of elders pushing back to maintain their own rank and power.

Symon and Jacob explained to me that all the *lmurran* (warriors) from the Lmasula section would attend, maybe 400 young men in all. And because the highlands was the center of the Lmasula clan, the ritual would be held right here. Each lmurrani would bring two steers so there would be plenty of meat to eat, and a big village would be built to house all the participants. The elders would bless the warriors, give them their section name, and install the launoni.

We were now in the first stage where the launoni was selected by the elders. The candidate had to come from a good family, be of strong character, be nonviolent, have both parents living, never have had a broken bone, and other very specific requirements.

"It's an honor to be chosen launoni," Symon explained.

"Yes," Jacob added. "And no one wants to be chosen."

"That's true," Symon clarified. "It's an honor, and no one wants it."

The launoni had considerable power. He also had serious responsibilities and prohibitions that conflicted with the life of a high-spirited warrior. For instance, he could never participate in a cattle raid or any dangerous activity for fear of harm coming to him. For lmurran, who spent all their time together, becoming the odd-man-out was a dubious honor.

"Actually, one was already chosen, but he ran away," Jacob offered.

"Yes, the elders have gone to Nairobi to bring him back. They won't reveal the date of the lmugit until they can get him here." As it turned out, the lmugit did not get going until August, and a runaway launoni was to be the least of their troubles. But that's a story for another chapter.

With all the wet-season activities came the steady need for market goods like tea, sugar, and ochre for body paint. This meant that my vehicle was requested more than usual. And by "request," I mean I'd hear BAM, BAM, BAM on my door and a polite but firm request that I drive whomever into town at that moment. On one such shopping run, I took several women of the Lentoijoni nkang. With the shopping done, we were leaving Maralal when I was surprised to come upon Letumba, who flagged me down on the road. He asked if I had room for his wife, as she was done with the hospital and well enough to come home.

"Wonderful! Absolutely," I said. Making a wide U-turn, I swung by the hospital to pick her up. Letumba, Symon, and Symon's five assorted relatives squeezed in the back, and we installed the now recovered patient into the coveted front seat. The young wife smiled weakly, but it was enough to ignite everyone in the car. The women passengers were so excited about the upcoming circumcision they were shopping for, and the healthy return of Letumba's wife and the coming lmugit, that they sang the whole trip back. They sang about me taking them to get tea. They sang about the circumcision. They sang about Letumba's healthy wife. They sang about everything current and happy. When we reached our first stop, Letumba's nkang, all of the young wife's children and assorted relatives ran out of the nkang, enveloping us in a cacophony of cheering and singing. It must have all been too much for Letumba's wife. Frightened by serious illness, grateful for recovery, and overjoyed to be home, she hung her head and sobbed quietly, unable to get out of the car. Gently, her husband opened the car door and helped her out and into the arms of her family, where she quickly disappeared from view. Turning back to me, Letumba beamed.

"Your Land Rover saved her life. Come back to my nkang tomorrow. I will give you a special gift." Well, that was enough to reignite the happy women in my car. They erupted in more laughter, more singing, and wild speculation about what the grand present would be! In case you are wondering, the gift turned out to be a heartwarming and extremely long speech and blessing, which touched me deeply but greatly disappointed the neighborhood women who sniffed disapprovingly when they heard of it.

I had just saved a woman's life, and that realization scared me. If I hadn't been there, would she have died? What about the little burn victim I didn't transport to the hospital last month? Was I lucky she had survived? Life was complicated, and my role as a "participant observer" in Samburuland was clearly weighing on me. Interviewing people, living with them, and hanging out with them over a prolonged period is what anthropologists do. The concept is that through living with people and participating in their community life, you gain a better understanding of the meaning and values behind sociocultural behavior—be it livestock marketing or any other academic question. Basically, it is all supposed to come together in the end.

The assumption is that the anthropologist knows how to do this. But how does one participate in the right things, how much participating is the right amount? And how does one participate and still maintain an outsider's perspective? "Hanging out" is such a slippery slope.

So far, hanging out had gotten me mixed up in all sorts of complications. I was supposed to study men's economic activities and specifically livestock marketing. Yet while studying this in the community context, I had been spending most of my time "in the context" and much less time actually studying livestock trading. When was the last time I even thought about The Market?! I was a guest lecturer at the elementary school. I made house calls as the resident nurse/doctor. I drove an ambulance. I took wedding pictures! I was getting sucked in and absorbed deeper and deeper into a tangled web of Samburu reciprocal relationships!

When I thought about it, I realized that this is what participating in a community is all about. It's how we survive physically and emotionally. We share. We share in the celebrations of birth, death, illness, and recovery. We share in the daily grind and in fortuitous events. We share our dreams and desires, anxieties and obsessions, proud achievements and gross miscalculations. What we don't do is participate while staying apart from it all!

Participating also brought up the problem of confusing individual variation with social norms. One woman squirreled away her earnings from selling beads in a small metal box, hidden behind layers of cloth and firewood, and secured by a giant lock. Was this a reflection of women's socioeconomic vulnerability, or of one woman's trust issues? The more I got to know the details of people's lives, the more I saw how individual "issues" were entangled throughout social behavior. This was especially true with the topic I chose to study: marketing behavior. *Who on earth doesn't have personal issues about money?!*

I was initially drawn to the highland Samburu as an example of a people in transition from a traditional to a commercial market economy. It didn't take long for that basic pattern to be a problematic oversimplification that failed to adequately explain what I saw in the field. Individuals were not on a linear trajectory. Nearly everyone, at some time in their lives, was simultaneously operating in several sectors—traditional, nontraditional, and commercial—sectors that themselves never stood still. Traditional, nontraditional, and commercial practices were continually changing. Well, not all of the practices were changing, and not all at the same pace, and not all necessarily in the same direction. And just where were the boundaries of these sectors!? Samburu women incorporated traditional, original, and foreign-inspired styles into their traditional crafts; junior elders bought and sold more livestock on the commercial market when they were younger than when they advanced to the next stage of their pastoral career.

Far from filling in the gaps of my neat theoretical framework, every answered question led me down a rabbit hole of new questions. For instance, take the widow Ratin. She was exasperated with the man who lived in the nkang next to hers. He was a belligerent drunk who was unpredictable and frequently threatened to burn down her house. So she packed up her mother, her children, and her belongings, and moved. Where did she move to? She built and moved into a new home just to the other side of the belligerent man's nkang! Then there was the case of high-land goats. Herd owners liked to keep goats because they were drought and disease resistant, easy to market for small cash needs, and they were the choice animal roasted and proudly served on special occasions.

"And they are delicious!" I added.

"Not really," replied one prominent elder. "The goats of the highlands are small, tasteless, hairy, and sad creatures."

What?!

An individual could be suspicious and risk-averse one moment, then driven by blind trust and greed the next. Some people had delusions of grandeur; others had self-esteem problems. Some people worked against their own self-interest; others lied for no apparent reason. Jacob told me the story of one boy who was mad at his father for giving away an animal he hoped to inherit. The next day, the boy went out and stole a bigger animal in broad daylight. "He must have known he'd get caught," I said. "Of course," Jacob replied. "That was the whole point."

Living with people and getting to know them as individuals was complicated and totally messing with my research hypothesis! When I first interviewed Lesewa, he asked me, "Do you want to hear our stories or our secrets?" Sometimes I felt like whimpering, *Can't you just fill in the blanks on my questionnaire?* The more secrets and stories I heard, the more odd bits and pieces of data I added to the "miscellaneous" pile. I both knew too much and didn't know nearly enough. At this stage of my fieldwork, the only thing I was sure of was that I was lost in the weeds.

Then there was the question of intervention. I helped Dorcas plan her wedding. I bandaged burns and bought Lekimorian's daughter medicine. I loaned stuff. I even—I'm ashamed to admit—gave marital advice to the school headmaster. The questions plagued me. *How much should I assist people in their daily lives? How do I ensure I do no harm? Should I take sides? Should I give people what they want, or what I think they need?* Lalaikiar wanted me to buy him a tractor and provide regular deliveries of petrol.

Finally, there was the guilt associated with the whole process. The concept is that, as an anthropologist, you live with the people as a trusted and participating member of their community. They know you are studying their ways. But it's not that simple. You become invested and engaged. They share their highs and lows, their plots and plans. You listen attentively, and at the end of every day you write it all down. You analyze every individual and deeply personal story for clues to better understand some higher sociocultural concept. But the more I got to know and care for these people as individuals, the creepier I felt about studying them. That was the hardest thing to do emotionally, and it was weighing on me in ways I had not anticipated. I was feeling overwhelmed.

I found myself spending more hours hiding in my room, reading *War and Peace*. Little did I know at the time, but life was about to get even more complicated.

April ended the same way the year began, with a fire. It was in the forest area near the school. But this time it was no small beehive that was burning. This fire was huge! Jacob raised the alarm and then enlisted me and my Land Rover to ferry in water and drive out any victims if the need arose. As we drove to the edge of the forest where the fire was centered, the first thing I noticed was the smell of smoke, which instantly ignited my fear response. I froze at the wheel and could go no further. With Jacob's urging, I pressed on as he jumped out of the car and ran into the fire zone. I could clearly hear the crackling and see the flames licking high into the treetops. I knew I should get closer in case they needed to carry out injured people. So I inched forward, feeling the intense heat through the closed windows. At one point I heard a sizzling sound and turned to see the rubber weather strips lining my car windows melt and shrink. *Far enough*, I decided.

Outside, I could see the warriors and at least one junior elder battling the base of the fire with palm fronds and other bundles of long branches. I could not imagine how they could put out the fire without water, but that's just what they did. Basically, they put this huge fire out with a bunch of brooms. These people never ceased to amaze me. After what seemed like an eternity, Jacob ran back to tell me that no one was hurt. I was also told that the blaze was started by the junior elder who lived there in a small nkang. He had lit a fire to burn the brush around his farm and then just walked away. *That's idiotic. It can't be true*, I thought. And really, the only thing that made it plausible was the fact that everyone else thought it was completely in character for the junior elder in question to do such a thing. Getting home at long last, I collapsed into bed without changing clothes and fell into a sound asleep. Even my resident cricket didn't keep me up that night.

The next few weeks passed like every other at this time of year. The rain made everything a bit easier. Symon and I made our rounds to various homes, conducting interviews concerning livestock issues and collecting milk yield data from the various households. If I couldn't exactly piece things together in my mind, at least I could collect tons of data and hope that sometime, with some distance, a thesis would emerge. My mental fatigue and warriors singing nearby put me to sleep at night. Maybe that's why in early May I slept through a major commotion that happened in the room at the end of my wing.

The first hint I had that anything unusual was going on was when I woke up to the sounds of a large group of people gathered outside my door. Dressing quickly, I emerged to see the schoolyard crowded with Samburu and police officers from Maralal and an official-looking vehicle. Evidently, two or three of the local elementary school teachers had gotten drunk the night before, and raped two Samburu girls.

The teachers were often drunk and loud. But things seemed to have gotten out of control over the last few days. It started when the headmaster caned several Samburu boys after class for misbehaving. The boys limped home, and one had trouble urinating for two days. When he began to piss blood, his father realized that this time the headmaster had gone too far. I drove the boy to the Maralal hospital while several enraged elders came to the school to confront the headmaster. Wisely, the headmaster ran away before they could catch him, and never returned. As second in command, Jacob, the only Samburu teacher, took over as headmaster until the situation was resolved. One of his first duties was to take public transport south to pick up the school's food supply. That was when all hell broke loose, while Jacob was gone.

With no official headmaster on the premises, the antics of the teachers were worse than usual, especially the two untrained teachers: Mwalimu and the Kisi man. It was not unusual for them to drink, sing, argue, and laugh loudly. But their behavior was usually confined to their rooms where they drank and played cards. Still, it was hard for me to imagine the people I knew attacking the local girls so violently. For the Samburu, this was a matter deeper than the assault on their girls. It was about the disrespect that outsiders, and in particular the Kikuyu, show the Samburu people.

The police stayed to question witnesses throughout the day and finally left with Mwalimu and the Kisi man in custody. But we were far from reassured. When the dust settled, we realized that Dorcas, one of the few witnesses named by the Samburu girls, had disappeared. This was the situation that greeted Jacob when he returned home the next day. Fortunately, he found Dorcas at her mother's nearby nkaji. Finding her was easy; getting her to return home was another matter. Jacob only managed to do this when she was assured that all the offending teachers had been taken away.

Once home, Dorcas explained to us what she witnessed.

"On that night I was alone with the young boy Solomon who stayed with us. Suddenly in the middle of the night, I heard screaming and pounding on my front door. We were so afraid!" The pounding was from the schoolgirls trying to get into her house. Not knowing who was screaming or what was happening, Dorcas and Solomon braced themselves against the front door to keep whatever was happening outside from getting in. As soon as it was quiet, Dorcas and the boy slipped out of the house and ran all the way to her parent's home. Being inherently shy, the idea of talking to the police terrified Dorcas. Patiently, Jacob comforted and counseled her.

"Dorcas, you must testify to what you heard and saw. It is the only way to justice."

It took a lot of convincing, but with Jacob by her side, she bravely gave her testimony to the police along with the other Samburu neighbors. The two teachers were jailed awaiting trial. And for days afterward there was a dark, tense pall hanging over the school grounds.

At the end of that dark week, I left for Nairobi to repair my vehicle and resupply. By my current calculations, my "participant observing" had gotten me further away from completing my study than when I arrived. I had not only strayed pretty far from livestock marketing, but Samburu culture kept getting more and more complex. There was so much going on. I really needed to focus. Focus. My mind was swimming. Turning left onto the main road, I went to roll down the window to get some air and was surprised to find that my window seals were melted to the glass. It had actually slipped my mind that I had recently driven into a forest fire.

Years later, I learned the fate of the two jailed teachers. They were caned and sentenced to four years in jail.

"They were caned four strokes on the bottom," Jacob explained with the calm voice of someone who has seen much. "Salt was put in the wound to make it hurt. Then the jailers would wait two weeks and cane them again. They became impotent. Mwalimu was lucky; he was broken out of jail after a few months and not sent back."

"And the Kisi man?" I asked.

"Who knows?" Jacob shrugged. "He was not released and probably died in prison."

Although Mwalimu lost his teaching job, I was to meet up with him one more time.

Chapter 8

A Delicate Condition

I spent the next two weeks in Nairobi: resting, resupplying, and repairing my Land Rover. The last two months had been particularly tough. And while I found no answers in the bottom of the guacamole dish, I found company and reassurance among my friends and fellow researchers. They knew just what I was going through. And they reminded me of another piece of advice I had received from Sally Falk Moore before I left Los Angeles—advice that made little sense at the time. Referring to the dark, confusing days of fieldwork she said, "Keep in mind that you know more than you think you know." It seemed like a pretty low bar to brag about. But I agreed to try and keep her words in mind.

Before I was ready, May turned to June, and I was on the road back to Samburuland. Some trips were harder than others. During this one, I cried throughout the first two hours behind the wheel. I was feeling sorry for myself—sorry for my wasted, sad, academic life—sorry and guilty for writing down everyone's stories and secrets. I cried and sang loudly, living the heartbroken life of each country singer blaring from the cassette player beside me. I passed Gilgil. I passed T. Falls. Slowly, imperceptibly, I began to feel better. By the time I reached the rough road beyond Rumuruti, I was singing along with happier tunes. One thing had always been true for me: through every hard period of fieldwork, driving in up-country Kenya never failed to cheer me up. I loved driving my big, hulking Land Rover; I loved driving barefoot; and I loved driving alone in the car, and in control.

Even when I picked up a passenger or two or five, driving was good, because the passengers never failed to surprise and fascinate me. As the hours passed, I felt stronger and my thoughts drifted further from feeling inadequate to feeling energized and excited to rejoin my friends in the highlands. Did Letumba's young wife fully recover from her illness? How was Jacob adjusting to being the first Samburu headmaster at the elementary school? By the time I pulled up and parked in front of my room, I was back, fully present, and ready to make some progress!

During the days and weeks that followed, I picked up the threads of these Samburu lives as if I had never dropped them. The stories of Letumba and Jacob resumed on their own paths, while Symon and I conducted our regular interviews and herd counts. As before, every interview revealed both answers and a bottomless pit of new questions. Meanwhile, the scuttlebutt from my ride-share program kept me up-to-date on miscellaneous gossip that might at any time reveal profound truths . . . or not:

- Jepi, Symon's younger brother, was preparing to become an untrained teacher to supplement the household income. How one prepared to be "untrained" wasn't made entirely clear.

- A hungry porcupine had been ravaging the string bean crops in a few gardens. Even though the passengers believed the shamba owners were entitled to compensation from the government, no one expressed the slightest concern for the crop or intention to circumvent future porcupine attacks.

Throughout all these interactions, I was determined to clear away the fog, focus on my research, and define some overarching patterns—specifically patterns related to moving livestock through the traditional and commercial markets. I barely made it through the month before, once again, my life was thrown off course. This time permanently.

It was beginning to dawn on me that I was pregnant.

I had been feeling sore, gaseous, and unusually tired. Also, I had been bouncing between extremes of joy, despair, and irritability. As time passed and I became more convinced of my condition, these feelings coalesced into one swirling, nauseous soup. At times I felt at one with every mother who ever lived on this glorious planet. At other times, I panicked. *No! Not now! I'm just getting the hang of things and I have so much more work to do!*

I was a mess. So to settle my mind I drove into the Maralal hospital to take a definitive pregnancy test. I knew that no Samburu woman actually got a pregnancy test, but I also remembered from a previous hospital visit that they had a French language pregnancy-test kit sitting on the shelf. At least they had it a few months ago. I was hoping no one thought it was valuable enough to pilfer and that it would still be there.

I told the receptionist at the front desk that I could read French, and if she'd let me use the kit, I could administer it to myself. Sure. No problem. She was evidently so utterly bored with clerking that she not only let me into the staff area, but she joined me, dragging an old male technician and another young nurse along. We assembled in the back of the dispensary, where modern-looking equipment, medicine, and supplies sat neatly crowded amid ancient scales, bowls, and unidentifiable medical stuff on worn wooden shelves. In the center of the room were similarly crowded wooden desks and tables. The technician and young nurse cleared off one of the tables, while the receptionist went in search of this mysterious pregnancy-test kit. Surprising us all, she found it easily and helped me lay out the components: two small test tubes, a plastic rack, a vial of solution, assorted parts, and instructions in French. Reading carefully through the instructions, translating as I went, I mixed a few drops of my urine into the solution. Then, we waited. They went back to work, and I read, or tried to read, while my mind raced.

Two hours later, we reconvened over the test tube rack. I peered at the urine closely—then at the instructions, then back to the urine. *Yes. Yes.* I gasped. They looked expectantly at me, searching for the translation.

"I'm pregnant." I whispered with excitement and fear. They beamed— the receptionist, the nurse, and the aging technician. And we embraced over the good news as if we had known each other since childhood.

By the time I left the hospital, my agitation returned. *Am I really doing this?* I asked myself. I was just starting my last six months of fieldwork. I wanted to have children eventually but not now. Now is not what I had planned. And speaking of plans, I didn't have any. I had dreams, but I'd hardly call them plans. I was exactly where I wanted to be, doing exactly what I wanted to do, and with whom I wanted to do it. I was in the moment. As I quickly learned, there is nothing like getting pregnant to zap one out of the moment and into planning mode.

Before I left Nairobi, having experienced the failure of a contraceptive device, David and I had talked about what we'd do if the *what if* came to pass. This included a discussion about where we might have a baby. Maybe it was the mandazis talking, but I really wanted to have the baby in Kenya. I was sure to find great health care, and it wasn't like I was having brain surgery. Babies are born everywhere. I probably didn't even need a hospital! How great would it be to have my baby in Samburuland! Not feeling the kumbaya spirit, David felt compelled to talk me down by reenacting every childbirth horror scene we'd ever seen in movies: the screaming, the sweating, the profuse bleeding, and the agonizing death of the birth mother. Okay, okay, so maybe having a hospital nearby wasn't such a bad idea. We continued to debate having this hypothetical baby in L.A. or Nairobi. But it always came down to the fact that David had completed his fieldwork and was determined to get back to Los Angeles in August. His decision was made, and I reluctantly came to terms with it.

But this was all hypothetical. At the time of these conversations, neither of us knew that I was actually pregnant, and it didn't seem particularly real. Suddenly, as I walked out of the Maralal hospital that afternoon, it became very real. So, without David even knowing that he was about to become a father, I started making plans.

If I was to have the baby in the States, I now had a deadline and needed to pick up the pace. I always thought I'd finish up my research around December with the option of staying longer if my money held out. With the clock ticking, that was no longer feasible. If I completed my work in early November, it would be the start of my seventh month; travel on the rough roads to Nairobi would still be manageable, and the airlines would still let me fly. Working from that assumption, my next step was to hire a second assistant, and I had just the person in mind—Lmariwan.

As you'll recall, Lmariwan was Symon's father's father's cowife's son's daughter's son, or Symon's nephew—a nephew about the same age as the uncle. Or by another account, Symon's father's brother is Lmariwan's mother's father's brother. In any case, Symon and Lmariwan were great friends, in addition to the uncle–nephew relationship, and their parents lived in the same nkang. Moreover, their personalities meshed perfectly. While Symon was the confident, outgoing leader and teacher, Lmariwan was soft-spoken and reserved. Although he was tall and muscular, Lmariwan tended to be the quiet one at the back of a group. There was considerable potential energy about him—an underlying eagerness, but he needed some encouragement to participate. He was quick to laugh at a joke and spoke English well. I felt that if I would only ask the right question, Lmariwan would love to jump into the conversation. Fundamentally, he was a good, smart, reliable kid. With Lmariwan on the job, I could do my rounds even when Symon was not available. And with both of them involved, I could potentially get deeper information, as more than one warrior in a conversation always generated an animated discussion.

With two assistants and a looming deadline, I really started to crank and pull in a lot of new data. I got my big break one fateful day when Lentoijoni asked me if I would like to review his diaries with his written livestock transactions over the past several years.

Say again?

It happened like this. We were sitting inside Lentoijoni's wife's house, discussing livestock marketing. I asked Lentoijoni to tell me about the different ways he moved his livestock. He thought about this for a while and then said, "I don't think I can recall all of them right away." Did he think I expected him to remember every sale, purchase, trade, loan, and gift he had ever made? These people have phenomenal memories when it came to cows! Still, I laughed at the very idea. Then he continued. "But if it would help, you can read my diaries of my transactions." I just stared at Symon, thinking: *No one, in the past 18 months, thought I might be interested in this?!*

"Yes, thank you," I told Lentoijoni, trying to stay calm and in control. "That would help." And it did.

Lentoijoni would not let me take the diaries, but he was more than willing to discuss them with me, which helped put the transactions in a social context. It was not clear how comprehensive they were. But I was thankful and astonished that they existed at all. It underscored yet another remarkable aspect of Lentoijoni's leadership: in a society that did not yet value education, he was one of the few elders who was literate.

Walking back to my room after leaving Lentoijoni, Symon, and Lmariwan for the day, I thought about the erratic family business of cattle keeping, the unwritten responsibilities that went along with each cattle transaction (given or withheld), and the rapidly developing commercial market. I thought about the diaries I was privileged to see and discuss. Did Lentoijoni just outline a Livestock Business Plan?

The Samburu have a saying: "*Ketuwana parakuo nicho la mali lchapu oa tii sesen*" (Wealth is like dirt on the body); it can wash away at any time, leaving nothing. While there were certainly areas of good grazing and market options throughout the region, unpredictability made the Samburu pastoral economy both vulnerable and volatile. Rainfall was localized and unreliable; you could get lucky or suffer the drought. Cattle raiders came by surprise from the north and west and were now armed with Kalashnikov assault rifles. *Lipis* (East Coast Fever) was a virulent tick-born cattle disease with no effective treatment (at the time), and it could kill 90–100 percent of a herd in two weeks! It could hit anywhere in the region, anytime, and spread like wildfire. As one herder told me, "Lipis is everywhere now. So there is no reason to send my animals to other nkang'itie. I would rather keep them with me. How are they? They are all dead. I just bought 20 animals and had to see them all die." Pretty grim.

Despite the risk and uncertainty of pastoral life, the Samburu were a surprisingly optimistic people. By and large, the Samburu were confident that if they could manage their herd and their relations well, they could benefit from both the commercial and traditional sectors. And there was some truth in this, because unlike farmers, who the Samburu noted could not move their farms, herders could move their cattle like chess pieces on a verdant board. The basic operation of pastoralism is to move livestock in a pattern from wet season to dry season grazing areas, visit watering points daily in the wet season and every two or three days in the dry season, with regular trips to a salt lick, and to a cattle dip for treatment during tick season, preferably one that is diluted to the proper strength. It was believed that a smart pastoralist could meet these and other livestock needs, manage raiders and disease, honor his social obligations, and hit the fluctuating cattle markets at just the right time.

Here is where all those social ties came in. For while the grasslands, water, and salt were not privately held, information was, and access to everything could be made easy or difficult. As an example, while water was not owned, a herder had certain privileges over a watering hole that he had dug and maintained. While he could not easily refuse access to another herder, he could share it first and more liberally with those he selected. In recognition of this, a herder would never approach another man's watering hole without first respectfully asking permission.

Each man was enmeshed in a spider's web of relationships that not only provided access to information and other scarce resources but could propel the man to success, catch him if he fell, and give meaning to his life. Sons managed and benefitted from their father's herds; clans intermarried and supported certain other clans; age-mates had a special bond across all of Samburuland; and a rich herder at times bonded with a poor herder in a patron–client relationship. Each social connection was cemented with the loan or gift of cattle. Loans had the added benefit of spreading a man's herd among individuals and locations to reduce risk. If disease or raiders hit one region, these misfortunes wouldn't wipe him out. And even if the animal died, the borrower would owe the lender a replacement. A particularly clever transaction is the trading of cursed animals. When a Samburu had to pay a fee or bribe to a non-Samburu official, he'd go to his relations or age-mates for a cursed animal to unload. If they didn't have one on hand, they'd acquire one from a friend. The bribe is paid without losing a valuable animal; one Samburu gets rid of a cursed cow and gains a little something for his trouble; and the official gains an animal he doesn't even know is cursed. Everyone's happy.

Arriving home, I sat cross-legged on my sleeping cot, and by the light and smell of a kerosene lamp I recorded my memories of the loan books before they evaporated. I had learned a lot about the business and value of cattle keeping, yet I knew so little about operational strategies. This was the value of these diaries. They let me leave traditional practices and market opportunities and think about a man's business over his lifetime. Reflecting on Lentoijoni's transactions over several years, it dawned on me that regardless of how a man got them, the hallmarks of success—the cattle, wives, children, friends, and respect—are only acquired over time. And Lentoijoni's goals and options clearly changed at each stage of his life.

I leafed through previous interviews and data about cattle sales, looking to see how they correlated, not to price, but to the age of the elder. Slowly, over the course of that long night, I saw strategies emerge, different marketing strategies at different phases of a man's social life. It went something like this: a young elder worked to exhaustion buying and selling to build up his assets in cash, cows, wives, and children; a firestick elder invested in the traditional sector to build his wealth, resilience, power, and respect in the community; and a senior elder ate his assets. Naturally, it wasn't that simple, but I was on to something. Moreover, I had a different way to analyze some perplexing behavior: like the young elder who bought high and sold low and then put all his revenue in a bank 31 hours away. Okay, so not everything made sense yet. But I felt myself moving forward.

Specifically, I felt my stomach moving forward, then up and over. I jumped up from my cot and raced outside toward the woods behind my room. *Hold it! Hold it!* I mumbled to myself as I passed a group of warriors. By now, the Samburu were used to me talking to no one in particular. They probably assumed I was cursing my female deity. I made it to the bushes, doubled over, and threw up. Feeling much better, I smiled into the inky forest. All in all, this had been a very successful day!

One of the side benefits of my pregnancy was it gave me access to another tangential—but fascinating—topic to explore: how pregnancy and pregnant women are regarded by the Samburu. The first thing I learned was that pregnant women requested and received milk and meat. Every time I drove into Maralal, Amer would send me home with milk, in whatever container he had available. In fact, Samburu men and women gave me milk whenever I visited their homes; people brought me milk whenever they visited my room; neighbors just dropped off gourds of milk outside my door when I wasn't home! I had never drunk so much delicious sour milk in my life. I loved it.

I also had begun to crave liver. 'Nuff said. I got liver. And getting good goat liver was hard to come by at that time, because so much of it was infected with worms. But somehow people found good worm-free liver. One fellow brought me liver all the way from Wamba, 108 km across Samburu District. "Please, don't go to so much trouble!" I pleaded. But they did anyway. And I was overwhelmed with the kindness and generosity of my neighbors. Finally, I was behaving in a way that made sense to people, because pregnant Samburu women also craved liver, just as they avoided fat, tea, and greasy meat. But these cravings were not always easy on the household, as one Samburu elder described in telling of his wife's pregnancy.

"She was pregnant, like you. One day, she pointed to my goat and said, 'Slaughter that goat for me. I need to eat meat!' So I slaughtered the goat and gave her all the meat. But she ended up only eating the liver. I slaughtered the whole goat for just the liver! The goat went before his time!"

Samburu women also wanted charcoal. It's taken by many pregnant women all over the world to relieve morning sickness, bloating, and nausea. I was given plenty of charcoal, which of course is always useful.

Other than craving liver and suffering from a bit of nausea and occasional vomiting, I felt great! I did, however, have one rather unglamorous fainting spell. It was the week a young British couple visited me in the field. She was a nursing student and he had grown up in Ethiopia. They were passing through and joined me on the plateau for a few days of sightseeing. I really enjoyed their company, and they were great to show around because I didn't need to babysit them and they knew how to drive a stick shift. The day I collapsed we were visiting a nkang near the school, standing in the kraal, which was covered in the usual dung and mud. Suddenly feeling dizzy, I plopped down on a nearby log and immediately fell backwards into the muck. I came to, once I hit the ground. Luckily, face up. The two visiting Brits nimbly got me into the Land Rover and took me back to my room to clean up and rest. It was great to have their help, because being the sole person who could drive was the only significant risk I worried about. I was fortunate that the one time I needed it, they were there.

The only lasting concern I had about the fainting spell was I feared the Samburu would brand me as a foreign girl in a "delicate condition." I didn't want people to exclude me from walking with them into the forest, heading out to distant nkang'itie, staying up late, or rising early because they thought I might faint again. And I didn't want people to withhold information they thought would upset me because I was pregnant. Evidently that was the case, at least once. I learned this the hard way when Jacob came to my door early one morning.

It was 2:00 a.m. Jacob woke me up, saying we had to rescue some poor lmurrani who was beaten up and thrown into the bush to die. Evidently, Lotuku had come by earlier, but the teachers chased him off, saying he should not disturb me. Knowing that it was urgent, Lotuku then woke up Jacob, who came to get me. After quickly briefing me, Jacob, Lotuku, and I jumped in the Land Rover and took off, stopping first at Letuno's nkang for reasons that weren't at all clear to me. Letuno was a firestick elder I did not know well, but his son was a gregarious warrior whom I had spoken with many times and knew quite well. The area outside the nkang was full of people—elders, warriors, women, even children. What were they doing awake at 2:00 a.m.? Where did they come from? I recognized Letuno, who was talking urgently to Jacob.

"Jacob!" I yelled, "Get into the car! We are wasting time here. Let's go!" It took forever to get the people out of the way so that I could get rolling. Too many warriors wanted to climb into the car. People kept climbing in and out. I couldn't get the door closed. Elders and women congregated all around the vehicle. Finally Letuno helped by getting people to move back, and people began to respond to me pulling them back from the car. We finally took off with Lotuku, three others, and Jacob in the front seat next to me.

There was no moon and no clear road through the bush, which made driving very difficult. My headlights seemed to make it worse. The lights bounced off each tree, and back in my face; everything else was engulfed in blackness. Jacob directed me as we wound round and round through the dark forest. I had absolutely no idea where I was, and the lights disoriented Jacob as well. But without them, we couldn't see a thing. We drove around for what seemed an eternity until we reached a spot in the bush that looked to me exactly like every other spot in the bush. I was directed to stop, and everyone jumped out of the car. This was evidently our destination.

Jacob told me to wait in the car while everyone else ran off into the forest. I sat there for a short time, listening to the warriors shouting instructions to each other, and to urgent footfalls through the dense foliage. Along with the tension in the air, the otherworldly night cries of the forest were jarring, especially the screeching of the tree hyrax that sounded like a bird being plucked alive.

Invited or not, I didn't drive out here at two in the morning to sit in the car. As quietly as I could I approached the noises coming from the darkness, until I could make out a group of men tending to a figure lying in the bush. As I stood behind them I could see it was a man, a warrior by his dress, lying on his back unconscious. Moving closer and bending over for a better look, I tried to make out who it was through his swollen and bloody features. Suddenly, I recognized him!

"Leshoo! This is Leshoo!" I cried. "Jacob, I know that warrior. Why didn't you tell me this was Leshoo?!"

"I didn't want to upset you, and risk you losing the child," was all he said.

Leshoo. I barely recognized him as his face was badly beaten. We quickly loaded Leshoo into the back of the car along with a junior elder, who had a horrendous slash on the top of his head. I put two of the other warriors in the back seat to take care of them, with Jacob up front to guide me. Retracing our route as best we could, we wound our way out of the forest and onto the road to the Maralal hospital.

On the way, Jacob told me what had happened. Early last night Leshoo had visited and slept with the wife of a junior elder named Lentowa. It was not unusual for a warrior to behave in this way. It was even understandable from one perspective. Warriors and teenage uncircumcised girls congregated together in groups, much like high school boys and girls do in America. Warriors had girlfriends and would woo them, give beads to them, and sing to them. The most popular girls—the bead girls—could be recognized by all the red beads stacked high around their necks. But all this fun and games would come to an end when the girls were circumcised and married. Bead girls were always married off to elders, sometimes many years their senior. It could be heartbreaking for the warriors and the bead girls who were not allowed to marry each other. Then again, love might have nothing to do with it.

Junior elders and warriors had a notoriously strained relationship covered by a thin veneer of respect and authority, independent of the conflict over women. Each age-set had a rival and potentially volatile relationship with the adjacent age-set. As warriors aged, they were pushing to become junior elders. Junior elders pushed back to keep the warriors from gaining power over women. At the same time, junior elders pushed upward to advance in power to become the ruling firestick elders, while firestick elders pushed back to retain their authoritative power. Like the ground in an earthquake zone, tension would grow and eventually a shift in power would occur, easing the stress temporarily. Until then, each group savored the rights and privileges of its rank and enjoyed competing with the adjacent age-set any way they could. For the warriors, this included seducing the elders' wives or, at the very least, making the elders worry about it.

Lentowa was off working in Nairobi when Leshoo paid a visit to his wife, or at least this was where Leshoo thought he was. Lentowa was actually just returning home. It was very hard to have secret affairs, especially when everyone lived so communally. For instance, Lentowa lived in a large nkang along with his two adult brothers and another relative, Lenairo.

Therefore, as soon as Lentowa returned home from Nairobi, his brothers told him what was going on.

"Standing before his nkaji," Jacob explained, "Lentowa shouted for Leshoo to come outside. Leshoo shouted back for Lentowa to come inside." Unbeknownst to Leshoo at the time, waiting outside the nkaji along with Lentowa were the two Lentowa brothers and Lenairo, who said they would kill Leshoo as soon as he emerged. They didn't have to wait long.

"I'll come out, but I won't die!" Leshoo yelled and came rushing out of the nkaji straight for Lentowa with his knife drawn. A fight ensued and Leshoo—being significantly outnumbered—got the worst of it. They beat him until he was unconscious, then plunged a knife deep into Leshoo's arm, thinking it was his chest. Finally, they threw Leshoo's body into the bush near the nkang, thinking he was dead.

"Shortly after that, Lotuku, who lived nearby, came to get me," said Jacob.

It took a while for Jacob to tell me the whole story, because every so often Leshoo would regain consciousness and he and the wounded elder in the back seat would start fighting. I had no idea why, until I learned the entire story and was told that the wounded elder in the back of my car— along with Leshoo—was Lentowa the aggrieved husband!

"Keep them separated!" I yelled back at the two warriors assigned to take care of them. "Keep them apart! NO FIGHTING IN MY CAR!" But it didn't do any good. Every time Leshoo regained consciousness, they started yelling and swinging at each other. Finally I slammed on the brakes, swerved to the side of the road, and stopped the car. I stomped back to the rear of the Land Rover and threw open the door that was hinged on one side. I was furious.

"Stop it! STOP IT!! If you two don't stop fighting, I will drag you out and leave you both by the side of the road to DIE!!" Then I slammed the door and stomped back to jerk the car into gear and continue to the hospital. What I neglected to see as I climbed back into the driver's seat was that Lentowa had managed to open the door, jump out the back, and run off into the bush. As I pulled away, I noticed him out of the corner of my eye, but in a moment he was gone.

"Why did he jump out!?" I asked Jacob.

"He went off to the west. He has family there, and he was afraid you would take him to the police."

Shortly after that, we pulled up to the hospital and Jacob and I walked Leshoo inside, while the others waited outside. The hospital ward consisted of two big rooms of beds, with an open-air hallway in between. I had expected a few technicians to run out and rush Leshoo into the ward on a gurney with the attending doctor hovering over him with an IV or something. Instead, Jacob and I stumbled in with Leshoo, sat him down on a wooden bench in the hallway, and waited. Finally, the attending nurse sauntered out from the back with a sleepy look and a clipboard.

"What is the problem?"

Are you kidding me?! I thought. Here was this boy, badly beaten and bleeding. He was conscious but kept passing out every few seconds, which made it doubly hard to complete the intake form.

"Name?"

This I knew, but not much else about this warrior, and Jacob had gone inside perhaps in search of the doctor. In any case, I don't recall any of the other questions because after the first one I put the pencil down. I was done.

"Please. I'll fill out the forms later. Just get a doctor to see him. Please!"

By the time we left the hospital at dawn, Leshoo was lying on a bare mattress, and the doctor said he should be all right, which I chose to believe as it was enormously reassuring. It was still morning when we returned home and were mobbed by everyone wanting to know how Leshoo was doing. No one knew what happened to Lentowa. Moreover, no one had heard from Lentowa's wife either. She had evidently been beaten, had run off into the bush, and had not been heard from since. Several days later I learned that Lentowa survived, but I knew of no other details. I was not even sure of the extent of his injuries.

Knowing I would not be allowed to take a nap, I decided to clean the blood out of the car, which was something I had to do before being able to drive anywhere. Equipped with a bucket of sudsy water, plenty of rags, and a scarf to cover my nose, I opened the rear door and set about cleaning the inside of the back section. There was blood everywhere, smeared all over the windows, on the seats, and the floor. Worse than the sight was the smell; it was overwhelming. The blood had a stomach-churning and pungent sickly sweet smell. By late afternoon, the car was acceptably clean, and everyone who needed to know about Leshoo had come by to be briefed. I slept that night undisturbed.

The next afternoon, I drove into Maralal to see how the poor warrior was doing and to drop off a few more people in town. Swollen, bruised, and bandaged, Leshoo was awake and healing remarkably well under the circumstances. But that was the easy part. A few days later, I was recruited to bring Leshoo home to face his father. It was a good thing Leshoo looked so beat up, or else his father would have surely laid into him. Instead, Letuno said nothing, nothing at all. But he said nothing in a brutal way. The father's words to his son would have to wait. For the moment, Letuno had Leshoo's legal troubles to address. A father not only controlled his son's livestock, but he also assumed the cost for his son's crimes and misdemeanors.

The day after Leshoo came home, Letuno went to the police station to deal with his son's case. It seemed to me that Leshoo had a good case against Lentowa as well, but evidently that was not how anyone else saw it. After some back and forth, the police officer requested an unspecified bribe—to be delivered the next day—as his price to have Lentowa drop the charges. With that deadline looming, an elder intermediary approached Lentowa directly to convince him to drop the police case and deal with this among themselves. At first Lentowa was unmoved. But eventually they settled on an amount outside the police and court system. Within two weeks, the case was resolved. Letuno paid Lentowa 2,000 shillings and Lentowa dropped the charges. I never did find out if Letuno also had to pay something to the police officer for his trouble.

As for Leshoo, he had to sell two prized *supat* (good) steer in Maralal. These were special animals that Leshoo received from a close age-mate during a promotion ceremony. One would never sell such animals. But Leshoo had no others, so off these went to market. Leshoo received 2,500 shillings for the two steers, enough to repay his father's debt.

In terms of Leshoo's physical recovery, he stayed at another nkang with a warrior friend to avoid his father's wrath. There he received plenty of support from his warrior mates who stayed with him constantly and gave him lots of meat. During this first week of recovery, they had eaten two sheep and a goat. As is the custom, water was withheld to dry out the wounds and avoid sepsis, and he was given seketet fruit to boost his immunity. Finally, a sheep's tail was cooked until the fat was rendered, and Leshoo was given the liquid fat to drink. I don't know how anyone ever recovers from that treatment. Perhaps it has some therapeutic effect; I remember my Russian grandmother giving me rendered fat to eat when I was sick. In any case, I can say from personal experience, it's best served on saltine crackers.

I checked on Leshoo once during that first week. His cut hand looked infected so I cleaned it, applied some tetracycline powder, and put on a fresh bandage. And although I knew it was not on the approved foods list, I handed him a juicy ripe orange before I left.

Another part of Leshoo's treatment included bleeding or wet cupping. This is a practice whereby the skin is lanced and "bad blood" is sucked out of the injured body part to relieve pain and swelling and promote healing. For this service, an expert was called in from Maralal. She was well-known all over Samburu District and charged—what I thought was a very reasonable—30 shillings per treatment. It was performed outside, with Leshoo lying on his stomach. In this position, the healer cut two small incisions with a razor blade over each swollen area, and using a two-ounce cow horn, she sucked out the blood. She did this by placing the base of the horn over the cuts and sucked through a tiny hole punctured in the tip of the horn. She drew out five horns filled with blood (about one cup), spitting the bad blood out onto a pile of dung at her side. I could not vouch for the effectiveness of the bleeding, but Leshoo seemed to be recovering smoothly. He was still pretty weak and frail, but it was nice to see him being nursed so attentively by his friends.

Another issue that worried me was the warriors' talk of taking revenge on Lentowa. They wanted to get together and beat up the junior elders who had tried to kill Leshoo.

"Lentowa had reason," they agreed. "But the other three who assisted Lentowa did not and should be punished!"

They were especially intent on getting Lenairo, who, throughout the fight, repeatedly yelled "Slit his throat!" I was hoping the warriors were just blowing off steam. In the past, a major fight had broken out between two age grade sections over just this sort of incident, causing the death of about 40 lmurran. In terms of Leshoo's case, Jacob kept his ear to the ground. Luckily, nothing materialized.

What a month! Leshoo nearly died, and I believe he would have if my Land Rover had not been there. Maybe he would not have died; maybe Letumba's wife would have survived fine without me as well. Maybe their traditional medicine was better than I gave it credit for, and maybe the body was more resilient that I thought it was. But it didn't feel that way to me at the time. I thought about the tiny heartbeat deep inside of me. I thought about its struggle to take root and grow. Life seemed so fragile, and death was too close for comfort. Looking down at my small belly—not yet stretched—I decided I wanted to finish my first trimester in Nairobi. I also had yet to tell David that he was going to be a father. A few days later, I was packed up and off to Nairobi for the next two weeks. I think the Samburu were a bit relieved to see me go, feeling as responsible for me as they did, and considering how I was currently in such a "delicate condition."

Chapter 9

The Government Is Not There

Back in Nairobi, I could get just about any fruit, vegetable, and delicacy I wanted, and the main thing I craved, other than goat liver, was fresh oranges. I remember one day, David brought home five oranges from the market. It was late in the afternoon, and he sliced them and put them on the table for afternoon tea for me, himself, and our housemates, Christie and Frank. I was ecstatically appreciative, until the moment he took a slice for himself.

Oh no! I thought. *There are four of us and only five oranges; that makes 40 slices. If David took one slice, maybe the others will follow suit. Maybe they will take more than one! How many orange slices will I get? Will they leave me any at all?* Self-preservation took over, and in one awkward lunge I scooped up all the remaining 39 orange slices and piled them on my plate. Hunching over my stash possessively, I glanced at the others to see if it looked like they would make a move. To their credit, they didn't grab for my oranges. They just sat there in stony silence and then slowly gave me a bit more room at the table.

Other than hoarding food, and resupplying for the field, a few other things filled my time in the capital: I informed David that I was indeed pregnant, broke the news to my family in the States, and got married. My mom was thrilled with both events, and even held a wedding shower for

me in absentia, requesting all the stuff she wanted. "I picked blue and yellow as the colors for your kitchen!" she told me proudly in a letter I got
two months later.

We held the wedding ceremony in our back garden. When the time
came and the guests had assembled, Christie, my maid of honor, came
into the back room to get me.

"Why are you still in bed?!" She cried. "Get up. Get up. You're getting
married!"

"I'm okay. I'm okay. I just might have to throw up."

"Well, do you or don't you?"

After waiting a respectful amount of time in silence, Christie continued. "Good. You're fine then. Forget your stomach and get out there!" She
threw off the bed sheet and helped me up and out the door, straightening
my wrinkled, white dress as we went. Outside, Lesley pulled some flowers
off of a nearby bush and shoved the bouquet into my hand. And somehow, in that glorious Nairobi sunlight, with several dozen friends all
together, happy and slightly preinebriated, I did feel better!

The wedding was officiated by the Assistant Senior Deputy Clerk, who
energetically assured us that he was 100 percent authorized to do so and
had us sign the marriage license as stated: *David William Caddis, divorced
social scientist marries Diane Catherine Perlov, spinster ditto.* I was 29 years
old. Whoever was in town at the time was in attendance, and everyone
seemed to contribute to the potluck lunch and subsequent dance party.
David looked handsome in an ill-fitting, three-piece grey suit, and I didn't
throw up once! If it wasn't the wedding of my mother's dreams, it was
close enough.

A few hours later, we left for a weekend honeymoon at nearby Lake
Naivasha. There, we hiked on Crescent Island, enjoying the water buck,
monkeys, dik dik, and other inhabitants. A special feature of the island is
no vehicles are allowed, and once reaching the shores by boat, guests are
encouraged to walk among the wildlife. The whole trip was enchanting.
Leaving the island, we rowed around the lake, above submerged hippos
that walked beneath us and below flocks of birds that flew overhead. The
only mishap occurred at the far end of the lake when we rowed under a
group of tall posts topped by nesting cormorants. Evidently, we got too
close. All of a sudden, THUNK! A dead fish dropped into our rowboat,
then another, and another. We stupidly looked up at the clear, blue sky.

THUNK! THUNK! THUNK! THUNK! They were coming from the cormorants' nests! Suddenly, we realized the birds were intently bombarding us with dead fish in an effort, we can only guess, to drive us back to where we came from! It worked. Dodging the aggressive air strikes, we rowed as fast as we could back to shore, leaving the rented rowboat on the beach. We never found the right opportunity to explain all the dead fish in the boat, convincing ourselves that once we were gone, the birds would most likely reclaim their fish, wrapping up the whole incident. Later that day, we left beautiful Lake Naivasha, not because of the cormorants—although they might disagree—but because we had to return to Nairobi, pick up two friends, and drive up to Samburuland.

It was at the end of July; I was finishing my first trimester, and my doctor gave me the green light to head back to the north. He had only two precautions. Oddly, they were the same two precautions I was given while recovering from my car accident concussion:

"Don't ride horses, and don't ride camels."

Again with the camels. Ok. No horses or camels. Got it!

This was the perfect time to be in the highlands. The lmugit lenkarna was finally scheduled to begin. The launoni was secured and brought back from Nairobi; the ritual village was built for the warriors; each warrior brought two steers to consume; and the weather was dry. It wasn't hard to convince David, Christie, and Abe (an American geography graduate student) to join me on the trip north to witness this mother-of-all ceremonies. After spending the first night in Maralal, we drove out to the plateau the evening of July 31 to learn that the lmugit was to begin any day now. Finally. The place was crowded with elders, some I had never seen before, congregating in their respective groups and enjoying the ample beer and latest news. Not far from the school where I lived, the mothers of the warriors had built the ritual village—the *lorora*—and the junior and senior warriors moved in. The current group was waiting for a few more warriors to arrive and for word from the elders to begin the rituals of the ceremony. I had been hearing that the lmugit was imminent since last March, so I couldn't wait until morning. That night it rained for the first time in a month, and it turned quite cold. It was an omen that things were about to change. And they certainly did.

Early the next morning, as I was heading out to the privy, I passed an elder—one of several who routinely hid from me—sitting by the school flagpole holding a radio. Very unusual. More unusual was there were voices coming from the radio. Somehow this guy had managed to score some batteries. He was listening intently with a bemused expression on his face.

"What's going on?" I asked.

"The government is not there," he said, pleased to be seen with a working radio.

"Come again?"

"The government is not there," he repeated.

"You mean, like on vacation?" I asked.

About this time David, Christie, Abe, and Jacob wandered out. As usual, I looked to Jacob for an explanation.

"It seems the government has fallen. But the Voice of Kenya (VOK) says everything is fine now and we should stay inside our homes."

"WHAT?!" We stood there processing this news and looked around to see if people were running somewhere in panic. There was no more information, because the VOK abruptly went off the air and did not return. No Samburu seemed to be the slightest bit concerned.

"This sort of thing doesn't affect us much here. And if it does, it will take a while before it reaches us," Jacob clarified. Then noticing the others, he added, "Are these your friends here to see the lmugit? Good morning!" I introduced all around. Then Jacob returned home to have his breakfast, and we shrugged and did the same.

After breakfast, with no more information about the government, we walked over to the lorora to join the festivities.

On the way, I proudly explained to my colleagues what they were about to see. The lorora would be arranged in a carefully prescribed fashion. The lead nkaji by the gate would be occupied by the family closest genealogically to the lineage founder. All the other nkajiji would be situated in a clockwise circle from the lead nkaji in descending lineage order.

"Hey, Sherlock," called David as we arrived at the lorora, "So, how come we've got two identical lororas sitting side by side?"

"Huh?"

Sure enough, right in front of us, spoiling my carefully researched description of the proper lmugit lenkarna ceremonial village formation, stood two identical villages. Fortunately, I spotted Symon nearby to come to my rescue.

"Symon," I asked, "What's going on? This lorora formation is making me look bad in front of my friends." The explanation for the remarkable configuration went something like this: Evidently, Letumbure's family disputed Lentoijoni's claim to having the closest relationship to the lineage founder. They had been arguing about it for years, with each family gathering supporters for their side. With no resolution in sight, they decided to build two identical lororas, next to each other, and agreed to disagree. Letumbure led one camp, and Lentoijoni led the other. It was another great example of the adaptive nature of resilient cultures. With the mystery of the lorora settled, and with permission to take photographs granted, we brought out our cameras and took some of the best photographs of our young academic lives.

Life inside the lorora was buzzing with restless anticipation, the smell of roasting beef, and the testosterone of hundreds of junior and senior warriors soon to be joined into one group. Throughout the day, the lmurran were singing, dancing, boasting, laughing, and eating, all while looking absolutely gorgeous.

Warriors are generally very particular about their dress and adornment, but this was the occasion to wear especially fine white and red cloth, beads, ivory ear plugs, bracelets, and carefully applied body paint. The Samburu were extremely proud of their body paint. It was made from the clay pigment ochre and applied primarily to the hair, face, and chest. Done well, the red ochre painted a clearly defined V on the warrior's chest. It covered the skin smoothly and evenly and was edged perfectly. Ochre on the face was applied in patterns that indicated the lmurrani's club. The warriors are known for growing their hair long—only cutting it when they become junior elders. They spent considerable time attending to their hair and inserting beads, feathers, buttons, and other adornments that were the fashion of the day. A thin board of wood was woven into the hair like a visor and covered with ochre. To protect the makeup and hair, they would sleep only on their backs, with their necks resting on a small wooden neck pillow so that they did not crush the hairpiece or the braids. I couldn't imagine getting a good night sleep that way—but then again, I'm no warrior.

Warriors were clearly aware of their high status in the community as brave and capable hunters and protectors of family and livestock. Ceremo-

Warrior at *ilmugit* ceremony with ivory earplugs. *Photo by David Caddis.*

nies such as the lmugit were key opportunities for them to posture, pose, and compete; bond with their fellow warriors; and impress the bead girls who gathered on the periphery. Each warrior was immersed in the moment and thoroughly owned the day. The only person standing apart was the ritual leader, the launoni, recently brought back from Nairobi. Dressed all in white, he had an enigmatic look on his face that may have been spiritual, or maybe just depressed.

Coup-wise, the VOK stayed off the air all that day and evening. Then at 11:30 p.m. they came back on with a short announcement to repeat that everything was back to normal, we were not to panic, everything's fine, and we were to continue staying indoors. Then the radio went dead again, and the VOK stayed off the air all that night. Somehow, we were not reassured. The next day, we decided to head back to Nairobi, which was the general protocol we learned from the US Embassy, the Peace Corps volunteers, and other US authorities. If there happened to be civil unrest in the country, get to the capital; from there, expats would be flown out, if it came to that. The capital was also where David, Christie, and Abe worked, so they were anxious to get back and check in with their offices.

However, with all communication dead, we had no idea if Nairobi was safe. As a precaution, we decided to first stop in Nakuru, a major town about one and a half hours north of Nairobi. Matt, an American friend who worked on an energy project in Nakuru, had a big house there, with electricity and access to more information than we had in the bomas. From highland Samburu we drove west along the Baringo Road, which was eerily still. We didn't see one other car on the entire trip. By 4:30 p.m., we reached Matt's house and his working radio. In fact by now there was news on the radio every hour.

From the VOK and the BBC we learned the following story: Sunday morning, August 1, rebel forces, led by members of the Kenyan Air Force (KAF), took control of the radio station, seized the airport, attacked army barracks, and aerial bombed Kenya's elite fighting unit, the General Service Unit (GSU). Most of Nairobi's commercial center was a disaster zone, as rebels, joined by students from the University of Nairobi along with discontented youth, engaged in massive looting and destruction of private property. The army and police remained faithful to President Moi and were able to arrest or kill most of the rebels by the next day. They were in the process of hunting down the rest who fled into the forest or hid within the civilian population. "Be assured," the authorities asserted, "everything is now back to normal. Shops are open. Stay home." It was a bit of a mixed message, but at least it was more than, "The government is not there." Further broadcasts clarified that more than 100 KAF soldiers had been killed and about 100 civilians died in crossfire, mainly when they came outside to see what was going on. A curfew was in effect from 6:00 p.m. to 7:00 a.m., and all incoming traffic to Nairobi was being diverted from the city. But again, "Things are being cleaned up. Shops are open. Stay home."

Everything was uneasily quiet in Nakuru, and the streets were empty as everyone was presumably glued to their radios like we were. Hungry for more reliable information, we decided to try calling a few friends living in Nairobi. Even in the best of times, the phones rarely worked in Kenya. But after numerous tries and through nearly unintelligible static, we were able to connect with two people. We first reached Caroline who worked for an aid organization and usually had a bead on current events.

"The BBC are a bunch of idiots holed up at the Hilton Hotel. Don't believe a word they say. It's a disaster down here. Stay in Nakuru." Click. Did the line just go dead?

Barbara, a colleague of David's at the International Livestock Centre, reported that soldiers were going door-to-door looking for rebels, and there was massive street fighting downtown, but most of the suburbs were okay except for Westlands (a tony suburb with a huge modern grocery store), which was totally trashed. "If you don't look like a university student, you should be OK." Well, that wasn't particularly helpful. Since we *were* university students, we decided to spend another night in Nakuru. However, we were a restless bunch and didn't like being cooped up for long. The next morning, Christie awoke to find David pacing up and down the small kitchen, waiting for the water to boil for his instant Nescafé.

"It's only been one day, David. Get a grip!" cried Christie. "And stop pacing! You're driving me crazy!"

There was a similar curfew in Nakuru. We could be outside until 6:00 p.m., but what should we do in the afternoon to get outside and pass the time? We had already seen the flamingos along the shores of beautiful Lake Nakuru. We agreed that the best idea would be to stock up on food, water, and batteries. But we decided that if there was a small chance we might be airlifted out of Kenya, we had better go shopping for cool leather jackets first.

There was a quick consensus, and we headed straight to a famous local tannery that smelled god-awful but had great deals on vests, jackets, and bags. All leather. All cheap. The merchant seemed as nonchalant about the coup as the Samburu had been. He figured that whoever won would still need leather goods. So he took the opportunity to offer some great *après-coup* sales. I bought a leather water bag and was seriously looking at a nice jacket trimmed in fur. The ends of the jacket weren't exactly even, but "this is the nature of handmade products," the merchant reminded me. Also it smelled pretty ripe, like a fresh sheep. I was assured that if I aired it outside for a few days, it would smell as sweet as those high-priced jackets made in Italy, and for a thousandth of the price.

"My mother will love this!" I said, and I bought two.

"Where's the food, water, and batteries?" Matt asked as we returned to his house with our bags of leather goods.

"We decided this was much more practical, given the fact that we wanted to buy leather goods," one of us replied. The others nodded. Matt just rolled his eyes and motioned with his head to follow him into the other room. We had company.

While we were out shopping, three other young women had joined our small group, figuring there was safety in numbers. Two were Peace Corp volunteers who were working in small villages around Nakuru. They showed up on Matt's doorstep looking like they had been put through the ringer, which was pretty much the current Peace Corps uniform: long, dirty hair, loose fitting T-shirts, and long skirts with sandals. The perkier of the two explained their situation.

"If you work for the VSO (British Peace Corps), they give you your own moped. If you work for the VSO Canada, they give you a vehicle, plus they airlift you out of the country if you get a bad cold. They really take care of their volunteers! The States? We don't even get a lift to our field site. We figured we're on our own, so here we are! Got any beer?"

The third newcomer was Stella, another researcher on a Fulbright scholarship like Matt, working in the energy sector. Short and wiry with curly black hair, she was a tight bundle of energy who got on everyone's nerves from the start. She was full of information. Although where she acquired it was a mystery, since she rarely listened to others and didn't seem to have the temperament to sit still and read reports. Naturally, she had her own account of the current situation.

"You're not going anywhere. There are over 3,000 KAF still at large, and the army is going door-to-door and all through the forest rooting out rebel students, looters, and KAF. There are roadblocks from here all the way to Nairobi. Some people are getting through, but I wouldn't count on it."

So, here we sat in Matt's living room: David, Christie, Abe, two Peace Corps girls, Stella, and me. By the time Stella finished her gloomy pronouncement, we were all pretty much resigned to staying put, helped along by the cool breeze and the beer. David was resigned but still pacing. Matt took the occasion to lay down the rules of the house, which consisted of two things:

"One: when you take a beer from the fridge, replace it with one from the pantry. Two: do not pet the dog. He bites."

Tiger was an ill-tempered German shepherd who was hard of hearing, which made him that much more unpredictable. Within five minutes, Stella had taken out a beer from the fridge without replacing it and had bent over to pet the dog.

"Oh, he doesn't seem so bad. You don't bite, do you sweetie pie?" Tiger immediately bit Stella on her lower lip and she came up howling. The bite left a huge gash across her entire lower lip, and blood streamed down her chin. Everyone rushed to her aid except Matt, who just sat there drinking his beer and shaking his head, because Matt knew precisely who would end up driving her to the hospital.

Wiping away the blood, it was plain to see that Stella needed stitches and probably a tetanus shot. Under normal conditions it would have been fairly routine to drive Stella to the local Nakuru clinic. However, these were not normal conditions; the curfew was in effect, and we had to assume the police and army officers were working on little sleep and lots of amphetamines or khat. Nevertheless, Matt loaded Stella, who was growing more annoying by the minute, into his Toyota Land Cruiser and headed to the hospital. By the time they returned late that evening, we were all crashed on various beds, sofas, and cushions and didn't even hear them get home.

The curfew continued through the next day. Spirits in the house remained remarkably relaxed under the circumstances, except for Matt, who was not used to being cooped up with so many people who talked so much. Poor Matt. We were depleting his pantry and wearing out his last nerve. He was fed up with restraining Tiger from eating his guests and moved a bit slower each time he had to tackle Tiger when he chewed through his leash. After a while, he stopped restraining Tiger altogether. Being the perceptive guests that we were, we decided maybe it was time for us to move on. So we packed up our stuff, took counsel on the safest route, and headed out on the highway to Nairobi. David was driving, I rode shotgun, and Christie and Abe were in the back.

We had just gotten to the outskirts of Nakuru when we met our first roadblock. There were about six soldiers stopping and searching every vehicle. Each soldier was armed and held his rifle close to the chest, our primary criteria for stopping. Armed traffic stops were not uncommon in Kenya at that time, especially in the northern frontier. Most consisted of armed soldiers by the side of the road, sometimes drunk, motioning for cars to stop so they could catch a lift. In general, I never stopped for armed soldiers when I was alone, as long as their weapons were leaning against a tree or far enough away to not pose an imminent threat. When soldiers looked like they were locked and loaded, as they did on the Nakuru road that day, it was another story.

We pulled over to the side of the road and were approached by a small, thin, and jittery soldier along with what seemed to be his commanding officer. The Commander was wearing the requisition Kenyan green and brown camouflage army uniform. The snappy dark beret and mirrored sunglasses conveyed he was clearly in charge of this parcel of road. The jittery soldier beside him was the one that worried me. He had augmented his army uniform with a red headband, like Rambo, and heavy metal bracelets. But it was his khat-stoned eyes that were the most striking. They were fully dilated, twitchy, and showed no mercy. I had been occasionally stopped by soldiers at gunpoint, but never had I felt in any real danger until then. This young man looked as if he would just as soon shoot us as let us go, and it made absolutely no difference to him which way this encounter ended.

When David rolled down his side window, The Commander spoke. Beside him, the jittery soldier, with both hands firmly gripping his rifle, could not stand still. It comforted me that we were all together and that we were clearly not the Kenyan Air Force they were looking for. All we had to do was keep cool heads, let them check our IDs, and get through. So when The Commander asked David for his passport, you can imagine my concern when it turned out that David did not have his passport. While each of us held our breath, David decided to try his California driver's license— his *expired* California driver's license—and casually flipped it into the outstretched palm of The Commander.

"What's this?" The Commander asked, looking as if he had just been handed a wad of chewing gum.

"It's my driver's license," David answered.

"No it isn't," pointed out The Commander.

"Well, you see, it's a California driver's license," David pointed out, as if this clarified the matter. There was a moment of silence as The Commander stared at the license, then at David, then at the rest of us one by one. I could sense he was working through his options. *Perhaps this laminated license was a meaningful form of identification*, he might have been thinking. *Moreover, this large, poorly dressed white man and his three friends might be more trouble than they are worth.* The Commander showed no emotion, while the jittery soldier drew closer to take a peek at the document in question. We silently awaited their next move. Then, with a heart-stopping, sudden jerk of his hand, The Commander threw David's expired California driver's license back to him and spat out these blessed words that I will never forget:

"Go! Get out of my face!" and he motioned with his arm for us to get the hell out of town. And get the hell out we did! We drove on, simmering in tense silence until we were well out of earshot of the soldiers. Then, Christie and I erupted in unison, directly at David.

"WHAT THE HELL, DAVID?!? YOU'RE DRIVING AROUND KENYA WITHOUT YOUR PASSPORT!? NOW?! WHAT IS WRONG WITH YOU?!"

David was actually quite proud of himself, and I think Abe thought the whole thing turned out just fine.

As an interesting aside, when David returned to the States a month later, he had a similar problem on a US highway. He picked up a beat-up 1972 AMC Matador from his sister's house in Memphis and was driving it back to Los Angeles. While driving through Oklahoma, the highway patrol pulled him over for speeding. Knowing his expired California driver's license wouldn't cut it this time, David casually handed the patrolman his Kenyan driver's license.

"What's this?" asked the patrolman.

"It's my driver's license," David explained.

"No, it isn't," replied the patrolman.

I'm not sure if David discovered a core characteristic of highway authority, or a core characteristic of himself. In either case, he once again talked his way out of trouble and was on his way.

Luckily, that first roadblock leaving Nakuru was the worst, and we arrived back in Nairobi later that day. Our neighborhood was empty, quiet, and still. There was only one scary moment late at night when we thought we heard gunfire coming from a few doors down. Immediately we rolled out of bed and onto the floor. It could have been fireworks, but no one was venturing out to check. Over the next few days we were dying to find out what was going on. It was like being in the center of an earthquake. All you know is what is happening right in front of you. Someone halfway around the world has a much better idea of the magnitude of the event. This was when we really could have used a working telephone system, or at least neighbors that we knew. Having neither of those, we had to get our news from the radio and the Kenyan newspapers, which were curiously still being promptly delivered as if the city was still functioning normally.

The VOK reported that the rebels caused 500 million shillings of damage and that 500 people were wounded. These were nice round numbers, but hardly believable. The radio further reported that the army was hunting down the remaining KAF rebels and that some were hiding in civilian clothes or even army uniforms. Soldiers, we were assured, were going door-to-door and through the forests mopping up all remaining civilians and military persons involved in the failed coup attempt, and police were going door-to-door recovering looted property. The newspaper stories were similarly reassuring. So with nothing to do for a few days, I kept busy cutting and organizing newspaper clippings. I arranged them into four piles. Each pile of clippings provided some insight into Kenyan shared beliefs and values, which went something like this:

There is no excuse for theft. If you beat up a person, the first question often asked was what the guy did to deserve it. Theft was another matter; it was considered a particularly inexcusable crime. Shortly after the coup attempt, police stormed the room of a cook living in the back of a friend's house. The police found stacks and stacks of electronic equipment floor to ceiling. When asked how he could afford the goods based on his meager salary, the fellow defended himself. "Some people are just better at managing their money than others," he replied. Despite his impressive guile, the unfortunate cook was hauled away. Stories about looting during the attempted coup and police efforts to return stolen goods, often itemized in remarkable detail, dominated the press.

> *Daily Nation—Aug. 4, 1982*
>
> 1,000 LOOTERS HELD BY POLICE. REBELS ASKED FOR COLOR TV'S
>
> Factory guard [W. W.] said three KAF men went to the factory and asked for colour television sets. But when he told them that they had none, they blasted open the main gate with gunfire.

> *Standard—August 6, 1982*
>
> CITY LOOTING: FIVE GET JAIL TERMS
>
> Five people out of a total of 327 who pleaded guilty [to looting] were yesterday jailed for 18 months each. Ramatu was found with a suitcase, a bundle of clothes, a pair of shoes, and a speaker, while Kanja had a jacket, a torch [flashlight], and two dresses. Wachira was found with three dozens of glasses, a white bag, a bowl, six sufurias [cooking pans], two tins of Blue Band [margarine], and 16 bars of Lux toilet soap. Kamau had a shirt, a mattress, and a suitcase. Omondi was found in possession of a pair of trousers.

Standard—August 6, 1982
POLICE SEIZE MORE GOODS
Police yesterday reported that they had seized more goods suspected to
have been looted in Nairobi and were being transported to Mombasa
and Eldoret. The items seized at a roadblock included several pairs of
shoes, towels, pillowcases, long trousers, ladies' dresses, a radio, children's clothing, bedsheets, shirts, calculators, and others. Those inter-
cepted at Gilgil included three Phillips radio sets, three long trousers,
10 neckties, five sweaters, one speaker, and two T-shirts.

Every citizen has a social responsibility. While Kenya is a firmly capi-
talist country, there is a strong belief that each person has a responsibility
to support the community, particularly to get involved in the name of
social justice. This comes as no surprise to anyone who has witnessed
"mob justice." If your purse gets stolen in the streets, don't yell *THIEF!*
unless you want the purse snatcher to be run down and pummeled by an
angry mob of bystanders.

Standard—Aug. 4, 1982
EXPOSE REBELS AND LOOTERS
Every individual in this country has a duty to report to the authorities
any of the rebels who have not surrendered or been apprehended.
They have a duty to expose those who support the rebels, the looters,
or those who sympathize with them. Our Armed Forces—Army,
Police or paramilitary—have demonstrated their loyalty to the Government and country. . . . We must support the Government in every
way possible, to ensure that Kenya will never be ruled by anarchy.

Stability is fragile. Stability is not taken lightly in young democracies,
as Kenya was, which remain divided by persistent land tenure issues and
ethnic tensions. The idea that the national government could be toppled
by a coup was taken seriously. So once the worst fighting subsided, Kenya's
ruling party worked hard to allay public fears and regain the people's confidence in the stability of the nation under the current administration.

Standard—Aug. 4, 1982
LIFE BACK TO NORMAL
Life in Nairobi returned to normal following the weekend disturbances.

Daily Nation—Aug. 4, 1982

NAIROBI ROARS BACK TO LIFE

Business in Nairobi went back to normal yesterday. Nairobi PC . . . had earlier appealed to businessmen to reopen their premises as security had improved.

The Nairobi Times—Aug. 6, 1982

DEATH TOLL PUT AT 129

The President put the death toll during the shoot-out in the attempted coup at 129 . . . most of the dead were rebels. The president said the furthest the rebels really went was the brief takeover of the broadcasting station in Nairobi, from where they issued disjointed and vague statements about their cause. He said the rebels appealed for support from University of Nairobi students, whose halls of residence they had already surrounded and were adjacent to Broadcasting House. President Moi declared: "My government regards the revolt as a serious form of hooliganism by misguided youth." He said the rebels were all young men, and they did not calculate the implications of their actions.

Loyalty is paramount. I have no idea when the Loyalty Oath originated in human history, but it sure became a big deal in the weeks following the aborted coup. It was promoted, organized, and publicized from Nairobi to the far corners of Kenya. Most people wisely jumped on the government loyalty bandwagon, except for those unfortunate few who bet on the losing side, like this Kikuyu official and his brother from Busia:

Nairobi Times—Aug. 5, 1982

LOOK OUT FOR SUSPICIOUS ELEMENTS

The Busia Town Council vice-chairman and his brother are being held by Busia police following reports that they took to the streets to celebrate the attempted coup. It is claimed that when they heard the announcement by the rebels they adorned their vehicles with leaves and flowers and sped around Busia town, chanting "chang'aa [a cheap and potent alcoholic brew] and magendo [contraband] are free now," stopping the whole population who were deeply shocked by the events taking place.

Standard—Aug. 4, 1982

MATANO CONDEMNS THE KAF REBELS

The Minister for Cooperative Development, Mr. Matano urged Kenyans to be grateful to President Daniel arap Moi for all he has done within the short period he has been President.

The Nairobi Times—Aug. 6, 1982

NAIROBI MP CONDEMNS ATTEMPTED COUP D'ÉTAT

MP for Dagorettu has issued the following statement: "On behalf of Kanu Nairobi branch, and Nairobi residents, I would like to congratulate President Daniel arap Moi, the President and commander-in-chief of the armed forces, for remaining triumphant over the misguided rebel elements of the Kenyan Air Force. Nairobi Kanu branch would like to express on behalf of the Nairobi people their loyalty to the President and the democratically constituted government of Kenya."

On August 6, based on the positive news reports, David and I decided to venture downtown to take a look around. Driving down one of the main streets, things looked pretty quiet. Shops were all boarded up where glass storefronts had been smashed, but the debris had been swept up. So far, so good. On one street, businessmen were walking around with briefcases. But where were they going with everything closed? We heard a rumor that the government had given men briefcases and ordered them to walk around and be calm. *That can't be true*, we thought. But that was exactly what it looked like. Every so often a truck loaded with armed soldiers would careen around a corner at full speed, abruptly breaking the odd stillness. Next we drove out of town to Westlands to see if the place was as trashed as Barbara said it was. Confirming her report, Westlands looked like a bomb had gone off. Debris and glass were littered everywhere. Broken windows were being repaired, but the fact that glass was being replaced by bricks gave us no confidence that businesses would reopen anytime soon.

The next day, the curfew was still in effect but scaled back to 9:00 p.m. through 5:00 a.m. Perhaps things were actually getting back to normal. We were friends with a group of researchers and expats who, when in Nairobi, lived in a wooded estate at the edge of town. The place had too many rooms to count and a large living room facing onto a lush garden. When we got word they were hosting a postcoup gathering that afternoon, we welcomed the opportunity to hear what was happening in other parts of the city. We drove out to the house with no mishap and were rewarded by a crowd of about 20 people all eager to exchange news of the past week. Sitting together until the approaching curfew sent us home, we heard some remarkable stories and tried to piece together a more comprehensive view of events. It was impossible to tell the truth from rumor-mongering, but there were certain consistencies. Clearly, it was better in some places than others, and timing was everything.

While the newspaper and VOK reported 129 dead, people reported seeing convoys of trucks carrying hundreds of dead bodies out of the university area. Jenny had a hair-raising experience of her own in that part of town. Driving by the university, she was highjacked by a few university students. They wanted lifts to different places in town. With a rifle pointed at her, she drove them around while they basically were looking around and being seen. She tried to just give them her car, but they insisted that she drive them. After a few hours, she was left unharmed and thanked for her assistance.

Tony, an Australian expat living in Nairobi with his Kenyan daughter, was robbed of his sunglasses. A young man on a motorcycle accosted him at a stop sign, stole his sunglasses, and sped away. A few miles down the road, Tony came across this same cyclist lying dead by the side of the road on his motorcycle. As horrific as this image was, someone did take Tony aside and ask him if he reclaimed his sunglasses. He did not.

A Swiss fellow working in Nairobi was injured but fortunately lived to tell the tale. According to those who heard from him, he was driving his Land Rover at the wrong time near the center of town when he was stopped by a soldier standing in the middle of the road. Without saying a word, the soldier leveled his gun and shot him in the arm, then calmly aimed and shot him in the other arm. The Swiss fellow managed to get away and was safely airlifted to Europe. He was expected to make a full recovery but would not be returning to Kenya anytime soon.

Throughout the whole first week, the VOK and the BBC were saying everything was fine and quickly getting back to normal. Where, we wondered, was this BBC reporter broadcasting from anyway? Evidently, as Caroline suggested, from the safety of his Hilton hotel room.

Eventually, things did settle down, but not without a price to pay. The entire Kenyan Air Force was disbanded. Three thousand people were jailed, including nearly 80 percent of the air force, and 12 people were executed. Reports also stated a new number of people killed—300. Kenya's ruling party and the government-controlled media were quick to put a lid on the matter and reassure the public that the "incident" or "weekend disturbance" by "hooligans" was over and everything was under control. In the end, President Moi prevailed to suppress any repeat of the 1982 attempted coup. But as a result, it would be 10 years before a multiparty democracy would return to Kenya.

Back in Samburuland, the lmugit finally got underway just as the attempted coup broke. It took a day before the repercussions were felt on the plateau, but it hit them hard. Because so many of the Kenyan Air Force were Samburu, when the army arrived they clamped down firmly on the Samburu citizens. They took the Samburu warriors, including all the Lmasula clan from the lorora, and led them onto the Maralal soccer field. There, the armed soldiers directed each warrior to pledge his loyalty to Kenya's ruling KANU party and to President Moi. By the time the warriors were allowed to return to their lmugit ceremonial site, they discovered that everyone fortunate enough to have been left in the lorora had consumed all the slaughtered steers! The distraught warriors were reminded that by custom the lmugit meat, once slaughtered, had to be consumed. Evidently their families didn't think the warriors would be back quite so soon.

Chapter 10

Not Enough Cake

By late August David had left for the States, the government was back firmly in control, and the roads up north were safe to travel. I drove to Samburuland as self-confident as a firestick elder in the rainy season. I turned off the dirt road and drove on the bush path out to the bomas. I was optimistic. I had the next two and a half months of work all planned out. Because I had such little time left, I reasoned, there was less chance of anything going drastically wrong. This time I was sure to stick to my schedule, and nothing could keep me from the swift completion of my appointed rounds.

Unfortunately, I wasn't a firestick elder and the rainy season was over. I was starting my fifth month of pregnancy and getting bigger every week. I had the looming deadline of November for leaving Kenya. I was nowhere near finished, and the clock was ticking. Moreover, another dry season was beginning, with its own aggravatingly slow pace and difficulties. The mood was quiet and the colors dull—far different from the exuberance of the wet season. The ill-fated Imugit ceremony was over, and the herders spent much of their time taking livestock to and from the dry-season grazing found at higher elevations.

Each year, this seasonal trek had gotten more difficult. The highland Samburu who owned individual ranches could sell their land to nonpastoralists who were seeking to acquire land in the area. The trend rarely happened in reverse, and the cumulative effect was taking its toll. Increasingly, the best year-round grasslands were being converted to agriculture, which meant less pasture was available close by. As a result, the Samburu had to walk much farther to find grass in the dry season, working with elders through reciprocal relations. This month, some elders had asked the chief of far-off Lorok for permission to graze there. The chief let in as many herds as he felt was reasonable and then closed off the pasture when the land reached its capacity. As it was too far to return each evening, the warriors and junior elders would stay with the cattle, building enclosures or camps, until the rains returned to the highlands in November. Other elders searched for similar deals in other regions, herding or sending their warriors and cattle off to other distant pastures. The upshot was that for the rest of my stay the warriors and junior elders of my region were widely dispersed. Symon and Lmariwan, like many other modern-day Samburu warriors, juggled their time among several different jobs. For my Number One and Number Two Assistants, this consisted of helping me, herding cattle, performing assorted warrior duties, and Symon teaching his adult education classes. Even when they were working with me, their thoughts were far away, leaving this region of the highlands a quiet and lonely place. Well, not completely quiet.

While the rebels had failed in their August attempted coup d'état, they had succeeded in one thing: they released all the prisoners from jail—not every jail, but many jails, including the one that housed the former teachers who had attacked the Samburu girls in our elementary school last May. I don't know what happened to the released prisoners during the government's "mopping up" operation, but evidently our once-incarcerated teachers were not high on the government's most wanted list because they weren't apprehended and sent back to jail. Luckily, they weren't returned to their former teaching posts either, and I never heard from them again, except for one who turned up on the plateau looking for me.

I found out about this when Symon casually mentioned one afternoon that a former teacher, Mwalimu, had come around asking for me. I'm not proud of it, but my first reaction was to run away.

"Symon, tell him I'm not here! Tell him I've gone back to Europe!" I thought that Europe was a good misdirection, since it was a whole ocean away from America and a continent away from Kenya. I was that scared. Mwalimu had to know that I helped talk Dorcas into testifying against him, and I figured he was not too happy about the whole thing. I kept up the hiding-and-skulking-around bit for two days. All the while, I could tell the Samburu were looking at me rather disdainfully. The Samburu, it seems, don't acknowledge the concept of fear.

"What is the matter with you?" Symon asked, confronting me one morning. "Mwalimu is [nothing but a] Kikuyu. What are you afraid of?"

"I'm afraid of him yelling at me or hitting me. I think he's mad at me." I said meekly.

"Pft!" Symon said, tossing his head in disgust.

Symon could not understand my cowardice. How could he? The Samburu were ridiculously brave. They'd go after a wounded lion with nothing but a flashlight and a spear. And I suspected that they really didn't need the flashlight. They'd blithely walk through a forest full of agitated lone buffaloes and trek hundreds of miles across the arid lowlands carrying nothing but that darn spear! It just wasn't fair for someone of that caliber to evaluate my level of bravery and fortitude, but I sensed that was exactly what Symon was doing. I also had a horrifying flashback to the first day I drove into the schoolyard and ran over those two kittens. "Take this kitten," the boy told me, holding up the one survivor. "It is a fine animal. Your father would be proud." Would he be proud if he saw me like this, hiding in my room? I felt my dad would totally understand. But I also felt it was useless to try to explain that to the Samburu. I realized that my behavior was not only disappointing Symon and friends, but I was further denigrating my family name. So, abandoning myself to my fate, I reluctantly decided to go ahead and face Mwalimu.

Based on ground rules set up by intermediaries, I agreed to meet Mwalimu in the schoolyard at noon the following day. I picked that place in particular because it was very public. I was sure there would be a ton of people milling around to witness the much-anticipated showdown and that my Samburu friends would have my back. Sharply at noon, Jacob knocked on my door to let me know that Mwalimu was waiting outside, and out I bravely stepped. Mwalimu was always a bit shy when sober, and he seemed especially so that day. That was a good sign. He was medium in height with short cropped hair and dressed in casual but dignified Western clothes. Nothing about him reminded me of a jailbird, or of the crime he had committed. That was also a good sign. As he waited for me, he stood looking down, with his hands in his pockets, kicking his foot in the dust. One quick glance around was all I needed to see that Mwalimu was alone. I also noticed that I was alone with Mwalimu; the place was completely deserted!

"Where is everybody?!" I whispered to Jacob—trying to keep the panic out of my voice.

"Who? Mwalimu is right there," Jacob informed me. "It is only Mwalimu who is visiting."

Remember when I said that the plateau was a quiet and lonely place in the dry season? Well, evidently my showdown with Mwalimu was only a showdown in my mind and did not rise above a "visit" for anyone else—a visit that was not even significant enough to draw children from the nkang next door. To be fair, the children were probably busy.

"Jacob, why don't you join us?" I suggested, walking him with me to the central area where Mwalimu was patiently waiting. Kind and proper Jacob, our resident scholar and philosopher, dressed in a white oxford shirt and Western trousers, Jacob was there to protect me. *Well*, I thought. *You go with the army you have,* and I had Jacob. So, I decided to make the most of it.

"Hello Mwalimu." I said cautiously. "You remember Jacob, don't you? He is the new headmaster of the school." *That ought to count for something,* I thought.

I don't know if it was the headmaster thing or if I had just misread the whole situation from the very beginning, but Mwalimu was not the remorseless sex offender I was expecting. He looked at me anxiously, and with a soft voice he asked for nothing but forgiveness.

"I know you must be ashamed of me, and I don't blame you. But I had to see you before you left, to apologize for my behavior. Please understand that I have never done anything like that before. It was the drink that changed me. And I will never do this again. I just had to come and tell you this."

I was not prepared for such a heartfelt apology and was really taken aback. I didn't know quite what to say. Yet he came to me with an apology in his outstretched hands, so I had to say something. In the end, I acknowledged his regret without accepting his apology, suggesting that the people he really needed to present it to were the girls he assaulted and their families. I don't know if he ended up approaching them, or if that was even a good idea to suggest. But it seemed to be the right thing to say, at least according to Jacob, who added that he was also pleased I had introduced him as the new headmaster, even though it was only an interim position, and he was planning to leave the highlands with Dorcas in the near future to enter the priesthood.

WHAT?!

Once again, before I thought the current discussion was finished, I was flipped into a whole new topic of conversation—a topic that seemed to come out of nowhere.

"You're entering the priesthood?" I asked Jacob. "When did this happen?"

"There is a school in Nakuru that will train me and find me a position. It is my calling," explained Jacob. I knew that Jacob felt a bit isolated among the teachers as the only Samburu and devout Christian, but this career change was a shock to me. I guess the church gave Jacob an offer he couldn't refuse—a way to succeed in his life's mission that had eluded him in teaching elementary school children.

And so it was, soon after I left the highlands, Jacob slipped away as well. As for Mwalimu, he left right after our meeting, and I never saw him again.

The rest of my days were filled with cramming as much work as I could into the hours available. Then, by late October, I had to begin preparing for my eventual departure in early November. How was I going to say goodbye? I had grown to love and respect so many people here, and I would miss them terribly. They had educated me and changed my life in profound ways. I saw the world differently because of them. Moreover, I had no idea if I would return in two years, 10 years, or ever again. I had been thinking of an appropriate way to honor and thank them but did not want to be presumptuous because they might have their own plans, and I didn't want to take that away from them.

I had discussed this with fellow anthropologists when I was last in Nairobi to find out what others' goodbye experiences were like. The only one around who had already been through it was a friend who had lived with a coastal community for two years. She had an amazing field farewell that I kept thinking about. On the day of her departure, the whole village gathered in a circle to see her off. Elder after elder stood to bless her and say how they were pleased to have her stay with them and learn all about them. Warriors and girls danced and sang, and a goat was roasted. Hours were spent giving speeches and presents, and I'm sure tears were shed by all. As she drove off into the sunset, they all stood and waved goodbye until her tiny Suzuki four-wheel drive topped the hill and disappeared from view. At least that's what I heard.

Hmmm, I thought. I wonder what the Samburu have planned for me.

My first clue that absolutely nothing was being planned for me was when I realized no one believed I was really leaving.

"Yes, yes, you are leaving. But you'll be back," everyone said. Even Symon didn't acknowledge that I was leaving. The more emphatic I got, the more he'd laugh at my histrionics. "You are funny, Diane, very funny!"

"How long does it take to get to your country?" Symon would ask.

"It takes about eight hours to fly to Europe, and then another 14 to fly to California. It's really, really far away. I cross East Africa, North Africa, and the entire continent of Europe. Then I fly over a huge ocean to New York, then across the entire United States," I explained.

"So, less than a day?" Symon replied.

"Well, technically yes. But that's because it's by plane," I said, scratching a big circle in the dirt. "You see, it's halfway around the world!"

Symon examined my small circle and the little airplane driving to the other side, but was decidedly unimpressed.

"You'll be back," he assured us both. And there the conversation ended as it always did.

I spent the last few days trying to say goodbye to everyone and give away my belongings. While no one was interested in saying goodbye to me, many were interested in my belongings—so interested, in fact, that as soon as I started dispensing the gifts, I knew I should have planned this out more carefully. The first to come by were people I barely knew. To them I gave away spoons, or a tin mug, maybe some sugar. I saved my pens, paper, books, desk, and chair for the elementary school, and I had already given items to Amer, Josephine, and Pascal. I knew I wanted to save my big stuff—folding cot, water barrel, sleeping bag, and typewriter—for Jacob, Symon, and Lmariwan. But handing out everything else was kind of haphazard and soon became a loud, unorganized free-for-all. My possessions were rapidly going out the door as more and more people were coming in. That's when the trouble started.

"Why do you give me just a plate when you gave her a spoon, a cup, and tea? I answered many, many questions and she did nothing!"

"How about a towel and matches?" I suggested. Clearly disappointed, she took her gifts and left.

"What about your water barrel? You can give me your water barrel," another woman suggested.

"I'm sorry, but I promised the water barrel to someone else." I explained.

"I will take your torch and the large pot," offered another.

"Where is Lentoijoni's elder wife?" I asked one woman. I really had wanted to say goodbye to her.

"She's by the lake, pouring in the milk," someone explained.

"What? What's this? Is this a ritual I know nothing about?"

"No. Everyone knows about it," the woman replied. It was the same reply I always got. But naturally, I knew nothing about it! What was going on? What were they doing, and why hadn't anyone told me about this? I can't leave! I'm not done yet! I don't know what's going on! I don't know anything! I need more time. I didn't get enough time!

"Why do you have so little left? Where are all your things?" asked another woman, pulling me out of my revelry of failure. She was clearly annoyed at the meager offerings so late in the day. It all happened so fast, with people coming and going from all directions. I barely had time to react. I ended up resorting to the only thing I could think of to deflect the anger away from me.

"Let's see," I said consulting my notepad. "Your name again?"

"You know me! Why do you need me to tell you my name?"

"Ah yes, *Ngoto* Paul (mother of Paul). Here it is. It says here that you get a tin mug and bowl."

"What? That's all? Look again."

"I'm sorry, that's all it says you are to receive. There is nothing more I can do."

"Humph." And away went *Ngoto* Paul with her tin mug and bowl. Not happy, but at least she was glaring at the notepad and not at me.

And so it went for some time until there was nothing left but the things I was saving for my three best friends—that is, if they ever showed up to see me off. With all the gifts handed out, I sat on the desk, alone, resting my aching back and feet. This had not gone at all as I had planned. Where were the speeches, the blessings, the dancing, the roasted goat?! And what were those women doing down by the lake?! As I surveyed my sad little room, my eyes welled up with tears, and I was just about to really lose it. At the perfect time, Lentoijoni walked in and stood by the desk next to me. He gave me a small smile and spoke gently, as a father comforts a daughter.

"I know you are leaving," he told me. "But I also know that you will return. You have conducted yourself very honorably while you have been with us, and for this I thank you and say that we are very proud of you. I am giving you my fly whisk as a gift so that you will remember us and return to your home with us."

It was a beautiful cow-tail fly whisk bound to a carved wooden handle, worn smooth with age and use. Through the small knob at the top of the handle was a short leather loop, reinforced at the end where it would hang on a peg at night. I knew what it meant. It was not just for chasing away the flies. Lentoijoni was given this fly whisk by his father. An elder never gives away such a fly whisk, and I was deeply honored. I took the gift and told him how thankful I was for everything he had done for me, for everything his family and the Samburu have given me.

In return, I gave him my prized Swiss Army knife with all the attachments intact—even the toothpick. He took it carefully in both hands, and I showed him what was tucked inside the handle, one blade at a time. As each new blade or tool was opened it was one remarkable surprise after another, and he carefully examined how each one worked. Although I worried it was so small by Samburu knife blade standards, I think he was pleased. I don't know what I said in my inadequate Swahili, but as a prophet who could read people's faces, I'm sure he could read mine and understood how grateful I felt.

In the end, it was enough. As I packed up my car, I was also finally able to say goodbye to Symon, Lmariwan, and Jacob. Symon laughed and said a quick "*Baadaye*" (see you later), the same as he did every time I drove off. And off I went. Glancing in my rearview mirror, I saw everyone going about their afternoon work. No one was waving. No one was chasing my Land Rover. It was as if I already wasn't there. As I drove around the corner and out toward Kisima, I noticed that the Samburu elder who lived by the road had looked up from his small garden and was smiling and waving to me. I stopped and rolled down the window, and he came out to my car.

"Goodbye, my child," he told me.

"*Ashe-oling apaiya*" (thanks very much father). I shook his hand and gave him my last roll of toilet paper and tin of Nescafé, which was about all I had left.

Well, my goodbye certainly wasn't one for the record books. But it was what it was. I took it as a sure sign that I'd be back. And next time, I'll plan the party.

Back in Nairobi, it was a mad dash to pack up all my stuff and arrange for boxes and trunks to be shipped to Los Angeles. I stuffed my most precious items into the two large yellow Amelia Earhart suitcases that I brought with me nearly two years before. There were two items I hated to leave behind: One was the spectacular mandible of an elephant—complete with teeth—that I had found in the forest near the school. I could hide the porcupine quills in my packed clothes, but the elephant jaw was so large; I wasn't sure if it was legal to transport, and I knew it was too big to disguise. I left it with one of the household Rendille guards, who looked perplexed by the gift but thanked me politely anyway. The second thing I had to part with was a large demonstration sign saved from one of the government loyalty rallies that read in Swahili: *Up with Moi. Down with the Vermin Rebels*. I tried to squeeze the poster into the box of artwork I was shipping home, but it just wouldn't fit, so the *Moi Juu* poster also stayed in Kenya—again with the same perplexed Rendille guards.

I was flying out on November 6, which happened to be my birthday. So Christie, Johan, and other friends took me out for a going-away/happy birthday dinner before seeing me off at the airport. The place they chose, inexplicably, was the Hotel Workers Training School Restaurant. Everyone working there, from the chefs to the servers, took classes during the day and practiced with patrons like us in the evening. We were a challenging group of 17 people around one large table. I wouldn't say we were demanding, but we were certainly loud and ordered many rounds of drinks and many courses of food. It was all delicious, and everything was going fairly smoothly until it came time to serve the cake. It was a beautiful chocolate cake that looked to me as if it could easily feed eight people, maybe 10. The problem was, we were 17.

For some reason, I became fixated on the size of the cake. Maybe it was because I had been doing a socioeconomic study for the past two years and had developed a crippling obsession with counting things. Maybe it was because I was pregnant and I had a primal fear of not getting enough cake for me and my unborn child. The group sang a rousing chorus of "Happy Birthday," and the servers began to cut and serve the cake to one and all. It was done in a strange way. One server held the cake while the other one cut out a wedge and served it to the customer. They began at one end of the table, not my end, and slowly worked their way around the table. From the first slice, I could tell that neither server had predetermined how to divide the circular cake into 17 equitable pieces. There was no indication they had even counted the guests. They just began cutting these nice healthy slices and serving them around the table.

I know people were talking to me, but I was only half paying attention. Instead, I was absorbed in the cake-cutting ceremony. I know these servers were just students, but how could they not realize their method of serving would only end in disaster? I could not avert my eyes, wondering at what point the servers would realize they either had too little cake or too many customers. It took much longer than I predicted. About halfway around the table, both servers stopped suddenly, counted out the guests, stared at the cake, and flung what seemed like heated accusations at each other. The cake slices got thinner and thinner, but even that could not save them. With five people left to serve, they finally ran out of cake. At this point they resolved the issue by shrugging and smiling sheepishly. Whose fault was it really? Had the restaurant not made a large enough cake? Was it our fault for being too many people? Perhaps the knife was not able to cut thin-enough slices, or the cake was just too small. Who could say for sure? In the end we made due by splitting up our pieces and making sure that everyone had roughly a fair share of cake. Problem solved by the community working together.

Wasn't this the perfect analogy to the pastoral condition? The Samburu normally strategize within both the traditional and commercial market sectors, and do so in different ways depending on their stage in life. But like their life cycle, other factors are in continual motion. For one thing, the once-abundant rangeland (the cake) was steadily shrinking, leaving the Samburu to survive on smaller and smaller slices. In many communities there was not enough left to feed all the livestock (us). The Samburu adapted to these conditions (sometimes resulting in unequal access to cake). In doing so, some family members quit the livestock business altogether. (I suppose some of us could have ordered tapioca pudding.) An interesting question is how these evolving strategies affect the Samburu culture over time—a culture based on pastoral cattle-keeping. (How can you possibly have a birthday party without cake?) And why should we go without cake, since the shortage isn't our fault? And since we did such a good job of redistributing the cake amongst ourselves, was there even a problem to begin with?

As I sat there eating my tiny sliver of cake, I got more and more absorbed in the mental task of forcing this analogy between cake and pasture, cattle and cake. *If I can't clear up my conceptual thinking how am I going to make sense of my hundreds of pages of typed, cross-referenced and neatly organized notes, my two years of daily journal entries, my log of cattle sales receipts, my binders of questionnaires, census data, rainfall charts, milk yields, and my forms filled out in duplicate?* I thought I was making progress. Now, I wasn't so sure. *I know more than I think I know. I know more than I think I know. I know more than I think I know.*

In any case, everyone else seemed to be actually attending the party and having a good time. They ate and drank everything available, sang several songs including one more round of "Happy Birthday," and whispered that my stupefied and distant stare must be due to the pregnancy.

After a teary farewell at the airport, I boarded the plane to Los Angeles and headed home via Europe and New York, with my mind churning and my stomach swimming. Like the Samburu bride, I was being moved by forces beyond my control over a landscape that was racing and changing beneath me—pushing and pulling me between the strange and the familiar—between leaving and arriving.

I had learned a lot about the Samburu. I had learned some of their secrets and stories. I had refined my research questions, found some answers, and had boxes of data to mine. Sometimes I was even confident I was on the right track. At the moment, however, the only thing I was certain of was that I came away with more questions than I started with. As I was speeding farther and higher away from my field site I felt an urgent need to be clear about something—to know I had figured *something* out. In the coming year, I not only had to finish my thesis and get a job, but I had to care for a new baby and a new husband. I knew nothing about any of those things! Like the restaurant cake servers, it dawned on me—when it was too late to change course—I hadn't planned this out very well at all. Now, from the distance of 35,000 feet above Kenya, nervously scarfing down bags of airline peanuts, I feverishly began to count the things I *did* know.

I knew the Samburu saw the world differently than I did. What was important to them was not always what was important, or even noticeable, to me. I also knew there was no one way to raise beautiful, healthy, and happy children or to express affection, grief, identity, and love of place. I knew each community considered itself at the center of a dynamic, resilient world, and that "others" lived "in the middle of nowhere."

Anthropologists seek to understand a foreign people in academic terms, for academic reasons. But when we are successful, we also shed a bit of light on this vibrant world as they see it, as it makes sense to them. We venture to the far corners of the globe and immerse ourselves in the center of someone else's world. While we look into that world from the outside, we also report from the inside and try to illuminate what makes it a home, a "home" in every sense of the word.

Yet I also saw how every individual behavior was so much more than an expression of family and cultural traditions, of environmental and societal forces. I saw how individuals were influenced by coincidence and innovation, personality and opportunity, skill and desire, and all the complexities of living. And through the individual stories of these Samburu, I saw the unfinished business that was their lives as they stretched and grew, challenged and chafed within their families and communities. I saw how a person called on an infinite combination of these morphing resources to navigate, negotiate, and go about the act of belonging and finding their place in the world.

While the differences in our lives broadened my view of the world, the similarities deepened it. There were times when our cultural and individual traits seemed to dissolve, when I stumbled on the familiar in the most unfamiliar setting, and I instinctively recognized an expression or a behavior we shared by virtue of our common nature. I saw these shared traits throughout my years in the highlands. I saw them in the way Letumba's young wife bowed her head and cried softly when she saw her family again after her long illness. I saw them in the way neighbors immediately rushed to the aid of the junior elder when his house was on fire, in the joyful singing and joking of the warriors during the lmugit, and in the pride on Symon's mother's face when she welcomed me into her home and served sweet milky chai. While many of the customs and regalia were strange, the underlying human condition of these moments resonated with me. I could see myself in them. They didn't seem odd or out of place. They seemed familiar. And when I reflected on my years in the highlands, what I remembered most, beyond the recurring flies, false starts, and dead ends, was the patient generosity shown to this bumbling stranger, the shared humor born of bizarre miscommunications, and the poignant moments when people of vastly different circumstances understood each other . . . perfectly.

Part Three

Promise

Keep in mind that you know more than you think you know.

—Sally Falk Moore, anthropologist
personal communication, 1980

Chapter 11

The Beginning
of a New Chapter

Things changed once I got back to the States in 1982. David and I had a wedding-themed dance party in my hometown. Then in rapid succession I: gave birth to baby boy Noah, got divorced (gut-wrenching yet so typical that the therapist couldn't even feign interest), secured a museum job and childcare, finished my doctorate, and started dating future beloved husband Dale. I was so frantically busy and so broke, that returning to Kenya wasn't even an option. But I kept in touch with my Samburu friends through letters, telegrams, and the kindness of those who hand-delivered the occasional package. In this way, news and photos rolled in several times a year, and I learned that Symon married a local girl named Malian, Jacob became a priest in the Anglican Church, and Lmariwan joined the General Service Unit (GSU) of the Kenyan Police Service and served as a presidential security officer.

Eight years slipped away before I knew it.

What I didn't consider during this time was how my two-year study had set into motion events and relationships that would evolve with lives of their own.

The first American to be entangled was my son Noah.

By 1991 Dale and I had saved up enough money, and it seemed like the perfect time, for a trip to Kenya. Noah was eight—old enough to remember what he would experience. Symon and the families all wanted to meet Noah and Dale, and I was excited to introduce my family to a people and place that helped form who I became and how Noah was being raised. It was a trip none of us would ever forget. I even think Noah has forgiven me for some of it by now.

Our first stop was Nairobi, where we rented a nice little Land Rover to take us on our own private tour around Kenya. When discovering that we were headed north, the car rental clerk kept trying to talk us out of it by stressing how dangerous the roads and people were. I could see Dale and Noah wide-eyed beside me as the clerk rattled on about bandits, wild animals, and potholes the size of trucks.

"Trust me!" I said, as I led my wary family out of the office. "The guy is just trying to sell us a package tour. We don't need that." I know Dale was trying very hard to believe me. However, it didn't help that the clerk just sat there, silently shaking his head in that *you're all doomed* kind of way. But not to worry. As soon as I adjusted to the left-side driving and found my way out of the city, it was smooth sailing. After an obligatory week touring the game parks, we headed up to Samburu District, our major destination. I booked the first night at the Maralal Safari Lodge so I could ease Dale and Noah into up-country life. While I lived in the highlands, I only visited the Safari Lodge to have drinks on the expansive veranda overlooking a zebra and buffalo watering hole and hide from my Samburu study sample. But now that I was an adult, I could actually afford to stay there.

"Hey, fieldwork isn't so bad!" Dale said as he turned on the tap and sparkling clean water came pouring out.

After asking around the lodge, I met up with a doorman named Samuel who knew of our pending arrival and said everyone was expecting us. So not wasting any more time, we drove out to the bomas that very afternoon, joined by Samuel who was still dressed in his doorman's crisp black suit, white shirt, and bow tie. Another lodge employee with local family connections also joined us. I had no idea how they managed to spontaneously walk off the job for the entire day. But after all, this was Kenya, and I

Dale, Noah, William (right), and Samuel who joined Diane's family at the *bomas* in his Safari Lodge uniform.

assumed this was arranged through some mutual agreement beyond my radar to detect.

I had no problem finding the beaten path to my old home. And soon I was parked in front of Symon's family nkang, had jumped out of the Land Rover, and was dragging my family with me. Symon, Lmariwan, and all the elders pressed around us along with the children—so many children—with the women clustered in the background, smiling broadly. When greetings were exchanged, and introductions were finished, Lmariwan abruptly asked the question on everyone's mind but ours.

"We see that your police have badly beaten Rodney King in Los Angeles. Why do your police hate black people in America?"

Huh?

It was impossible to claim we didn't understand the question. But they gave us a reprieve when I asked if we could *at least sit down first.*

Led by the men, we all filed into Symon's mother's nkaji for a welcome glass of tea and some food. Bending over and winding our way through the short, narrow, entrance, we emerged onto the small inner chamber of the nkaji. Noah, Dale, and I sat on one of the beds beside the central fire. Everyone else sat on a stool, on the ground, squeezed onto the bed opposite us, or stood in the doorway. All total, I think we had about a dozen people in the place. Soon our eyes adjusted, and we could see that Ngoto Symon was handing each of us a brimming glass of chai and a bowl of rice with meat. There was food for others, but not all, and I knew she had gone to a lot of trouble to prepare this meal for us, so this was a special honor. I explained to Dale and Noah that tea in the highlands was made with rich black Kenyan tea leaves, heated cow's milk—never diluted with water—and lots of sugar. It was absolutely delicious, so thick and sweet. I had really missed this over the years, and just the smell of it nearly brought tears to my eyes. Noah and Dale looked a little less enthralled, so I discretely whispered to them that they would have to drink the entire mug of tea and eat all the food—all of it.

While we were eating, Symon and Lmariwan mainly talked, catching us up on all the news. When we got to the issue of Rodney King, Lmariwan repeated his questions, and we let them know what had happened since the video's release. The only problem was that while this conversation was going on, there was something else happening with Noah and Dale. Evidently, when Dale sat down after accepting his bowl of food, he accidently bumped the central pole hard enough to shake loose the bugs—that were minding their own business—on the post or ceiling overhead. Dale kept brushing off his head and shoulders as politely as possible, and Noah kept staring at his bowl of food.

"Noah. Stop staring and eat your food," I whispered.

"But Mom, there are spiders in my bowl!" Noah looked up at me pleadingly. I looked into his bowl, and sure enough, there were about three big black spiders crawling around on top of the rice and chunks of meat. I decided not to inform Dale, who was busy enough with his shirt.

"Well, just eat around the spiders, honey," I told him as lovingly as possible. I could not imagine offending Symon's mother by not eating her food, or by picking out soggy bugs. And it wasn't as if they were scorpions. These were just spiders and not such big spiders after all. Besides, we were having such an interesting conversation.

"But Mom," Noah continued. "It's so dark. I can't tell what's meat and what's a spider!"

"Just eat the things that aren't moving," I told him helpfully, and reassuringly patted him on his knee. Noah made a heartfelt attempt, and in order to get on with the day's plans, Dale and I helped him finish his meal down to the last piece of meat. All that was left were the spiders—hopefully the same number we started with.

After the meal, we went outside to meet more elders as well as Symon's wife Malian and their three children, including the youngest infant daughter named Diana. I was so touched! For the record, I didn't learn until much later that this baby was actually named Lucy. However, Symon and Malian did name their next baby after me (Diana). So now everyone is happy, especially Lucy—who eventually got her rightful name back.

While I was cooing over my presumed namesake, the elderly Leshomo approached Noah for a special blessing. Traditionally the Samburu elders would greet each other and bestow blessings by spraying each other with a fine stream of their spittle—spit out between their two lower teeth. The two central teeth on the lower plate were pulled out for this purpose. Not surprisingly, this custom is not commonly done with foreigners. But Leshomo was an old and traditional man, and he was determined to bless my little boy properly. Because I didn't know this was coming, I didn't have the chance to warn Noah. So it was a surprise to both of us when Leshomo walked right up to Noah, pulled him in close, and sprayed a mist of spit over his face while uttering an incomprehensible (to us) Samburu blessing.

"Mom! He's spitting on me!" Noah cried out.

"That's OK, honey. He's blessing you," I explained.

"But I don't want him to spit on me!" Noah pleaded.

"Honey, just let him spit on you. It's a blessing. Really, it's an honor!" It actually went on a bit longer than I expected because Noah kept moving back and jerking his head while Leshomo kept pulling on Noah's shirt and edging closer to land a shot. It probably wasn't my finest hour as a mother. But after the fact, I tried to put it in perspective, explaining that this was just a custom like hugging or shaking hands. Dale helped the most when he put his arm around Noah's shoulder and put it another way. "Look," Dale offered. "She didn't make you eat the spiders."

"No, no," I corrected. "You are both looking at it all wrong. It wasn't a challenge. The point was to enjoy the meal and wonderful company and realize it would not have hurt you if you accidentally ate a few spiders along the way!"

"What?!" cried Noah. "That doesn't make me feel any better. That doesn't make me feel any better at all!"

"What?!" agreed Symon, having walked into the bewildering conversation and sympathizing entirely with Noah. "We do not eat spiders?! If there is a spider in your food in America, you would leave it? You eat spiders? I am not going to America!"

While neither Symon nor Noah appreciated my cavalier attitude about the spider incident, they both cheered up when I suggested we get Noah a real Samburu bow-and-arrow set to make up for it.

But before we got to that, we had our presents to hand out. There were hats, jackets, and shirts for the elders, scarves and cloth for the women, and, among other goodies, Teenage Mutant Ninja Turtles for the kids. While that may seem like a culturally odd gift, the Turtles were durable, they had swords, and we just thought, *they'll love these!* It turned out to be the biggest hit from the whole suitcase. Every time we turned around, someone else was playing with the Ninja Turtles. And by the end of the day, they all belonged to the elders.

Symon, Malian holding Lucy (AKA Diana), and their two sons standing outside their *nkang*. Ltangires (front) holding up his new Teenage Mutant Ninja Turtle toy.

Over the next few days, I continued introducing Dale and Noah to the beautiful countryside and the people of highland Samburu. We visited the Rift Valley escarpment north of Maralal, enjoyed some wildlife at the hotel veranda, visited more with Symon and family, and took an ambitious camel ride with Samuel's cousin who was starting up a new venture.

We were his first (and possibly last) customers. It was quite an experience. The first mishap was when Dale tried to mount his camel and the animal bolted and ran off into the bush. The second minor setback occurred when my saddle broke as I gingerly sat on it. It had to be repaired—on the spot—as there was no other. "No problem. No problem," we were told. Eventually, Noah and I managed to make the jury-rigged saddle work and we shared a very agreeable camel. Dale managed on the last remaining camel, a willing but hardly enthusiastic animal, who seemed to glance longingly into the bush after his escaped comrade. In the end, the ride and picnic received our highest ratings. And we would have thanked Samuel's cousin personally, if he were not still in the bush tracking down his third camel.

I didn't want to leave the area without taking Dale and Noah to see my old room at the school, the reservoir, and the forest. On this wonderful excursion, we were accompanied by a group of about six to eight people who told us what to look for in each spot. In the forest, we saw hornbills, ibis, and, thankfully, no lone buffalo, forest elephants, or black leopards. What we did come upon were porcupine quills, dozens of them. Noah and a Samburu boy his age collected as many as they could and started a long conversation around those quills. The boy began to show Noah all kinds of things in the forest, including how he used his six-inch knife and how a warrior carries his rungu over his shoulders in a particular way. I have no idea what language they were speaking, but they communicated easily as children do. By the end of the day, I could tell that Noah and Dale were feeling much more comfortable. They came out of the forest, deep in conversations with our Samburu hosts, and with my eight-year-old Noah wearing an African bracelet and carrying a rungu just like a warrior.

But it was the bow-and-arrow set, presented to Noah by Symon, that truly sealed the deal. The bow was crafted from fine flexible wood with a tightly coiled sinew drawstring, sized for a newly circumcised boy—just about Noah's size. The arrows were made of the same wood, with bird

feathers stuck in place by tree sap resin. The whole thing was so tight and gorgeous. *All well and good*, I thought. But, being the attentive mother that I was, I drew Symon aside and asked, "Are the arrow tips poisoned?" I knew the Samburu used a type of plant-based poison on their arrows that could bring down an elephant, and that was where I drew the line.

"No," he replied slowly, adding, "But we can get some. Do you want the poison ones?"

"No! No poison!" I said emphatically.

I guess Symon wasn't entirely sure what kind of mother I was.

"Ah, Mom!" was Noah's response. But what we took away from Noah in deadly poison, we delivered in archery lessons. Symon, Lmariwan, and a few others, including Samuel—still in his Maralal Safari Lodge suit and tie—joined us as we walked to a clearing in the forest. Symon and Lmariwan took turns teaching Noah the proper way to shoot a bow and arrow, while young boys ran out to retrieve the arrows shot blindly into the woods. Although Noah may not have hit all of his marks, you wouldn't know it by the proud expression on his face whenever he let the arrows fly.

The trip ended with the exchange of more presents, warm goodbyes, and our pledge to return next time with more "turtle dollies." And while it seemed doubtful that I was raising an anthropologist, Noah may be raising one himself. As a young adult, now married with two children of his own, Noah still wears his Kenya bracelet on special occasions. He tells his two young children, Matilda and Leo, bedtime stories of searching for the black leopard in the highlands, collecting porcupine quills in the Karisia Hills, and shooting arrows with the warriors. And as she often does, Matilda—the oldest—asks her father as he tucks her into bed, "Papa, will you take us to Africa one day?"

"One day, sweetheart," he whispers. One day.

[*Facing page*] Lmariwan and Symon (in cap) teaching Noah to shoot arrows like a warrior.

Chapter 12

A Plot Twist

While I had been sharing my stories of Kenya among friends and family, my Samburu friends had been apparently doing the same thing. It would take years for their version of events to inadvertently reach my ears and for me to realize the profound implications.

For the next 20 years, I continued to stay in touch with Symon. I had established myself in a California museum, and Symon had established himself as an influential elder with a large and growing family. It wasn't until Symon's two eldest sons and Diana (the real one) became young adults that we connected through social media. Suddenly, what took weeks or months to communicate took seconds. And while the distance between us shortened, it was not Symon I was texting with, but his sons and daughter—strangers who described a community I didn't recognize—strangers who looked a lot like Symon, but who were of a different world. I had been away too long.

Dale and I finally made it back to Kenya in 2016. Diana was at Mount Kenya University, "scaling," according to the University, "the heights of education." She was studying livestock health and production and was on course to land a good job when she graduated. We timed the trip to coincide with her school vacation so that she could join us up north. I had been communicating with her and had also heard about her from her brothers and from Symon's letters. But this was the first time we would meet. That early morning in July, Diana was to take a matatu to Karen—just outside Nairobi—then take a taxi to where we were staying. Where we were staying was in the home of Christie, my British friend from those early days in Kenya who was now living and working there. From there we'd transfer to a Land Rover and head straight up north. A lot was riding on us getting along, so I was a bit nervous as we waited for her arrival.

We heard the taxi before we saw it, coughing its way along the narrow dirt road. As it rolled to a rough stop, Diana alighted from the back seat with a smile that immediately melted our hearts. It was love at first sight. I was thrilled to discover she was as sweet, bright, and engaging as I knew her parents to be. Over the next few weeks I learned Diana was also highly adaptive, sociable, and quick. She was fluent in at least three languages, laughed easily, and moved seamlessly between a conversation in front of her and one on her cell phone. Like many modern Kenyan women, she was as at ease in her parents' nkang as she was on the cosmopolitan streets of Nairobi. She knew exactly who she was—wherever she was—and showed respect for her elders but didn't fear a fight. I saw her stand toe-to-toe with her mother's friends, debating the merits of the persistent ritual of female circumcision. "It's dangerous, outdated, and completely unnecessary," she argued. She even gained some traction on her last point: "Moreover, it reduces female sexual pleasure!"

While I figured I could get by speaking English and my rudimentary Swahili—improved with a quick audio course—I soon realized my self-declared language competency was sadly overrated. Thank goodness for Diana's assistance. More than a mere translator, she gave me a new perspective on Samburu culture. She revealed both how things had changed since my last visit, and—to my uneasy surprise—how memories of me among the Samburu had evolved in my absence.

Maralal had changed considerably since I was last there in 1991. It was no longer a loop of two dirt roads, one high-end lodge, and one low-end hotel. Most of the development had occurred in just the past five years. Maralal now sprawled in all directions with some of it even paved. It was the same noisy, bustling town. Only now newly constructed shops and homes sat next to the old colonial buildings. Gated housing complexes lined the road into town, and a gleaming four-story glass office building was under construction. Locals boasted of having five working petrol stations, restaurants, health clinics, banks, a post office, a stockyard, a daily market, four hotels listed on Trip Advisor, and waves of new tourists, residents, cars, *boda bodas* (motorcycle taxis), and pedestrians who filled the streets all day and night. The population had ballooned from 8,962 in 1989 to 15,860 in 2009. Cell phone coverage was ubiquitous and electricity was no longer supplied by private generators; it came all the way from Rumuruti via transmission lines that ran alongside a half-paved highway actively under construction. Once completed, the roadway would provide an all-season pipeline for commerce and investment, shops, homes, people, and money. It was said that future economic development would even bring electricity out to the bomas where the Samburu lived.

Other changes came along with the boom in population and building. The urban landscape that once included rolling hills, forests, grasslands, and clumps of slow moving livestock and zebra around the town was gone. Standing on Ngari Hill north of town, I had a clear view of Maralal and the surrounding region. It was beautifully green after the rains, yet human activity had transformed the landscape into a patchwork of small farms, wood and wire fences, and concrete-block houses. Everywhere I looked, the land was cut into small chunks, proclaiming an entirely different kind of land ownership for a district that was once held by community trust.

The large herds of cattle were also gone. In the 1980s the cattle population was slowly climbing back from the last disease epidemic, while at the same time herders were experimenting with agriculture. That trend continued over the subsequent decades. But working against this was the steady decline of rangeland available for pastoralism. The Samburu still had access to the forest in the dry season and could pay to graze their stock in the forest in the wet season. But the days of vast grasslands available outside the cash economy for grandiose herds were clearly over.

"Diana," I said as we toured around town. "I don't recognize anything in Maralal. The place is completely different."

"Yes. Everything has changed," she nodded. "Everything. We now have money, electricity, and education. It is very different from when you were last here, especially the education."

It's too much of a stretch to say that the benefits and risks of education were accepted by everyone, but clearly it seemed to be at the tipping point. Schools were everywhere. There were church schools, government schools, private schools, a school for "deafblind children," elementary and secondary schools, boys and girls schools, and Laikipia University. The Samburu had developed a fever for education that had spread throughout the region. Elementary school was no longer considered primarily for dull boys and unmarriageable girls. It was for ambitious children and families who saw in education an avenue to cash-money jobs and a broader definition of what it means to succeed. And they weren't wrong. In the past, when a boy went to school or took a job in town, he risked losing his inheritance of the family herd. It was simply not considered feasible to finesse the social relations and management of livestock as an absentee herd owner. Now it was no longer unusual to see a traditional highland Samburu family keeping cattle, sheep, goats, and a shamba while running a rural shop, hiring labor, and working in the civil service, the financial sector, health care, politics, the military, or the police force. Moreover, they did this while still identifying as Samburu.

On the trip out to the bomas, I asked Diana to remind me of the names and ages of her brothers and sisters. You'd think this would be easy. But it's not always so. This is a culture where men have multiple wives and numerous children each. Moreover, no one celebrates birthdays and everyone has several different first names depending on the context.

For the record, Diana got all 18 names, which mother they belonged to, and eventually their approximate ages. Not that I could actually use this information. There was always such a swarm of children running in and out of every Samburu home—being fed and/or disciplined by whichever mother was nearest—that I could not have differentiated them if I tried. The important thing was they all seemed to know exactly where they belonged.

Prior to reaching Symon's nkang, I carefully considered how I would greet him for the first time in 25 years. I knew Samburu men did not embrace women in public, so I had rehearsed the proper handshaking etiquette. I'd lay my left hand lightly over my right forearm as we'd shake hands. This would not only indicate respect for him, it would also indicate that I hadn't forgotten all my manners while I was away in the wilds of America. When we pulled up to his home, Symon was standing outside the nkang of his second wife, dressed in a Western shirt and trousers and wrapped in the brightly colored wool plaid blanket of a venerable elder. I jumped down from the Land Rover and have no memory of covering the ground between us. The photographic evidence shows that we did indeed shake hands in some awkward fashion and then Symon embraced me in a big old American bear hug!

The younger wife's home was similar to the traditional version with several welcome updates. In place of the thorn bush fence, surrounding the nkang was a fence of tall wood slats. The low, domed, mud and dung nkaji was replaced by a taller one with straight walls and more exposed wood around the base. In place of the dung roof was one of corrugated metal. The inside layout was much like the nkaji of the old days. The younger wife, Kotina, seemed about 20 years younger than Symon, with the shy look of a girl who was raised to not speak in front of her husband.

It was a reflection of Symon's high community status and investment in the traditional sector that he had multiple wives and so many children. In addition to keeping about 50 cattle and assorted sheep and goats, Symon had held—like his father before him—a series of local government positions. As his eldest son described him, "My father remains a very traditional Samburu man." Yet Symon also declared his belief in educating his children both to improve their chances in life and to diversify his own portfolio. He was betting that educating them would pay off with salaried jobs.

The gamble was whether Symon could control his children's educational aspirations once he opened that door and whether educating his children would pay off before he ran out of cattle to pay for it all: twelve-year-old Tuman wanted to be a doctor, Nasinya a nurse, Cindy a teacher, Diana a livestock scientist, Musarini an administrator, and Ltangires—the eldest—wanted a job at the university or maybe a museum. "I love archiving," Ltangires told me. Certainly this was something I never thought I'd hear from a Samburu pastoralist. Then there was the issue of who tended the cattle while the children were working for wages or were in school. For the most part, Symon solved this the way his father before him did—he hired labor when he was feeling flush, kept one or two sons out of school when he wasn't, and relied on his wives to pick up the slack.

Despite Kotina's silence, we had a joyous reunion at the nkang, exchanging gifts, photos, and stories over a delicious roasted goat. Our next stop was to visit Lmariwan and eat more goat.

Lmariwan had also done well for himself. He had one wife, four children, cattle, sheep, goats, and several fat chickens. The family lived in a fine concrete-block home with concrete flooring. The living room was furnished with a couch, chairs, coffee table, and a hefty battery in the corner for some in-home electricity. The backyard had a vegetable garden and my favorite modern convenience: a spacious, clean, and private two-stall outhouse, supplied with a toilet and rolls of toilet paper! Lmariwan had left the presidential security service and was now a very successful traffic officer, working in the Samburu lowlands. He split his time between his policeman's job on the other side of the district and at home on the plateau, while his eldest son—now a senior warrior—managed his father's small herd of cattle. He said he planned on educating his daughters as well as his sons.

"Through college?" I asked him.

"As far as they can go," he responded.

"So, who tends your livestock while your children are in school?"

Like Symon, Lmariwan hired labor when he could afford it, and when he could not, his wife tended the cattle, along with the sheep, goats, chickens, garden, and household. I glanced at his wife, who stood impenetrably silent by his side.

"Diana, a few days ago you said that everything here had changed," I said, picking up the dangling thread from our previous conversation. "Let's look at it another way. What has NOT changed?"

"Oh, nothing has changed," she quickly replied. "Everything has stayed the same. We are still very much Samburu, and in many ways we live as we have always lived."

I reflected on Symon's modern traditional life, with his livestock, traditional nkang, civic duties, educated children, and two traditional wives. I thought of Lmariwan with his modern home, shamba, livestock, vehicles, in-home electricity, and a traditional wife at home to tend it all. Finally, I recalled another Samburu family with one educated daughter living in town and the other daughter living a life much like her grandmother's. "Hunh," I grunted. "Everything has changed, and everything has stayed the same."

"Precisely," Diana confirmed, in a way that generously assumed I was beginning to catch on.

The next day I met with Symon and Jacob at the Anglican Church where Jacob was now the district's Anglican bishop. We spent a long time reviewing the draft of my book, reminiscing about the old days, filling in the gaps, and arguing over our memories. For instance, Jacob was intent on correcting my story about taking the warrior Leshoo to the hospital. According to Jacob's recollection, when we arrived at the hospital I passed out and had to be carried to a hospital bed where I recovered.

"Me? Fainted? No, no. That never happened!" I said.

"Yes, you did. I was there!" Jacob said emphatically.

"You are MISTAKEN. I was there too!" I countered.

"No, YOU are mistaken!"

This could have gone on forever and was only resolved when I promised Jacob that I'd add his version of the story to the book. So here it is. Personally, I don't believe a word of it, but such is the nature of shared memories.

We did, however, agree on most things and laughed about the now distant frustrating times and the close scrapes we narrowly escaped. We also talked about how much we meant to each other, or perhaps I was the one talking about that.

This was the first time Symon, Jacob, and I were together in decades, and the occasion made me reflect on our relationship in ways I had never expressed before, but which came effortlessly to the surface now.

"You changed my life," I told Symon and Jacob. "You changed the way I think about the world, how I think about family. You influenced how I raised my son." This was true. It's hard to work and live closely with people for two years and not come away influenced by their thoughts and ideas, values, and how they live their lives. With the passage of time, it's often easier to see the influence of particular events and particular people. That was what I was reflecting on now. I wondered if Symon and Jacob had given any thought to this from their perspective.

"What about you guys?" I asked them. "Did I have any impact on your lives?"

In retrospect, I most certainly should have expressed myself more clearly or not have asked the question at all, because I didn't hear what I expected to hear. What I heard was Nothing. Crickets. I waited for their response. I probably looked a little pathetic as I waited. Symon and Jacob searched my eyes for my meaning, wondering what I was worried about. What was I really asking?

Finally, Symon broke the silence. "No! No! You caused no trouble. When you left, it was all as it had been before." Jacob nodded in agreement.

"One thing that you could have done better, was you were too generous with your vehicle," one of them added. "You gave everyone rides in your Land Rover when you could have been working. People can walk. Why did you give everyone so many rides? But that was not too bad. Over-all, you integrated well, were sociable but proper, and lived very simply." And they both relaxed back in their chairs, feeling confident that they had found the answer I was cryptically searching for.

"How'd everything go?" Dale asked me. I had joined him, Diana, and Joe (our driver) on the trip back to our hotel for the evening. I said every-thing went well, but they could undoubtedly tell that I looked disturbed. We drove along the winding, rutted road up Ngari Hill in silence while I thought about my conversation with Symon and Jacob. On the one hand, I was glad my research had not been a problem for Symon and Jacob in the community. As an anthropologist, that was ideal. On the other hand, I had to admit that I was slightly disappointed. It was hard to face a one-way emotional investment. Reflecting on how much the Samburu had affected me, I wondered, *had I left no mark on my closest friends? Had I sparked* no *interest in learning about California, Europe (or wherever they thought I came from), the continent of Asia, women drivers, cats, anything?* I must have been musing aloud about this because from out of nowhere, but pre-cisely from the back seat of the Land Rover, came a firm female voice.

"You are talking to the wrong people."

It was Diana. I turned to face her.

"What?" I asked. "I am talking to the wrong people about what?"

"You are talking to the wrong people about your impact on the com-munity. You need to talk to the women."

"The women? But the women never spoke to me. I never spoke to them. My research focused on the men's economic sector. I mean, I spoke with women, of course I did. But not that much," I said defensively.

"That may be the case. But they were watching you, and they talked about you."

"They were? They did?"

Diana didn't respond, but she didn't need to. Her expression—those raised eyebrows, tilted head, and tight mouth—clearly communicated that I was an idiot for not noticing the obvious.

Well, I thought. *This is certainly a plot twist.*

"Tomorrow we will talk to my mother," she stated definitively.

And we did.

As we drove out to meet her mother the next morning Diana explained further.

"Many girls go to school now. Women can make money, and we have more control over our lives. There are Samburu women now who lift their voices against the early marriage of their daughters and in favor of their education. But this is a recent thing. When you were here, they could do none of this. A woman could not speak in front of her husband. In the 1980s, all a girl thought about was getting married. There were a few girls going to school, but people thought, *what's wrong with them? Why go to school? It's only to learn the ABCs and counting, and we all know how to count.* Women in those days didn't even know that secondary school existed! But there you were. And even if they did not talk to you, they were watching you and talking about your life. You had an impact on them and consequently on me. Maybe my mother would have sent me to school anyway, maybe not. But she remembers you as awakening her to the things you could do with an education."

I worked assiduously during my original two-year study to be aware of my presence and do no harm. And while I expected to have had some impact on the personal lives of those closest to me, I never considered that the Samburu I briefly interacted with or those whom I never met could be influenced by my presence in any lasting way, by ideas attributed to me, or by observations of me. It never occurred to me the extent to which cross-cultural *observing* is a two-way street. But of course it is. And that's what occurred to me now, as we turned off the highway and followed the dirt road out to Malian's nkang. While I had been exploring their world, the Samburu had been exploring mine.

We found Malian at her temporary home in the ceremonial lorora, the large circle of nkajiji built for the lmugit warrior promotion ceremony that was going on at the time. The lorora consisted of about 65 traditional domed nkajiji, one for each family. As in every traditional lorora, these nkajiji were placed in order of their family's descent from the clan founder. Other than the colorful plastic tarps over the roofs to keep out rainwater, the lorora looked pretty much the same as the ones I had seen 35 years ago. While all the nkajiji looked identical from the outside, knowing the rough lineage lineup enabled Diana to pinpoint the location of her mother's home.

"*Kodi!*" (May I come in?)

As was the custom, we announced ourselves outside the doorway and waited until Malian called to us to enter. The Samburu used the Swahili word "*Hodi*" (May I come in?) but put their own spin on it, pronouncing it "Kodi." Stooping slightly to clear the doorframe, I entered and wound my way through the entrance to the central room. There I joined two other Samburu women friends of Malian already seated on the stretched-hide beds.

Over cups of piping hot Kenyan tea, Diana translated as Malian told me about her life, how it was getting better, how it was getting worse, and what our intersecting paths have meant to her.

"Symon's father and my father were both from good families and wanted to arrange their children to marry," Malian began. She spoke softly in Samburu and looked deep into my eyes, wanting to communicate with me directly. I understood nothing and cursed my poor language skills. She bent over to tend the fire, handling hot logs gingerly with her bare fingers, to give Diana time to translate. Then she continued.

"My father had several sons already, but when my mother was pregnant with me, Symon's father, who was a prophet, said *this child will be a girl and will marry my son*. It was a girl—me. So from birth I knew I was to marry Symon. In those days, we did not argue. And Symon's father was a powerful man. I was married at 15, or perhaps I was younger. It was around 1985.

"At first, things were good. I opened a small shop with Symon's help and sold sugar, cloth, beads, tea, and other things that I bought in Maralal and Kisima and sold here in the bomas. We used the money to invest in our growing herd. We planned on selling some animals for primary school education expenses—uniforms, books, things that young children need. It wasn't easy running a shop for Samburu by a Samburu. There were always neighbors—friends and relatives—who wanted to buy things using credit. But I soon got to know those people who were good at paying what they owed and those who were not. It became easier for me to speak plainly to them. I would say, 'I am not a bank. I cannot loan you money. You need to bring me cash if you want to take sugar!'

"When you came back [in 1991], it was the first time I saw you, although I knew of you before that from Symon and the others. I wanted to talk to you, but I did not know how to approach you. I was not afraid of Symon, but my Swahili was very bad then. I remember thinking, if only my father had educated me, I could move around like you. I wanted you to stay so I could learn from you. But you left so soon. You said that you'd return in 1995, so we waited."

"What?! I didn't say I'd be back in 1995." I tried to clarify.

"Yes, you did. You said 1995," Malian corrected. "While you were gone and in preparation for your return, I told Symon to enroll me in the adult school at Maralal where he was teaching. I wanted to be better at Swahili to talk with you directly, and I wanted to be educated like you. I loved going to school and learning things. Symon and I talked a lot after you left about the benefit of education, and we could both see how this was a path to improving ourselves and our children's lives.

"Then it was 1995 and you did not return. We were very concerned. I learned about the big flood in America [which was in Louisiana], and we thought maybe you had died. I urged Symon to write you to make sure you were alive, but still we heard nothing. You cannot imagine how worried we were!"

"I answered every letter I got from Symon. Honestly!" I whined. But honestly, I wasn't altogether sure if that was the case. I racked my brain for what I was doing in Los Angeles in 1995 that was so important that I would ignore a letter desperate to know if I had survived the devastating floods in Louisiana! I came up blank and began to feel terribly guilty. Luckily, the conversation was interrupted by a neighbor's grown daughter who popped into Malian's nkaji to ask if she carried automotive brake fluid in her shop. It did not appear to be an unusual request, which was what startled me.

"What on Earth does she need brake fluid for?" I asked after the girl had left. "Does she even know anyone with a car?"

"No. That is precisely her problem," the woman seated next to me answered.

"Huh?"

It was then explained to me that brake fluid was found to be the only remedy to effectively treat a persistent skin rash, which reminded me how often questions and answers have failed miserably to clarify things.

Meanwhile, Malian had moved on.

"Things started to get bad around 1997," Malian was saying. "There was a terrible drought, my shop failed, and Symon lost many cattle. We have still not fully recovered. But I've reopened my shop, and my two eldest boys, who are educated, have good jobs in Maralal, they help us. If I think about what is most important to me, it is to educate my children. It is not easy to keep them all in school. Symon wanted to pull one of the young boys out of primary school to herd the cattle. But we agreed that if I do the herding instead, we can keep him in school. I moved another young son to my parents' nkang. There he would be protected and can go to school."

Keeping children in school was a problem for many families. It was not only an issue of needing them for herding cattle and saving on school fees; not everyone saw the benefit, especially of educating daughters. Diana explained to me that girls in Samburu culture are supposed to marry early to gain cows for their fathers; they are not supposed to go to school. While more Samburu parents than in the past said they wanted to educate all their children, girls still faced an uphill battle over resources. Those same parents were also likely to say *this is not a good time* when faced with the reality of selling off livestock for school fees. And many feared that educated girls would get pregnant and drop out of school and/or marry outside the community, *wasting the money parents have put into their heads*, as one elder told me. It was a common theme.

"You ask Lepilian," chimed in the old woman sitting next to Diana. "Lepilian will tell you. She sold a cow to pay for her daughter's secondary school education. The girl came back pregnant and dropped out of school. Now Lepilian says '*what use was it to send that girl to school? I wasted a good cow!*'" While the conversation was going around simultaneously in English and Samburu everyone seemed remarkably on the same page.

"Yes," Diana agreed. "My mother argued hard to keep me in school. It was because I performed so well in school that I gained my father's approval to continue."

"Life was easier when I was a girl and we lived on milk," Malian concluded. "We had no need for money. Now, even if you have a large herd of cattle, there is no place to graze them. No one has large herds anymore; we all rely on money. On the other hand, the roads, petrol, and electricity have brought more products and people for my shop. And we can go to school to improve ourselves. When I met you I saw how a woman could be educated, independent, and drive a car. It was too late for me but not for my children. I want to educate them to the highest level. All of them!"

Malian's optimism and determination were palpable. She had opened, closed, and re-opened her shop after countless setbacks, led a greenhouse cooperative, sold crops in several markets, cared for livestock, and raised 10 children in her spare time. I could only imagine what she might have achieved if she had been fed with the primary, secondary, and college education she craved.

"My mother works hard, and never gives up," Diana said proudly. "In fact she named me after you because she saw that you were hard working and determined as well. She wanted me to be like you and to be educated. And she thought that if she named me after you, you would help me with my education." The second old woman, whom I'd never met, had been sitting patiently next to Malian and Diana the entire morning. Now she spoke up. She thanked me profusely for paying for their petrol and lodging for a trip the women took to sing in Wamba, a trip I knew nothing about, and I was certain I never paid for.

As various neighbors filed in and out of Malian's nkaji that day, and as I moved around, I heard several other stories from the women of the bomas—stories created around my Land Rover, my "work," my imagined escapades, and my freedom that I took for granted. For instance, I learned that the women *did* think I was somewhat of a slut, but evidently "not in a bad way." To this day, there is a cooking pot called Diane's *sufuria*, with stories attached to it, which is passed around when anyone needs a laugh and a pot. I don't even remember giving it away. In nkaji after nkaji I saw the metal trunk, cups, and other bits and pieces of my past field life spread throughout the bomas, with stories attached to each one. Lord knows where my two flashlights ended up or how many wounded lions they have killed.

I flashed back on an earlier conversation with Jacob's wife, Dorcas, where she casually mentioned that watching me helped her find her voice and gave her the confidence to speak up loudly when she had something to say. I wasn't sure what she had meant, but in light of these conversations, it took on greater meaning. Dorcas was about 15 years old when I met her, a skinny, shy girl from the plateau south of Maralal. Her family kept cattle, goats, and sheep. She was so young when she got married, 16 years old, if that. In those days, girls did not have a voice in their marriage. Dorcas, like many girls of her day, was not educated beyond a few primary school years.

"Did you know that I was the last person Jacob spoke to about our marriage?" she told me.

The process went like this: Jacob asked Dorcas' father if he could marry her. Then the father took it to the elders to get their permission.

After all the negotiating for bride-price cattle was done, and everything was arranged, only then did Jacob ask Dorcas to marry him. She was the last person he asked.

"Things are different now," Dorcas explained. "Now the woman is the first person to be asked in marriage, because she can refuse. She can refuse marriage. She can even refuse circumcision." In the days when Dorcas was married even Christian girls were circumcised, as the church did not interfere with Samburu traditions.

Thirty-five years later, I still recognized Dorcas' small round face, slight frame, and perfect crescent-moon slice of a smile. But the close-cropped black hair was now flecked with grey and the painfully shy girl of her youth had transformed into an elegant woman and community role model. Also, the plastic shoes and the well-worn dress were replaced by a stylish ensemble with matching sandals. She still moved with slow precision, but now she was clearly leading the way rather than trying to hide.

"Watching you, I saw that women, other women, have a voice. I eventually found my voice in my marriage. It was not easy; it was an adjustment for Jacob."

"And what do you say with this voice?" I asked her. Dorcas replied without hesitation in the frank and calm manner of a woman in a good marriage. "Now I can tell Jacob 'No, this is not right. This is not *my* fault. This is *your* fault.'"

Over the years Dorcas has acquired the poise and wisdom of a church elder. She taught herself to read and write, and taught herself to speak English fluently. Along with Jacob, Dorcas is an ardent believer in educating women and has been committed to serving her community. She teaches reading and writing to Samburu women in the evenings and is the leader of the Mothers Union in the Maralal Anglican Church. Dorcas now speaks with a clear and confident voice before groups on a variety of issues from education to intertribal peace, and child health and literacy. At the same time she has raised three strong children who have each inherited their mother's faith, inner strength, and dedication to community service.

Dorcas and Jacob's eldest daughter, Naisula, entered politics after a high-profile career in journalism, with her mother being her greatest female mentor. In 2013 Naisula became the youngest woman to serve in the Kenyan Senate and was elected vice chair of the Kenyan Women's Parliamentary Association. She left the Senate in 2017 to run for a seat in the Parliament's lower house, the National Assembly. The prevailing opinion at the time was that the Samburu in her district would never elect this young woman over the popular male incumbent. The Samburu begged to differ, and Naisula won handily, becoming the first female member of Parliament for this constituency and confirming her position as one of Kenya's rising stars.

Life has stayed the same in many ways for Samburu women. They retain primary responsibility for home and family, health care and education. For many, female circumcision and marriage remains the only path for girls to become adult women and marry within the culture.

Life has also completely changed. Samburu women today have opportunities and voices their mothers could only dream of. Female circumcision has been outlawed and attitudes are changing to help enforce it. Kenya's 2010 Constitution requires more rural development and female representation. Women have significantly greater access to education, participation in government, and more independence in business. Electricity, cell phones, banking, and paved roads have contributed to opening up the wider world for them.

In the early days, before this period of rapid change, what seems evident is that for some of the women I crossed paths with on the plateau, I became a personification, unwittingly, of what one could do with things like an education and a driver's license. The story of these women is a story of personal transformation that has run parallel to my own and completely under my radar. While I was observing and analyzing the Samburu and their world, they had been observing and analyzing me and mine. We each became windows through which we saw and changed our assumptions of "the other," of the world, and of the possibilities within that wider world for ourselves and for our children. Some of these women, like Dorcas and Malian, have embraced the possibilities of a wider world as only an optimistic people can. And whether they have been lucky or smart, they are striking examples of how individuals can change life dramatically in a single generation. Other women have tried and quietly failed. Still others, like the Samburu bride, may lead their lives in relative obscurity but have never forgotten a singular encounter with an audacious stranger that advanced their dreams in ways perhaps only the two of them would ever know.

Namayian was electrified by the car ride I had given her on her wedding day, and 35 years later, she could still recall the details.

"I was still in pain from my circumcision, so the ride you gave me in your car was so good," she told me. "I had seen cars, but I had never been so near to one. It was the biggest thing in my life to get inside. All of a sudden, we started to move and the trees started to move around, and then they started to fly! I was excited, but I was also scared because you were driving so close to the flying trees, and I was worried that the trees would hit us. I didn't dare to move.

"After that, I wanted to ask you for another ride in the car, but I couldn't. But I saw you. I saw that you were free to associate with anyone and move around as you wished, asking people questions and writing things down. Mostly, I dreamt about driving like you and moving around freely. But, of course, I had no idea how to get a car.

"Now I know about school and getting a job that pays money. And with money, you can buy cars. But at the time we thought the only people who were supposed to be educated were the men. I didn't know that women anywhere were educated. I didn't know that you were educated. I just knew you had a car and I thought that was because you were white."

Namayian's husband is dead now, and so are her husband's brother and mother. She lives with her seven younger children, selling fire wood and fence wood, and digging gardens. To supply her family with milk and small change, she keeps 10 sheep and goats and one cow.

"I would like to educate all my children, but that is not possible."

A twinkle came to her dark eyes as she glanced over at my Land Rover.

"But the oldest boy, he is educated and doing very well," she said proudly. "He went to primary school, then to driving school. Now he is a Professional Driver. And whenever he comes home, he brings his vehicle up to my nkang, and he drives me wherever I want to go."

Chapter 13

Definitely Not the End

On December 6, 2019, Diana graduated with a Bachelor of Science degree in animal health and production from Mount Kenya University. I had arrived in Kenya a few days earlier and hired a car and driver to get me around. It was hard adjusting to not driving my own vehicle, but there were key advantages, such as not having to worry about parking and car maintenance, and I quickly adjusted. My go-to driver, who I had used on a previous trip, was a Kenyan, Joe, who had his own safari service and could drive his way around any obstacle, out of any mudhole, and never lose his perspective or humor.

Mount Kenya University was in the town of Thika, 50 miles northwest of Nairobi, where Joe and I set off early in the morning to attend Diana's official college graduation ceremony. Arriving two hours late due to Nairobi traffic, we were met at the gate by a friend of Diana's, Nelson, who led me to my seat while Joe parked the car. My seat was evidently on the stage, next to Nelson, a few rows behind the speakers, along with about 100 other VIPs. Nelson told me he was on the dais representing his home country of Uganda. How Diana had arranged all of this, and how she knew Nelson, was a mystery I forgot entirely by noon.

The ceremony was held in a distinguished setting on the graduation grounds of the university. The outdoor stage was covered with a red carpet and adorned with flowered garlands and bunting in the school's blue and gold colors. The 6,000 graduates, resplendent in caps and gowns, sat in the stands around the quad that was similarly draped in blue and gold.

I joined the graduation already in progress, missing the academic procession, several introductions, and a Somali dance performance. What I did catch were the speeches by the Chairman of the Board of Directors, Cabinet Secretary Ministry of Education, Chancellor, and Deputy Vice-Chancellor. The 13 Deans of each academic school then announced their graduates, who stood and cheered when the last person in their group was named. In their own words, each speaker praised the work and mission of the graduates to make their mark in the world, contribute to society, and extend a hand to those who follow in their footsteps. It was a heady responsibility for these young adults, and one they seemed to enthusiastically embrace.

As soon as the trumpet sounded an end to the ceremony, everyone rushed onto the grassy field of Graduation Square to congratulate each other amid dancing, singing, balloons, and streamers. Diana found me easily and we embraced for a long time. She was beaming and could hardly stand still. Surrounded by her good friends and classmates, she glowed with pride and relief! Diana also stood out, because of the 6,000 graduates, she was the only one I saw wearing the dazzling jewelry of the Samburu people across her forehead and face. I was so proud of her and took tons of photos to capture the moment.

I felt bad for the thousands of family and friends of the graduates who had to wait outside the square that was fenced off throughout the entire ceremony. Only now—four hours later—could they join their students. While Diana's parents were not able to make the trip to see her graduation, her cousin Rebecca who lived in Nairobi had attended. Rebecca soon found us, looking radiant and ready for the after-graduation party to begin. I had wanted to take Diana and her friends out to lunch to celebrate. I had planned to give a speech and everything. I quickly realized this would have to wait. The graduates had their own plans and the day was theirs.

After about 30 minutes of wandering around the university aimlessly in search of food, we gave up and left the girls to party with their friends. Nelson stayed with me and Joe, hitching a ride to Nairobi; he had generously agreed to do an errand for Diana before returning to Thika later that day.

Walking to the carpark, we joined everyone else, tens of thousands of people heading off-campus at the same time. Finding our car was easy; leaving the carpark and merging onto the narrow two-lane road out of town was another matter. Luckily, there was much to see while we waited to exit the carpark—inching forward—in the congestion. There were elegantly dressed parents and siblings, stylish university students in the latest sunglasses, hawkers weaving through the cars and crowds selling balloons, diploma frames, sodas, water, garlands, streamers, meat pies, and newspapers. Unfortunately, we got stuck behind a matatu with a few more spots to fill. While the already-crowded vehicle rolled forward, one of its passengers was crawling over others to get out—deciding she'd rather walk—while the makanga was simultaneously cramming two new customers in through the same door. Horns honked. People yelled. Pedestrians and cars alike were intermingled, grabbing every available space between one another and not going anywhere. And we hadn't even left the carpark!

"We'll never be able to turn right!" I shouted over the din to Joe. "Why don't you just turn left and we'll find our way back by some other road?"

"There is no other road," he shouted back. "If we go left we end up in Garissa." Turning to face me in order to emphasize the nonchoice before us, Joe added sarcastically, "You want to go to Garissa?" his implication being, *that is nowhere you want to be right now.*

We eventually turned right. Hours later we dropped Nelson off in Nairobi, and finally we made it back to Karen, the Nairobi suburb where I was staying with Christie. I don't even want to remember how long it took.

One of the highlights of the drive was getting to know Nelson better and, after we dropped him off, speculating with Joe about Nelson's relationship with Diana. Nelson would graduate in June with a degree in economics. His home was in Kampala with his Ugandan father and Rwandan mother. Both Joe and I had liked him immediately.

"Nelson seems like such a wonderful person; he's so bright and thoughtful," I said. "Do you think we can get him and Diana together?"

"They already *are* together," said Joe. "I'm sure of it."

"You think so?"

"Look, he traveled two hours to Nairobi just to pick up Diana's iPhone. He'll turn right around, take public transport back to Thika to deliver the iPhone and join what's left of the graduation after-party. Doesn't that seem like a very special friend to you?"

I was impressed with Joe's sleuthing and analysis of the clues. If he was right, we both hoped the very best for them. On the other hand, it reminded me that this presumed relationship was exactly what some Samburu fathers and mothers feared would come of educating daughters.

They feared their daughters would marry outside the culture and with-
draw from its network of relations and responsibilities. The university was
not only an opportunity for academic learning; it brought together young
people of very different backgrounds and ethnic affiliations to mix and
learn from each other. Diana's father wanted to see Diana succeed in her
education and career, and to gain independence. At the same time, he was
not likely to appreciate her getting too friendly with a Ugandan–Rwandan
classmate and risk his control over her future marriage. I wondered wist-
fully if Symon would become another father pacing under an acacia tree,
living in a culture that was changing way too fast in a direction he didn't
fully understand. In a reassuring voice, Joe wisely pointed out, "Diane, I
think you are getting ahead of yourself."

Several days later, with Dale joining us, we left for Samburu County
where the celebration would continue, and where we would honor Diana
individually. It was such a pleasure to leave the urban traffic for the rural
highlands, even though, as we noticed on our last visit, it was not the vast
forest and plateau of yesteryear. As we turned off the main road toward the
bomas, Diana and her brother Ltangires were pointing out one particular
feature of the landscape that had come about only over the past three years:
wood fences now surrounded and expanded the area of nearly every nkang.
    "People are getting ready to claim title to their land," Diana's brother
explained.
    While the highland Samburu had collective ownership of their range-
land through group ranch membership, families had never had individual
title to their land. In other pastoral districts of Kenya the group ranches
were being subdivided into individual parcels. Evidently, this major land
reform was expected to come to this part of Samburu County any time now.
    The Maasai were among the first pastoral groups to receive individual
titles to their land in the 1980s, and while I could tell the Samburu were
excited for land titling, there were lessons to be learned from the Maasai
experience.
    The desire for individual land ownership was certainly understand-
able. Over the past 35 years the Samburu, like the Maasai before them, had
become increasingly tied into the commercial economy and national values. As many Samburu had told me many times, "Today, money is everything!" And the cash needs were considerable. Extended families were

often called upon to contribute money for relatives in trouble due to anything from hospital bills to bail. One elder's wife was battling cancer; another elder had a younger brother in jail in Nairobi for allegedly, although accidentally, burning down his girlfriend's house. Then there were the periodic family expenses for livestock, medicine, and government fees. Plus there was the continual cash needed for modern living: home construction, furniture, gas and electrical power, school fees, cell phones, and "incidentals." Elders used to sell off an animal to meet urgent cash needs, but with smaller herds and the demand for cash more prevalent, this was no longer sufficient. Sons with jobs in town could cover some expenses, but not when they were the sole wage earner for a large family.

The Maasai experienced similar problems and also looked to the subdivision and titling of group ranches as part of the solution. Anthropologists John Galaty (2013), Carolyn Lesorogol (2008), and others have studied this extensively. Their findings are disheartening. Like the Samburu of today, the Maasai strategy was to gain title to their group ranch allocation with the idea that, if needed, they could sell the land to pay for short-term needs as well as invest in future growth. Investment took the form of buying more cattle, purchasing more land at a lower cost, educating their children, starting a business, buying a plot of land in town, or any other number of opportunities. In reality, those short-term expenses kept coming, and the investment opportunities too often never materialized. Little by little the Maasai land was sold until too little was left to support even a reduced pastoral herd. And who bought the land? For the most part, land was sold to nonpastoral people residing in the expanding nearby towns.

"You just need to look at the Ngong Hills outside Nairobi," points out anthropologist J. Terrence McCabe. "Land that was nearly all Maasai 30 years ago is now nearly all Kikuyu" (personal communication, August 7, 2020).

Overall, the Maasai experience warned us of the impoverishing impact that land subdivision and titling could have for a pastoral people, despite thoughtful planning, high hopes, and the best of intentions. It was something to keep in mind. At the same time, there were success stories that fueled the inherent ambition of an optimistic people. Everyone in the highlands knew of young Samburu who balanced a government job with a modernized home on the plateau and a viable herd, as well as of young educated Samburu women who had entered business and government in Maralal, Nairobi, and beyond.

I saw this hope and aspiration in Ltangires' eyes as we drove slowly through the rural area. He pointed out how each family, in anticipation of the impending titling, was installing boundary fences. The fences staked out what they saw as their rightful share of the group ranch, often expanding the territory around their nkang. They might have to justify the allocation to the group range committee, but they were prepared to do so. We all gazed out the car windows at nkang after nkang surrounded by tall timber fences strung together with wire.

"With title deeds," Ltangires continued, "people will have the ability to sell off portions of their land to get money for school fees or business . . . and many will!"

The sentence hung in the air, each person silently taking in the fenced landscape, alone in their vision of the future. My thoughts took me back three years when the son of a prominent Samburu elder told me he always wanted to keep some cattle, even if he worked in a city office. "It is what makes us Samburu," he said. "And cattle are always a good bank account to have in case of emergencies." Three years later this same young man, who had moved even farther away, said he could easily live without cattle. "I *am* Samburu. I don't need to keep cattle to be Samburu." I know that cultures are continually in transition, but that simple declaration startled me, and I kept coming back to it. I don't know how many elders at the time shared his sentiment, but I could not have imagined hearing this only a few years ago.

My mood brightened considerably when we arrived at our destination. This was, after all, a celebration. Party-central was at the home of Diana's older brother, Musarini, who was a local politician and generous host. He had built a cozy two-bedroom home of Cyprus wood, concrete block, and plaster, with a green corrugated metal roof and internal kitchen and bath. While electricity had yet to come to the Samburu homes, Musarini had set up a solar battery on a living room corner table to run the TV, stereo, lights, and cell phone charger.

Roasted goat and potatoes were served to early arriving guests as about 80 family, friends, and neighbors convened in the large backyard. The elders sat on the ground in the grassy corner under a shade tree while women, girls, and dozens of children sat together on the opposite side of the lawn. In the only chairs available, all lined up along one side of the backyard in the place of honor, sat Ltangires, Malian, Symon, Diana in her university cap and gown, me, Dale, and a Ndorobo elder. One more chair was added at the far left that was shared by the wives of Ltangires and Musarini. The young men, in the fashion of warriors, wouldn't sit but milled about, with most of them congregating around the goat being roasted in the side yard. A large group of women gathered in the opposite side yard, chatting and laughing, while they adjusted their beaded jewelry in preparation for the dance.

Waiting among the gathering crowd in our designated seats I asked Diana about her next move. I knew she was scheduled to begin a government-paid internship in the public or private sector, but I hadn't heard what internship she'd accepted or where she'd be situated for the next year.

"Last year I had a three-month internship with Kimetrica, a nongovernmental organization (NGO) working to promote economic growth in northern Kenya. I worked for 11 days in the field interviewing people around Maralal, gathering data about their economic livelihood. I like to work in the field, to go out and talk to the people. If I get a government internship, I can help my community learn about the medicine, vaccinations, and other resources available to them so the people can better care for their animals and their families." I had previously suggested she take an internship with a company in the private sector. Diana had some pretty good arguments for both options and clearly was giving them a lot of thought.

"Do not worry about me," she said confidently. "I will look at my options and make the best decision." She gave me a long look that said *I got this*, which, as I sat back in a chair normally reserved for senior citizens, made me feel both comfortably reassured and uncomfortably old.

Without any announcement, the formal program began, and those with iPhones recorded the performance. First up were the women who stepped around the side of the house, singing and dancing in unison. Leading the way was Diana's mother, Malian, dressed in a bright orange wrap with a white cloth tied like a shawl over her shoulders. Like all the women, she was adorned with beaded earrings, a headband, ankle bands, and stacks of her best necklaces. Samburu women used to wear rows and rows of single stranded red beads. But those days were long gone as accessories had evolved over the years. The fashion essential of modern Samb-

uru women was the broad, flat disc of beadwork, often with short strands
of beads and sequin-like discs hanging over the edge. The necklaces were
wired to stay stiff, as if you were wearing a large beaded LP record around
your neck—stacks of them. You can buy such necklaces in the marketplace, but trust me, the most beautiful ones are kept and worn by the
women for special occasions. They are elaborate and beautifully made, in
part because they are essential to the performance. As the women sang,
they stepped and bobbed to make the necklaces dance up and down for a
clapping sound and to catch the light. The sound, color, and light of the
dance harmonized with the voices singing in unison. While each song
began as a group performance, or a call and response, there were plenty of
opportunities for women to break out and compete with each other to
show off one's individual style, message, humor, and talent.

The singing and dancing competition, while good-natured, reminded
me of another one brewing right in front of me, one that didn't look like it
could be resolved quite as harmoniously. Previously that morning, Diana,
Musarini, and a bunch of us had stopped off in town to buy sodas for the
party. It was decided—not by me—that two cartons of twelve Fantas
would be plenty. This hardly seemed adequate for the crowd. But it was
explained to me that the Fantas were not for everyone. They were to be
reserved for the dancing women who would work up quite a thirst.

Diana—the honoree, cohost, and person who cared more than anyone
else—had the Fantas placed on the grass between us where she could keep
an eye on them. Now, I'd thrown enough parties to know that this was just
asking for trouble, especially as the Fantas were on the lawn in plain view
of everyone. Sure enough, shortly after the dancing began an elder came
over and reached for a bottle. "No." Diana waved him off. "These are for
the women after the performance." While he backed off without a word,
this set up an interesting problem. On the one hand, elders are not accus-
tomed to being refused by a girl. On the other hand, Diana was not only a
girl, she was a university graduate and the party's honored guest.

While the dancing was captivating, I was somewhat distracted by the
simmering tension—a tension I was convinced was not only in my mind.
Educated girls were a big part of the changes swirling around the highlands. What kind of influence would this educated girl have in a system
ruled by elders, and just how was she going to distribute 24 Fantas in a
crowd of 80 thirsty guests?

As it turned out, Diana's system for guarding the Fantas worked remarkably well. That is, until she joined the dancing and passed the task on to me. Somehow, at some point I lost track of the Fantas I was assigned to guard, because when I next checked them they were all gone. One by one they had disappeared quietly into the crowd of elders. *Of course*, I thought. Patience is indeed a virtue, and in times of change, people (in this case the elders) find ways to adapt.

"What were the women singing?" I asked Diana as she returned to her seat.

"They were praising God and praising education," Diana explained, exhilarated and breathless from the dance. She continued, having thankfully forgotten the Fantas and my dereliction of duty. "They sang that we should educate our children because they are the future and will reduce our burden. They also sang about how proud they are of me, that other girls will see me and know that they can make it, and that now that I am educated I cannot leave the other girls behind. They emphasized that I must see to it that the girls don't get pregnant at school and waste their parents' money."

"Wow! That's a big responsibility to lay on you."

"I'm fine with that," Diana said instantly. "I want a bigger platform. I want to help my family and community, and especially my sisters. Maybe I'll start a savings group where women of the community contribute a little money each month, like the other cooperatives we have here. Maybe I'll . . ."

Our conversation was interrupted when the elders began their speeches. Diana's older brother Musarini opened the event. He was a forceful speaker and everyone listened respectfully, even the small children. His message was direct, and he quickly got to the point, which underscored what the women had conveyed in song.

"We have seen the benefit of those girls like Diana who are educated. You all know them. They are independent and they are stable in life. And now their father, mother, and extended family can enjoy the fruits of those girls. But the reality is that I am disappointed by our community, especially when it comes to educating our girls. From the 1970s up to now, you do not see more than 20 girls who have transformed like Diana. There are too few. So, emulate her example! And you, Diana, go out into your community. Go and get those girls. Hurry! Talk with them! Let them not be cheated by boys, get pregnant, and have all those issues." Musarini continued to congratulate Diana and call the audience to action. The speech was surprisingly brief and ended with a few very well-received jokes before he passed the stage to his father.

Symon moved to the center of the lawn. He was wearing a Western shirt, cloth wrap, and, on his left wrist, the solar digital watch I had given him in 1982. After a short blessing, Symon thanked Dale for supporting Diana's education and her success. With those words, Diana and I shot each other a glance and a broad smile. It was a look between women to communicate a shared experience that required no translation. That's alright, we shrugged. We knew we were on the right side of history and were thus able to appreciate the grand and heartfelt accolades Dale received for the work Diana and I had accomplished. Then Symon presented Dale with his grandfather's flywhisk which is traditionally passed down from father to eldest son. It was an incredible honor and not the only one bestowed. Symon also gave Dale a milking cow named Napiruk, with the first calf going to his son Noah.

The next up was Namasa, Malian's sister-in-law and the wife of Symon's brother. As Symon spoke, she presented me with a beautiful long traditional beaded necklace. I was actually wondering why Namasa was making the presentation, but it was later explained to me that the gift was from Malian who was too overcome with emotion to present it herself. Dale was then called up to join me, and Symon blessed us while wrapping Dale and me in our final gift: a green and black checked traditional blanket.

It was a lovely celebration, and when it was my turn to speak, I was finally able to give the speech that I had long planned for. I congratulated Diana on behalf of myself, Dale, Noah, and the rest of her extended family in America. I also thanked Diana's family and community for supporting her through rainy seasons and drought. While this was a short visit, I assured them that we would return before too long to see how our cow was getting on. Joe had helped me draft the speech in Swahili. And while I can't be certain I said all of that, people laughed at the right times, and my gracious friends said I was clearly understood by all.

Finally it was Diana's turn to say a few words of gratitude to her guests. She was generally a confident speaker, and certainly started out that way. However, on this emotional occasion, Diana managed only a few words before she suddenly choked up with tears. She tried again, but all she could manage was laughter and tears at the same time. With a few appreciative gestures she sat back down, shaking her head and covering her mouth with a chagrined hand. She had truly said all she needed to say, and everyone clapped and laughed along with her.

The day ended with group and individual photos, a few more gifts, and blessings for Diana that flowed from honeyed voices. For something thrown together rather quickly, the event was incredibly successful and came off looking quite organized. In it I saw common elements from every celebratory party I'd ever attended. It was prescribed by culture and tradition with modern and foreign bits woven in as they made sense. Most everyone knew the songs, when to sing them, and who gives what speeches. It was a joyous celebration of individual achievement, family and community, continuity, and change. It rippled with unspoken pride and aspiration, and undoubtedly with some envy and drama that I was totally unaware of.

Malian had been a quiet presence throughout the party. She joined all the dancing but after the first number, was rarely in front. She sat quietly next to Symon for the speeches but did not give one herself. She did not smile for the cameras but stood by Diana's side, and with fingers interlocking, they held hands throughout. *It is too late for me*, she had told me long ago, *but not for my daughters*. At one point, Malian whispered a few private words to Diana, and in Diana's nodding response I remembered what Diana had said earlier without hesitation: *my greatest role model is my mother*. When Malian looked up, she caught me staring intently at this interaction between her and her daughter. A bit embarrassed, I looked away, but not before Malian reached out and embraced me with her radiant smile.

It dawned on me as I was sitting outside Musarini's modern home a few steps away from my now demolished 1982 room that this was the goodbye party I had longed for 35 years ago. This celebration, however, was not for me. It was not intended to say I would be remembered, as I had fantasized in 1982. It was so much better. This party was to recognize someone I loved and that I had earned a place in her story not because of any one thing I had done or because I was leaving, but because I returned and would continue to be a part of their lives. I had a designated spot on the lawn, along with my husband, son, and even grandchildren. We had speeches to give, speeches to hear, dances to join, a fly whisk, a necklace, a cow, and the promise of a calf.

Some things just take time.

The impact and expanding scope of my relationships with the Samburu has been only gradually revealed to me over time. I started with a few cross-cultural partners so long ago, partners who were not particularly interested in starting a relationship with me. But they did. Over the past 35 years, I have come to see that the relationship, which began tentatively—*my father says I must help you*—has spread out with irrepressible force and morphed into something that continues to grow in ways I can neither control, stop, nor predict. It is surely nothing my Aunt Helen ever imagined when she dropped that elephant-hair bracelet into my restless hand nearly half a century ago. It seems that wherever we go, whether we intend to or not, we absorb traces of the people we spend time with and leave traces of ourselves behind. It can be a cooking pot, a strong voice, or a ride in a car. What we leave behind and what we take away can last a lifetime and percolate down to subsequent generations. How they are used is not up to us. I felt profoundly grateful that, like my childhood make-believe stories, this particular chapter had such a happy ending.

"I am so proud of you," I told Diana as the last guests were leaving. "You did it! And I think you are already an admired role model for the young girls. Did they come up to you at the party to ask you about college?"

"NO, THEY DID NOT!" Diana snapped, shaking me out of my reverie. "None of them came up to me. None of them asked me anything. They are thinking *I need to do my work, why should I listen to you?* They are not interested in anything I have to tell them!"

For once, I knew just what to say.

"Ah, but they will," I said, slipping her the last Fanta that I had squirreled away just for her. "They are watching you, and they are talking about you. This is how it begins."

Glossary of Words Used in the Text

ashe	thanks, *ashe-oling* (thanks very much)
apaiya	father
baraza	meeting, or place of meeting (Swa.)
boma	settlement or homestead (Swa.), *bomas* (pl.)
duka	shop (Swa.)
hodi	May I enter? (Swa.) Expressed as *kodi* among Samburu
githeri	a traditional Kenyan dish of boiled maize and beans (Swa.)
kabisa	completely (Swa.)
launoni	spiritual leader of an age-set
lchapukera	best man
lmugit	age-set ritual for warriors passing through warriorhood to adulthood
lmurrani	warrior, *lmurran* (pl.), *moran* (Swa.)
lorora	ritual village built for *lmugit* ceremonies
maiyolo	I don't know
makanga	*matatu* driver's assistant, a young man or adolescent boy, whose job it is to hustle business, collect fares, and pack the vehicle (Swa.)
mandazi	East African-style fried donut, usually in triangle shape (Swa.)
manyatta	settlement or homestead, also *nkang*
matatu	privately run, multipassenger taxis, often minibus or converted pickup (Swa.)
mira'a	plant, chewed as stimulant (Swa.); also *khat*
muratina	local beer made from honey
nkang	settlement or homestead, *nkang'itie* (pl.); *boma* (Swa.)
Nkai	God
nkaji	Samburu traditional house, *nkajiji* (pl.)
ngoto	mother of, e.g., *Ngoto Paul* (mother of Paul)

rungu	wooden club carried by warriors
shamba	garden plot (Swa.)
shuka	decorative length of cloth worn around the body (Swa.)
sotwa	special friend among men, *sotwatin* (pl.)
sufuria	handleless saucepan (Swa.)
supat	good
ugali	cornmeal porridge, popular in Kenya (Swa.)
wazungu	people of European descent, white people (Swa.), *mzungu* (singular)

The spelling and definition of Samburu words are based on Mol's *Maa Dictionary*, Elliot Fratkin's glossary in *Laibon*, and my Samburu assistants and teachers.

Bibliography and Suggested Reading

Baker, R. 1980. "Sociological Factors in the Commercialization of Cattle in Africa." Discussion Paper No. 61, Institute for Development Studies, University of East Anglia, UK.

Brokensha, David W., and Peter D. Little, eds. 1988. *Anthropology of Development and Change in East Africa*. Boulder: Westview.

Cronk, Lee. 2004. *From Mukogodo to Masai*. Boulder: Westview.

Dahl, Gudrun, and Anders Hjort. 1976. *Having Herds: Pastoral Herd Growth and Household Economy*. Stockholm: University of Stockholm.

Domingo, Pilar, Aoife McCullough, Florence Simbiri, and Bernadette Wanjala. 2016, March. *Women and Power: Shaping the Development of Kenya's 2010 Constitution*. London: Overseas Development Institute.

Equipe Ecologie. 1979. *Pastoral Production and Society / Production Pastorale et Societe*. Cambridge, UK: Cambridge University Press.

Evans-Pritchard, E. E. 1940. *The Nuer*. London: Oxford University Press.

Fillo, F. 1981. Livestock Marketing in the Development of Maasailand and Samburu. Nairobi: International Livestock Centre for Africa.

Fratkin, Elliot. 2001. "East African Pastoralism in Transition: Maasai, Boran, and Rendille Cases." *African Studies Review* 44, no. 3 (December): 1–25.

———. 2012. *Laibon: An Anthropologist's Journey with Samburu Diviners in Kenya*. Plymouth, UK: Altamira.

Fratkin, E., and T. Sher-Mei. 1997 "Maasai and Barabaig Herders Struggle for Land Rights in Kenya and Tanzania." *Cultural Survival Quarterly Magazine*, September.

Galaty, John. 1982. "Being 'Maasai,' Being 'People of Cattle': Ethnic Shifters in East Africa." *American Ethnologist* 9:1–20.

———. 2013. "The Collapsing Platform for Pastoralism: Land Sales and Land Loss in Kajiado County, Kenya." *Nomad Peoples* 17, no. 2: 20–39.

Galaty, John, D. Aronson, and P. Salzman (eds.). 1981. "The Future of Pastoral Peoples." Proceedings of a conference held in Nairobi, 1980. Ottawa: International Development Research Centre.

Goldschmidt, W. 1969. *Kambuya's Cattle*. Berkeley: University of California Press.
———. 1971 "Independence as an Element in Pastoral Social Systems." *Anthropological Quarterly* 44:132–42.
———. 1976. *The Culture and Behavior of the Sebei*. Los Angeles: University of California Press.
Helland, Johan. 1980. Five Essays on the Study of Pastoralists and the Development of Pastoralism. Occasional Paper No. 20. Bergen, Norway: University of Bergen.
Hodgson, Dorothy. 2001. *Once Intrepid Warriors: Gender, Ethnicity and the Cultural Politics of Maasai Development*. Bloomington: Indiana University Press.
———. 2005. *The Church of Women: Gendered Encounters between Maasai and Missionaries*. Bloomington: Indiana University Press.
Hjort, Anders. 1979. "Savanna Town: Rural Ties and Urban Opportunities in Northern Kenya." *Stockholm Studies in Social Anthropology*, vol. 7. Stockholm: University of Stockholm.
Klopp, Jacqueline, and Odenda Lumumba. 2017. "Reform and Counter-Reform in Kenya's Land Governance." *Review of African Political Economy* 44, no. 154: 577–594.
Leo, Christopher. 1984. *Land and Class in Kenya*. Toronto: University of Toronto Press.
Lesorogol, C. 2008. *Contesting the Commons: Privatizing Pastoral Lands in Kenya*. Ann Arbor: University of Michigan Press.
McCabe, J. Terrence. 2004. *Cattle Bring Us to Our Enemies: Turkana Ecology, Politics, and Raiding in a Disequilibrium System*. Ann Arbor: University of Michigan Press.
McPeak, John, and Peter Little. 2006. *Pastoral Livestock Marketing in Eastern Africa: Research and Policy Challenges*. Rugby, UK: Practical Action.
Mole, Frans. 1978. Maa: A Dictionary of the Maasai Language and Folklore English-Maasai. Nairobi: Marketing & Publishing.
Ngugi wa Thiong'o. 2015. *The River Between*. New York: Penguin Books. (First published in 1965 by Heinemann.)
O'Keefe, P., and B. Wisner (eds). 1977. *Land Use and Development*. London: International African Institute.
Perlov, Diane. 1984. "Exploiting the Forest: Patterns and Perceptions in Highland Samburu." In *Wood, Energy and Households: Perspectives on Rural Kenya*, edited by C. Barnes, J. Ensminger, and P. O'Keefe. Uppsala, Sweden: The Beijer Institute and the Scandinavian Institute of African Studies.
———. 1987. Trading for Influence: The Social and Cultural Economics of Livestock Marketing among the Highland Samburu or Northern Kenya (unpublished doctoral dissertation). University of California, Los Angeles.

Schneider, H. 1980. Livestock and Equality in East Africa: The Economic Basis of Social Structure in East Africa. Bloomington: Indiana University Press.

Shell-Duncan, Bettina, and Y. Hernlund (eds.). 2000. *Female "Circumcision" in Africa: Culture, Controversy, and Change.* Boulder: Lynne Rienner.

Spencer, Paul. 2003. *The Samburu: A Study of Gerontocracy in a Nomadic Tribe.* 2nd edition. London: Routledge Classic Ethnographies.

———. 1973. Nomads in Alliance: Symbiosis and Growth among the Rendile and Samburu of Kenya. London: Oxford University Press.

———. 1977. "Pastoralists and the Ghost of Capitalism." Paper presented at the 1977 conference organized by the International Livestock Centre for Africa, Nairobi.

Talle, Aude. 1988. "Women at a Loss: Changes in Maasai Pastoralism and Their Effects on Gender Relations." *Stockholm Studies in Social Anthropology,* 19. Stockholm: Department of Social Anthropology, University of Stockholm.

Veit, P. 2011, March. *Rise and Fall of Group Ranches in Kenya.* Washington DC: World Resources Institute, Focus on Land in Africa.

Werner, David. 2017. *Where There Is No Doctor.* Berkeley: Hersperian Health Guides.

Western, David. 1997. *In the Dust of Kilimanjaro.* Washington DC: Island.

Western, David, and V. Finch. 1977. "Cattle Colors in Pastoral Herds: Natural Selection or Social Preference?" *Ecology* 58: 1384–1392.

Woodhouse, Emily, and J. Terrence McCabe. 2018. "Well-being and Conservation: Diversity and Change in Visions of a Good Life among the Maasai of Northern Tanzania." *Ecology and Society* 23, no. 1: 4.

Acknowledgments

While the material for this book was collected from my fieldwork in Kenya from 1981 through 1982 and subsequent trips through 2019, its development has involved the assistance of innumerable friends and colleagues. I cannot claim credit for this work without acknowledging the many individuals who have been central to its formation.

I am deeply grateful to Robert Gottlieb, Peter Wiley, and Emy Thurber who provided critical and moral support from the earliest days of this project, and to their fellow authors, publishers, editors, reviewers, and friends in the literary world who guided me along the way: Ann Gray, Sukey and Gil Garcetti, Jennifer Lawrence, Dennis Jenkins, Susan Heeger, and Sara Crasson. I particularly want to acknowledge and thank Sukey Garcetti for her astute and gracious editorial review and advice, Jeni Hentschel for her patient and expert copyediting, Terry McCabe for his insightful content review and expert guidance, and Tom Curtin for his support and tremendous leadership through every stage of the process. Their suggestions, words of encouragements, friendship, and wise advice kept me going in more ways than they will ever know. I thank graphic artist Betriza Inglessis for the beautiful map of Kenya, and my son and senior visual effects artist Noah Caddis for his expert contrast and color correction of my digitized photos.

Many of my colleagues from the old days in Kenya remain close friends, as do their children. Several went over and above, and I appreciate their generous assistance in reviewing and advising on the manuscript: Frode Storaas, Johan Helland, Christie Peacock CBE, David Caddis, and

Peter Hetz. Thank you for your wisdom and enduring friendship. It means the world to me. I am also grateful to my colleagues at the California Science Center who provided steadfast moral support as I completed this project with a full-time workload at the museum.

Walter Goldschmidt left me with more than advice on tennis shoes. As a wonderful writer and observer, he taught me to be attuned to the fortuitous event and to the power and educational value of storytelling, exemplified by his book *Kambuya's Cattle*. I remember with gratitude his confidence in me and his years of encouragement. To sustain me through the dark days of fieldwork, anthropologist Sally Falk Moore once told me to keep my perspective and realize that I knew more than I thought I knew. At the same time, my Samburu friends were there to correct me when I knew considerably less than I thought I knew. I am deeply indebted to Symon, Jacob, Dorcas, Naisula, Lmariwan, Malian, Ltangires, Musarini, Ndipama, and especially to my personal hero Diana! Thank you for giving so graciously of your time and trust, day and night, and memories of our days together. Your warmth, humor, and wisdom continue to inspire me, and I can't wait to see what you and your children accomplish in the new Kenya. While I cannot name everyone, I am also grateful to the Samburu people of the highlands for their always warm hospitality and cooperation.

Finally, to my husband Dale, who read, reread, and advised me on this manuscript in all of its iterations. Thank you so much for your incredible patience, understanding, and unsinkable encouragement. And to our son Noah and his family: Maria, Matilda, and Leo. You are my north star and inspire me every day. For you and all my children (adopted and biological), grandchildren, nieces, and nephews, I pass on this final bit of wisdom: when I was a child my mother told me to beware of strangers; when I was an adult she reminded me that if it were not for the kindness of strangers, including the ones in this book, I'd be dead by now. This book is for them and for you, and the hope and the dream that one day you will find each other.

DIANE C. PERLOV serves as Senior Vice President for Exhibits at the California Science Center in Los Angeles, where she has overseen curatorial research, collections, and exhibit design and development for the past 20 years and currently oversees special exhibit projects. She has lectured in the US and abroad on museum work and on her field research, including on livestock marketing in Kenya, and women's economic activities and social mobility in Bolivia. In 2008, she received the International Service Citation from the U.S. National Committee of the International Council of Museums for her outstanding leadership and invaluable service to the international museum community. While she has curated six major exhibits and codirected four ethnographic films, this is her first solo book and her most fearless work to date. She lives in Los Angeles with her husband Dale Weaver and a cat named Oscar Purple.